# Europe and Its Interior Other(s)

# Europe and Its Interior Other(s)

*Edited by Helge Vidar Holm,*
*Sissel Lægreid and Torgeir Skorgen*

Aarhus University Press |

*Europe and Its Interior Other(s)*

© The authors and Aarhus University Press

Cover by Jørgen Sparre

Cover image: Magritte, René (1898-1967): "La reproduction interdite", 1937

Rotterdam, Museum Boijmans van Beuningen. Oil on canvas, 81 x 65 cm

© 2014. BI, ADAGP, Paris/SCALA, Florence

© René Magritte, The Estate of Magritte/billedkunst.dk

Typeset by Anette Ryevad, Ryevad Grafisk

Printed by Narayana Press, Denmark 2014

ISBN 978 87 7124 128 0

ISSN 0065-1354 (Acta Jutlandica)

ISSN 0901-0556 (Humanities Series/15)


Aarhus University Press

*Aarhus*

Langelandsgade 177

DK – 8200 Aarhus N


Published with the financial support of

The Department of Foreign Languages, University of Bergen

INTERNATIONAL DISTRIBUTORS:


Gazelle Book Services Ltd.

White Cross Mills

Hightown, Lancaster, LA1 4XS

United Kingdom

www.gazellebookservices.co.uk


ISD

70 Enterprise Drive

Bristol, CT 06010

USA

www.isdistribution.com

# Contents

## Part 3:
## Variations on the Interior Other(s)

# Introduction:
# European Notions of Identity and Otherness in Times of Crisis – Present and Past

*Helge Vidar Holm, Sissel Lægreid and Torgeir Skorgen*

"Is there a European Identity? Is there a Europe?" These questions posed by Václav Havel (2000), have been asked time and again by European politicians and researchers in order to find ways of dealing with the ever increasing problems of integration within an expanding European Union currently facing its biggest financial and political crisis since its foundation. Though the answers to the question of European identity vary, the importance and relevance of both asking the question and realizing its impact seem in essence to have been summed up by Václav Havel (2000), who more than a decade ago stated:

> By inquiring about it; thinking about it; by trying to grasp its essence, we contribute to our own self-awareness. This is immensely important –especially because we find ourselves in a multi-cultural, multi-polar world in which recognizing one's identity is a prerequisite for co-existence with other identities.

Since 2007 the European crisis referred to above, has not only driven the younger generation of Southern Europe into collective agony about its own future in terms of work, an independent existence, and the possibility of raising a family. It has also led to a large scale political, economic and cultural polarization along a south-north axis, which appears both new and old at the same time, appealing to certain Protestant stereotypes of the economically backward, lazy and morally irresponsible Southerners, as expressed in the debate about the 2013 financial crisis of the Cypriot bank system.

Northern European clichés about the 'lazy Greeks' and the 'criminal Russians' only lead to new hostility towards the financial EU elites, recently in particular towards Germany, the financially and politically most powerful member of the EU, now held responsible for the harshly prescribed medicine for members facing the current crisis, like Greece, Italy or Spain. In these countries anti-German attitudes represent a new trend, since parts of the older generation of these countries spent many years of their lives working in the German industry during the prosperous post-war German economic miracle

(*Wirtschaftswunder*). As so-called guest workers (*Gastarbeiter*), immigrants from South-Eastern Europe, earned good money. This in turn was invested in new establishments in their native countries.

In the wake of the international oil crisis in 1973, German authorities had declared that Germany was no immigration country, a statement which was repeated and confirmed both in the 80s as well as in the 90s. In the present situation, however, German authorities have had to invent a new and more inclusive terminology for the new generation of guest workers from Southern Europe, as Germany finds itself quite desperately in need of new skilled employees.

What is required in the current situation of crisis in Europe, is a new mind-set, realizing that many guest workers have developed and will develop a feeling of belonging to their European immigration country. They are therefore planning to stay in the new country and bring their families along. This leads to a new demographic situation in many European countries: In Germany for instance, today more than 11 million Germans are immigrants or children of immigrants. Nevertheless, many employers, and even some authorities, continue to refer to them as guest workers, who like visitors, would soon be leaving to return to their native countries.

In this sense both the German term *Gastarbeiter* and the Norwegian *fremmedkulturell*, the term mostly used to describe non-European immigrants and refugees to Norway of foreign cultural origin, are symptomatic indications of the kind of ambivalence, which the resident population throughout history has felt towards people coming from countries far away. As strangers looking, talking and behaving differently, they were and still are generally thought of as individuals or groups not really belonging, but as people only being here today and (perhaps) gone tomorrow. However, since they tend to stay on in their new country, they become interior other(s), who are still rooted in their old countries and as such at the same time asymmetrically defined as 'out-groups' by the dominating, and more or less, resident 'in-groups' in their new country (Koselleck 1989).

The complex relation between the stranger and the local community was addressed by the German-Jewish sociologist Georg Simmel (1858-1918). In a short essay in his book *Soziologie* called "Exkurs über den Fremden" (1908), he presented the stranger as a unique sociological category. Since then, Simmel's *Fremde* has become a rather intriguing concept in modern sociology, through its emphasis on the paradoxical opposition between liberty to move on and fixation to a limited space:

> If wandering is the liberation from every given point in space, and thus the conception opposite to fixation at such a point, the sociological form of the stranger presents the unity, as it were, of these two characteristics (Simmel 1996: 37).

Different both from the 'outsider', who is not related to a specific group, and from the 'wanderer' who comes one day and leaves the next, the stranger is a member of the group in which he lives and participates and yet remains distant from native members of the group:

> The stranger is thus being discussed here, not in the sense often touched upon in the past, as the wanderer who comes today and leaves tomorrow, but rather as the person who comes today and stays tomorrow. He is, so to speak, the *potential* wanderer: although he has not moved on, he has not quite overcome the freedom of coming and going (Simmel 1996: 37).

Unlike other forms of social distance and difference (such as class, gender, and even ethnicity), the specificity of the stranger has to do with his origins. The stranger is regarded as extraneous to the group even though he is in a more or less constant relation to other group members. Often his distance is more emphasized than his nearness, and his situation is characterized as being simultaneously close and far away. Since he once came from afar, there is always a possibility that he might be leaving again at some point. Therefore a kind of inherent mobility and fluctuation seems to stick to him as a distinctive mark.

On the other hand, because the stranger is considered not to be committed to the kind of life-long community constituted by work and permanent residents, he may approach it with some kind of objectivity. And due to his contact on a daily basis with a number of individuals living in the local community, he also participates in it. But since they see him as not really belonging and therefore expect him to be leaving sooner or later, the locals tend to tell him their innermost secrets. Being conceived as a visitor whom they might not see again at all, he would have no particular interest in misusing them. Their secrets, they think, could only be misused by others who are more organically connected to the community and its particular interests. Paradoxically it is the same quality of mobility and distance which makes the stranger suspicious to the resident population. For the same reason, the stranger is considered an objective observer watching the local community from a kind of bird's-eye perspective.

However, his position makes the stranger vulnerable to hatred and to the local population's need for a scapegoat, in case a misfortune should occur. In this sense, despite the freedom of the position of the stranger, his position is a dangerous one, since "in uprisings of all sorts, the party attacked has claimed, from the beginning of things, that provocation has come from the outside, through emissaries and instigators" (Simmel 1996: 39).

The scapegoat function of the stranger as described by Simmel is similar to that of the European interior other, which is the topic of the present volume and which throughout history especially has been the experience of the European Jews. Since antiquity, Judaism and the Jews have represented a major challenge to the Christian communities, a challenge which was intimately linked to the role of Judaism as the 'mother' of Christianity and the origin, from which it had developed and seceded in a constant tension between nearness and distance, succession and competition.

When Christianity was declared state religion of the Roman Empire, an initial Christian attitude of anti-Judaism was turned into real prosecution: Synagogues were destroyed, Jews physically attacked and new laws were adopted and carried out, prohibiting the conversion of Christians into Judaism or marriages between Jews and Christians. During the Middle Ages however, the traditional hostility towards the Jews became part of Christian popular piety, incited by the Crusaders. Hence anti-Judaism became an integral part of the medieval social norm. And their imperial or princely protectors often withstood them only as long as they could exploit them or benefit from their financial or administrative resources. Since they were also excluded from the guilds, which were organized as Christian associations, they were confined to making their living as hawkers, moneylenders or pawnbrokers, thereby violating the Christian ban against gaining profit from borrowing rates.

According to the IV[th] council of the Catholic Church in 1215, the Jews were banned from several state offices and imposed to wear certain clothes, such as hats or yellow circles, identifying them as Jews. As a consequence, they were not considered equal citizens, although they were under imperial protection. Moreover, during the black death pogroms, entire Jewish societies in Europe were devastated by pilgrims murdering and burning all over the European Continent. Seeing themselves as part of a larger Christian *Europeanness*, the pilgrims confirmed their own Christian piety by hating and murdering Jewish infidels.

A tragic example of this was the expulsion and slaughtering of the Spanish Jews and Muslims by the Catholic Inquisition, which became known as the purification of the blood (*limpieza de sangre*). This expression was in fact anticipating essential parts of the vocabulary and imagination of modern European anti-Semitism, which was launched in the late 19th century by the German publicist Wilhelm Marr, who, holding the Jews responsible for Marxism, liberalism and the entire process of modernisation, called for a racially and pseudo-scientifically based political movement against Jews and the Jewish emancipation.

Throughout history, the notions of both Europe, Europeanness, and the historical self-images of the Europeans were pre-conditioned by diverse cultural, mental, meta-geographical and aesthetic borders such as those between included and excluded, between culturally dominating and dominated or between center and periphery, natives and exiled, nomads and resident population groups. In all cases we find asymmetric counter concepts of in-groups and out-groups, where the out-groups often were in no position to define themselves, but were defined by the dominating in-group (Koselleck 1989).

The feeling of being defined as others by a hegemonic in-group has without doubt formed the self-image that many European minority groups have developed over the years. The problem has illustrated and debated by a number of writers and intellectuals in various ways. In *Les Identités meurtrières* (1998) Amin Maalouf for instance, holds the identity struggle responsible for the great majority of genocides and wars in Europe in the last hundred years, and he stresses the overall tendency to make the other seem like a group of foes to fight against or worse, to eliminate, be it for ethnic, religious, cultural, territorial or language-related reasons. Frantz Fanon (1952) explains this tendency from a psychiatrist's point of view, where the inferiority complex of the members of dominated group makes them want to hide, or even to get rid of, some of their identity marks.

Fanon is inspired by his philosophical *maître*, Jean-Paul Sartre, who in his famous post-war essay reflecting on the Jewish question, *Réflexions sur la question juive* (1946), explains how the image or the 'spectre' of the Jew is a constructed one, made by the anti-Semite's way of thinking in synthetizing categories. In this essay, Sartre makes his point by distinguishing between four paradigmatic models: the anti-Semite, the democrat, the inauthentic Jew and the authentic Jew. The greater part of his essay discusses the anti-Semite's personality, how his fundamental choice of hatred as a basic existential category develops into a passion that blocks his ability of rational thinking and creates an attitude of impermeability to any arguments contrary to his synthetizing 'comprehension' of Jewishness: nothing Jewish can be positive or good, because it is related to Jews. Opposed to this synthetizing attitude, we find the analytical way of thinking, incarnated by the Democrat, who regards the Jew just as anybody else, as good or bad people according to their merits, and to whom Jewishness has no particular meaning as a personality category. Sartre points out, however, that the Democrat is not an especially good ally to the

Jews, as the Democrat thinks in universal terms and sees no reason to preserve Jewishness as such. The authentic Jew will therefore need other allies than the Democrat, whereas the inauthentic Jew may find important reasons to trust the Democrat.

Sartre's analysis of how people think of the other, especially how passionate hatred against a particular minority group tends to block any rationality regarding the subject, is still of great value, be it in discussions about today's growing anti-Semitism in Europe, or in any other debate on European minority groups, such as the gypsies/Roma people, or on the issue of Muslim communities in Europe. Interpreted in the context of Sartre's phenomenologically based existentialist philosophy, where *l'impact du regard d'autre*, the way you feel that people define you, is decisive for your self-understanding, Sartre's essay helps us understand how terrorist movements may develop today, in Europe and elsewhere. *Stigmatization* is a key word here. If you feel excluded because of your religious or ethnic identity, you may respond by emphasizing the identity features that you feel part of and therefore may want to defend. Maalouf puts it like this: "When you feel that your language is despised, your religion attacked, your culture devaluated, you will react by showing your difference with ostentation …" (Maalouf 1998: 53, our translation).

So what is identity? Can it be fixed as a 'true' entity or is it a mixture moving between construct, fact and fiction? And what about the relation of the individual or psychological aspect to that of the collective identity?

As suggested by Vacláv Havel (2000), the two categories may be seen as entities co-existing within a dynamic dimension, where the one is the prerequisite to the other. In so far he was in line with Balibar (1991: 94), who on his part stated that:

> it is not a question of setting a collective identity against individual identities. All identity is individual, but there is no individual identity that is not historical or, in other words, constructed within a field of social values, norms of behaviour and collective symbols. The real question is how the dominant reference points of individual identity change over time and with the changing institutional environment.

Since identity constitutes itself in relation to social action, it might be fruitful to see identity more as a form than a concept (Delanty 2003). The idea is that since no categories of identity begin as fully formed and articulated entities expressing an underlying consciousness or essence, but are created in action in the course of a lifetime, identities can in truth never be fixed. As a creation the identity of the self is constituted in symbolic markers or signs, based on the principal of difference and co-existing in a relational context. However, even though all categories of identity relate to each other in different ways, and may therefore be referred to as multiple identities, as overlapping, mixed and co-existing, this is especially the case with individual identities, since they rarely have one single identity (Maalouf 1998). And as such they may be conceived as narratives people tell about themselves in order to bring continuity to their own existence; in other words as a kind of narrative identity in the sense Paul Ricoeur coined the term in order to come to terms with the complex question of identity.

The term implies either the individual or collective entity addressed by questions such as who has done this or acted in such a way, and to whom certain things happened (Ricoeur 1988). Essential to this notion of identity is the fundamental temporality of being, where the 'who' as a being in co-existence with others in a common world, transforms him- or herself in the course of a life history and only becomes who he or she is always already in the course of becoming him- or herself. In the Freudian sense this may be conceived as becoming aware of oneself as a consciousness, which, according to Freud, comes into being instead or in place of the memory trace: "das Bewusstsein entstehe an Stelle der Erinnerungsspur" (Freud 1982: 235).

To conclude this quest for identity, it seems fair to argue that, whether or not the notion of identity is analysed from a universalist or existentialist perspective on identity (Habermas 1976, Ricoeur 1988, 1990), from a sociological (Giddens 1991) or a psychoanalytical perspective (Freud 1982), as stated by Jacobs and Maier in their paper on European identity as construct, fact and fiction (Gastelaars 1998: 13-34), no form of identity, collective or individual, can ever in truth be fixed, since it is never complete or stable. Still, rather than being conceived as 'a loose patchwork', it should be seen as a more or less integrated symbolic structure, forming a narrative with the dimensions of a past, present, and future, thus providing both the individual and the collective with the feeling of the continuity and consistency needed. In line with Freud's description of the talking cure as a kind of construction work (Freud 1982: 398), where the analyst makes suggestions to the analysed in search of his (true) life story, identity, conceived as a narrative with the dimensions of a past, present, and future, is therefore never final, but a piece of preliminary work (*die Vorarbeit*).

## Narratives of Europe and Its Interior Other(s)

Who were and who are the European other(s), and how has their socio-cultural situation been aesthetically expressed and commented upon in works of literature and art throughout the history of Europe? These are questions which are reflected upon in various ways in the present volume written by members of "The Borders of Europe", an interdisciplinary group of international researchers in the field of the humanities based at the University of Bergen. In sum the volume offers a discussion of various aspects of our European past and their impact on the present situation for various minority groups in Europe.

As indicated above, the situation of the European interior other(s) has been constantly undergoing transformation throughout history, and today one of the most important problems is that of integration. As a consequence of the present situation of financial and economic crisis, migrating people in search of better living conditions than their home countries can offer them, create a totally new demographic situation in Europe. In the wake of the Schengen Convention and the European Economic Area Treaty, and in a situation where the outer borders of the European continent are still objects of theoretical discussion, its internal borders are undergoing a practical transformation on a daily basis, as the national frontiers have lost parts of their importance. New regulations permit Europeans to move freely all over the continent in search of economic prosperity and survival. As they bring their cultural heritage and customs, this very often results in integration problems as well as new constellations of in- and outgroups, and thereby in ever changing narratives of identity and otherness.

The present volume highlights these narratives and the nine chapters in its three sections offer a wide range of approaches to the historical and cultural background of the on-going change. Bearing the historical dimension of the situation of the interior other(s) on our continent in mind, its focus is on a variety of aesthetic expressions of the situation of its 'out-groups', either through the analysis of literary works or through discussions of architectonic and scenic landscapes.

The opening chapter of the volume's first section addresses the European Middle Ages. Jørgen Bruhn takes his cue from the art historian Michael Camille's *The Gothic Idol*, in which Camille claims that medieval Europe divided the other into three categories: the internal other (Jews), the past other (Greek/Roman non-Christianity), and the external other (the Moslem threat just outside the borders of Christianity). Doing a cross-disciplinary reading, using both Camille's ideas from the history of art and more conventional historical works, Bruhn discusses what is considered a high point of medieval French literature, namely the work of Chrétien de Troyes from the second half of the 12ᵗʰ century. A main point argued by Bruhn is that since woman, nature, insanity, and beastly otherness are parts of the violent economy of Chrétien's chivalric universe, one of the oft-mentioned sources of European civilization turns out to have an otherness attached to it that should not be forgotten.

In the second chapter of the first section, Øyunn Hestetun starts from the premise that although the European colonies established in the wake of the Age of Discovery were geographically located on different continents, they were – legally, as well as for all practical purposes – considered part of their mother countries. She then proceeds to discuss the migration to North America of a group of British Puritan separatists known as the Pilgrims in 1620, and a text by Robert Cushman, who acted as an agent in negotiating the contract for the passage to the New World and who comments on the various implications of their venture. Hestetun shows that by relocating to the outskirts of the British Empire, the Pilgrims, representing Europe's interior others, secured not only the possibility of preaching and practicing their religion amongst themselves without the threat of persecution, but also a way to spread their gospel to the indigenous population, representing Europe's external others.

Michael Grote concludes the historical section of this book by a chapter on Heinrich von Kleist's poem "Germania an ihre Kinder" (1809). One main point argued in the chapter is that, due to its paradoxical rhetorical structure, the poem cannot be integrated into any form of historical or discursive knowledge. Comparing the Kleist text with Schiller's "Ode an die Freude" and Kleist's play "Penthesilea", Grote shows how the rhetorical function of Kleist's ode permanently undermines the logical discourse of the text. He then argues that on the basis of this comparison we can consider Kleist's propagandistic activity in the Napoleonic wars as an artificial, rather than an actual, political practice: aesthetics, not history, moved Kleist to his harsh engagement in the war against Napoleon, and it is aesthetics that organizes his literary production even in its most violent and aggressive nationalist manifestations.

In the second section of the present volume, which focuses on the situation of the Jews in Europe, Torgeir Skorgen starts off by presenting the reader with reflections on the history of the concept of tolerance in a European context. Focusing on the genre of utopia and centring his discussion on key works by Erasmus, More, and Lessing, and with reference to Henrik Wergeland's poem *The Jew*, Skorgen shows that for centuries, ideas of interreligious tolerance were considered a heresy in Europe and could be punished by death. For this reason utopian ideas of tolerance had to be projected upon some imagined undiscovered island. Interestingly, however, Skorgen finds that in the works of Lessing and Wergeland, interreligious tolerance does not appear to be some utopian end of history, but rather utopian episodes on a dystopian backdrop of hate and bigotry, or as fictions within the fiction.

Taking her cue from the relative absence of homosexual victims in Holocaust studies, Željka Švrljuga in her chapter discusses two musical texts that in different ways pay tribute to the silenced internal other of the Nazi era: Ståle Kleiberg's *Requiem for the Nazi Persecutions of Victims* (2004) and Jake Heggie's chamber opera *For a Look or a Touch* (2007). As she shows, their different musical idioms and formats, as well as underlying textual practices (Edwin Morgan's poetry versus Marvin Levin's journal and his lover's oral testimony), provide a paradigmatic shift from monologism to dialogism, from the general to the particular, from the poetic to the historical, never losing sight of the underlying alchemy of pain. Her chapter constitutes a significant example of discussions of 'rememory' (the repressed memory of others) and ghosting (the staging of memory that we find in tragedy and opera), and exploring different experiences of victimhood and ways to overcome it.

In the next chapter of this section Sissel Lægreid starts by conducting a discussion of Max Frisch's "The Andorran Jew". This is a prose sketch in which a young man is treated by the Andorrans as a Jew and, though in actual fact he is not, accepts and insists on his 'false' identity as the other, thus eventually getting killed for allowing himself to be what he is not. Drawing on theories of identity proposed by Freud, Kristeva, and Ricoeur, and the point made by Frisch, that each individual carries the responsibility of preventing a future Holocaust by accepting and affirming every person's unique being, Lægreid explores narrative ways in which the traumatic experience of estrangement have been depicted in post-war European literature looking back on the Holocaust. With special reference to Ricoeur's concept of narrative identity, she focuses on texts by Georges-Arthur Goldschmidt and W. G. Sebald retracing the tragic history of Jewish identity and otherness, and in so doing shows how the traumatic experience of estrangement is kept from being forgotten by narrators telling the story of a life, which in the Ricoeurian sense can only be told because there has been human activity and suffering.

Closing the section on the European Jews, Helge Vidar Holm continues the path opened by Lægreid, in treating the question of Jewish identity in literature, especially in cases where neither ethnic nor religious belonging makes the 'Jewish' character genuinely Jewish. Holm analyzes the Jewish element in some of the novels of Marguerite Duras, especially in *Abahn Sabana David* (1970) and *Yann Andréa Steiner* (1992). Referring both to Ricoeur's concepts of sameness (*idem*) and selfhood (*ipse*) and his model of a *triple mimesis*, he argues that Duras' strong engagement in the cause of justice for minority groups, and especially for the Jewish cause, has its roots in the *préfiguration* influenced by her upbringing in a French colony and by experiences in her close family during and after World War II. Moreover, he claims that Duras' uses of narrative silences characterize her style of writing, together with a deliberate confusion of identity marks in the presentation of her fictional characters. The chapter focuses closely on the complicated yet extremely important relationship in Duras's writing between literary language and the historical reality to which, however indirectly, it refers.

Lillian Helle opens the third section of the volume by discussing how Russian literature and cultural thinking construe the Russian people, the 'narod', as a highly ambivalent and mythologized inner other. In this myth, developed by the Eurocentric Russian gentry and intelligentsia, the Russian working-class was thoroughly exoticized and imagined as a kind of internal Rousseauésque wild man. They thus became an object of orientalization in a process of internal colonization that has been described as 'white on white' imperialism. This self-colonization takes the form of a secondary colonization by the westernized state of its own territory and population, and it is a process that partly coincided with the country's external colonization, in a highly complicated and interchanging relationship. The chapter shows that in Russian literature and cultural thinking the orientalising binarity is often undermined. As a result, the borders between the europeanized classes and the country's rural masses become rather unstable. Like the Caucasian external other, the 'narod' as Russia's internal other, is an image that in the westernized Russian evokes feelings of both sympathy and shared identity. Consequently, the peasantry, the muzhik, as an internal alter is regarded, in many cases, as a hidden and ambivalent ideal. He becomes the Westernized Russians' own *noble savage*, or a more authentic and pre-Petrine part of the national psyche, thought to be more compassionate, sincere and genuine than the sophisticated, disillusioned europeanised ego.

Focusing on landscape-oriented perspectives in cultural exchange situations, Knut Ove Arntzen in the next chapter discusses the interplay of scenic landscapes and Nordic light, with reference to the changes in the landscapes and cultural meetings in coastal theatre and in drama reflecting the other, as in Knut Hamsun's drama *Play of Life*. Considering the landscape as a dialogical space of cultures in remote areas, the chapter argues that a Northern gaze is marked by a search for identities and typical features of the relation between nature and culture. One tentative conclusion reached by Arntzen is that there is a paradox in creating Nordic viewpoints between cultures which traditionally collide, like the Sami and the southern Scandinavian cultures.

In the concluding chapter of the present volume Siri Skjold Lexau discusses Istanbul's architecture in literature from Le Corbusier to Orhan Pamuk, and in a sense turns the question of otherness around. Focusing on the city of Istanbul, and noting that a number of novelists including Ahmed Hamdi Tanpınar, Orhan Pamuk, Yachar Kemal, Pierre Loti, and Abdülhak Şinasi Hisar have used the physical outline and structure of Istanbul as a way of defining the city as different, she asks: different from what? As she observes, although the oriental difference was about to disappear in the mid-twentieth century, often nothing came to fill the void, and the drive to westernize the city amounted mostly to the erasure of the past. Referring to Pamuk's use of the word *hüzün* to describe the melancholy connected to this cultural and physical loss, Skjold Lexau, by conducting a wide-ranging discussion, shows how the loss of difference may be intrinsically linked to that of otherness.

The proposed link between the loss of difference and otherness, if read as a kind of loss of identity characteristic of the stranger (Kristeva 1991), may serve as an illustration of what this book is all about: Its intention is to contribute to both reflections on and awareness of the dangerous dynamics of othering and the traumatic experience of estrangement. It follows this goal by making a mental, time-space journey across and beyond internal and external borders of Europe, moving from medieval times to the present, from Istanbul to the northernmost tip of Norway, and even embarking on a historical voyage made by European Puritans from England via the Netherlands to America, where, after settling down in New England, the dynamic process of othering between true believers and heretics, now representing in- and out-groups, went on.

In accordance with the opening lines of the German traditional folk song and poem[1] "Wenn jemand eine Reise tut, so kann er was verzählen", indicating that travelling people will have significant stories to tell, mainly unheard of narratives about the strange life of the others, the book's main focus is on various narratives of otherness. The contributions of the book illustrate that, since the stranger and other may be the hidden face of our identity, our mutual challenge is to recognize the stranger within ourselves and become aware of our own difference. Only then shall we be able to accept the strangeness of others. This requires the kind of self-awareness, which Václav Havel, as already cited, declared as "immensely important – especially because we find ourselves in a multi-cultural, multi-polar world, in which recognizing one's identity is a prerequisite for co-existence with other identities."

---

[1]     Opening lines from the poem "Urians Reise um die Welt" by Mathias Claudius (1740-1815).

# Bibliography

Balibar, E. and I. Wallerstein (1991): *Race, Nation, Class. Ambiguous Identities*. London: Verso.

Delanty, G. (2003): "Is there a European Identity?". *Global Dialogue*, vol. 5, no 3-4.

Fanon, F. (1952): *Peau noire, masques blancs*. Paris: Édition du Seuil.

Freud, S. (1982): *Sigmund Freud. Studienausgabe, vol. I-X*. Mitscherlich A. et al. (eds.). Frankfurt a. M.: Fischer Verlag.

Gasterlaars, M. and A. de Ruijter, eds. (1998): *A United Europe. The Quest for a Multifaceted Identity*. Maastricht: Shaker.

Giddens, A. (1991): *Modernity and Self-Identity*. Cambridge: Polity Press.

Habermas, J. (1976): "Moralentwicklung und Ich-Identität". In: J. Habermas: *Zur Rekonstruktion des Historischen Materialismus*. Frankfurt a. M.: Suhrkamp Verlag.

Havel, V. (2000): "Is there a European Identity, Is there a Europe?". Project Syndicate, www.project-syndicate.org.

Koselleck, R. (1989): *Vergangene Zukunft: zur Semantik geschichtlicher Zeiten*. Frankfurt a. M.: Suhrkamp Verlag.

Kristeva, J. (1991): *Strangers to Ourselves*, trans. Roudiez, L. New York and London: Harvester & Wheatsheaf.

Maalouf, A. (1998): *Les Identités meurtrières*. Paris: Édition Grasset.

Menocal, M. R. (2002): *The Ornament of the World: how Muslims, Jews and Christians created a Culture of Tolerance in Medieval Spain*. Boston / New York.

Poliakov, L. (1974): *The History of Anti-Semitism*, 4 volumes. London: Routledge & Paul Kegan.

Ricoeur, P. (1988): *Time and Narrative*. 3 volumes, trans. Blamey, K. and David Pellauer. Chicago: University of Chicago Press.

Ricoeur, P. (1990): *Oneself as an Other*, trans. Blamey, K. Chicago: University of Chicago Press.

Sartre, J.- P. (1946): *Réflexions sur la question juive*. Paris: Éditions Gallimard.

Simmel, G. (1996[1908]): "The Stranger" and "The Web of Group Affiliations". In: Werner Sollors (ed.): *Theories of Ethnicity. A Classical Reader*. Hampshire & London: Macmillan Press.

Simmel, G. (1971): *"The Stranger" in Georg Simmel: On Individuality and Social Forms*, ed. by Donald L. Levine. Chicago: University of Chicago Press.

Simmel, G. (1992): *Soziologie: Über die Formen der Vergesellschaftung. Gesamtausgabe,* vol. 11, Frankfurt a. M.: Suhrkamp Verlag.

Valdes, M., ed. (1991): *A Ricoeur Reader*. Toronto: University of Toronto Press.

# Part 1:
# The Historical Dimension
# of the European Other(s)

# Meeting the Other in a Medieval Chivalric Novel

*Jørgen Bruhn*

Most of us feel familiar with the European Middle Ages: knights and virgins, plague and scholasticism, monks and mystical cathedrals are all parts of the European dream, or nightmare, of the period from ca. 500 A.D. – when the Roman Empire collapsed – and until sometime round the fifteenth century when Italian scholars began seeing the preceding thousand years as a mere interregnum, a dark period of intellectual, technological, and spiritual decline, a *medium aevum* between antiquity and the Renaissance. The dream, or the various post-medieval fantasies, of the middle ages (to use a term by Umberto Eco 1990) can be infinitely recycled, for instance in the books by Tolkien, a relatively unknown scholar of medieval philology, who was also to become a world famous author of fantasy fiction – or in the innumerable science fiction films that seem to represent a future that strangely resembles (some of our visions of) the Middle Ages. But modern medieval scholarship has during the last forty or fifty years disclosed a dynamic or even 'luminescent' version of the so-called dark middle ages (for an engaging overview of research on the Middle Ages, see Cantor 1991); these scholars have shown that the birth of modern science, the concept of Europe as a geographical, political, and cultural entity, the focus on individualism and the budding money economy and capitalism can be traced to the Middle Ages. And we probably owe even the cherished ideas of art as the source for enjoyment, and love as the most crucial part of human life, to this period too. In this article I wish to first give a sketch of the Middle Ages from two different perspectives, and then offer a reading of one of the well-known writers of French medieval literature, Chrétien de Troyes. I intend to show that even in a seemingly 'innocent' chivalric and courteous context we may detect signs of a threatening other. My point of departure in my sketch of the Middle Ages will be the concept of the other.

If we consider medieval man as immensely preoccupied with meeting and confronting the other (below I shall specify Michael Camille's ideas on this question), it may lead to two different interpretations an optimistic understanding and a more negative or pessimistic vision. We may interpret European identity and mentality as the positive result of meetings with the other and proponents of this trend has stressed all the 'positive' cultural meetings: the writings and thoughts of Aristotle (known by the name of The Philosopher in medieval texts) were reintroduced by Arabic commentators and interpreters; Jewish scholars were instrumental in producing revolutionary theological ideas in the 12$^{th}$ century; the crusades were indisputably bloody and cruel, but they also instigated cultural meetings that became crucial to the development of European mentality, and the crude and primitive knights that went southeast met a sophisticated court culture that they brought home and made their own. So, as a result of the meetings with the others, modern enlightened Europe could slowly arise, partly through the so-called "renaissance of the twelfth" century. We find an example of such a view in one of the most influential books in modern research on the Middle Ages, R. W. Southern's *The Making of the Middle Ages* from 1953. The work was an important breakthrough due to its stress of the aspects of medieval thinking leading directly to 'modern' phenomena of rationalism and modern aesthetic and philosophical sensibility based on the relations between – 'us' (Western (Christians)) and non-Christians/Westerners considered as 'the others'.

There exists, however, another and more pessimistic interpretation of European medieval history which finds Southern's perspective to be idealizing and anachronistic. In this view, some of the most negative aspects of modern European history are actually foreboded in the Middle Ages. According to an optimistic viewpoint, twentieth century Europe is the result of the struggle for freedom and equality, often inspired by meeting 'others'. A contrasting position would claim a fundamentally opposite conception of Modern Europe, claiming instead that the most negative aspects of modern Europe are the result of the medieval heritage. This is, for instance, the thesis behind the work of the British historian R. I. Moore. In *The Formation of a Persecuting Society*, 1987, Moore provocatively claims that the processes of exclusion and persecution who in his view is so typical of twentieth century civilisation can be traced back to the same centuries that for Southern were the source of modern enlightenment and freedom.

According to Moore, execution and persecution (and not scholarly development and religious devotion) formed the ways in which a stumbling and as yet uncertain political and religious identity was formed. These are the kind of 'meetings' Moore is interested in investigating; the destructive and bloody meetings and persecutions of heretics, Jews, lepers/the sick, three of the significant persecuted groups in the early-modern history of Europe. For Moore, these groups made it possible for the representatives of the power structures of the time – the church and the aristocracy (both were internally divided, though) to show their unity as opposed to these divided (and dividing) groups.[1] Moore stresses that the persecution of these groups was not the result of the workings of the church or the aristocracy basically feeling threatened (related to economy, power, or the risk of losing of souls); for that role heretics and Jews were all too small groups. When it comes to the results of the 'persecuting' mechanisms of medieval societal structures Moore is clear: investigating the twelfth century is, according to him, actually a part of establishing a genealogy of the GULAG-camps and Auschwitz of the 20th century. Historians argue about this (see for instance Nirenberg 1996, Bouchard 1998, Jordan 2002) but as a literary scholar I will try not to lose myself in the complicated historical arguments that are partly beyond the reach of my academic competences. Instead I intend to find traces of the destructive dialogue of the power and the other in a specific literary representation of the period. By way of a literary example, I wish to show that signs of the threatening 'other' of medieval European mentality pop up in relatively unforeseen places. Before I do this it might be useful to specify the idea of the other or the others.

Tzvetan Todorov has conceptualized the importance of 'others' in general terms: "I can conceive of these others as an abstraction, … as the Other – other in relation to myself, to *me*; or else as a specific social group to which *we* do not belong. This group in turn can be integral to society: women versus men, the rich versus the poor, the mad versus the 'normal'; or it can be exterior to society, i.e., another society … outsiders whose language and customs I do not understand" (Todorov quoted in Camille 1989: 353).

Michael Camille, specifies this comprehensive, and rather abstract, model in *The Gothic Icon*, 1989, where the medieval fear of the other is divided into three categories: the 'others of the past', the 'geographical other', and the 'internal other'; to these three terms I wish to add a fourth category, the 'social other'. Below I will briefly present the categories.

Both the learned scholasticism and the popular imagination were much concerned about the other of the past. Medieval man admired, feared, and despised Greek and Roman culture which had at least one thing in common: namely the fact that a multitude of gods prevented them from understanding the absolute moral necessity and logical structure of monotheism. Medieval

---

[1]    Dante, in this sense, is a typical medieval thinker: in his *Divine Comedy*, reserved severe punishments for those historical figures that were supposedly 'dividing' and 'splitting up' coherent and organic religions/societies.

man was also deeply worried about the geographical other; he worried, from a certain historical point about the competition from Byzantine culture, a relation that reached the climax in the crusade of 1204, where Christian crusaders sacked the (Christian) city of Constantinople, capital of the so-called second Rome (see, for instance Heer 1991, Runciman 1951, Riley-Smith 1991). And at least as important were the impressions of Islamic culture, for instance found in the Moorish culture of the Iberian peninsula. The Christian fear was of course very real because Islamic warriors did indeed develop into a conquering military force that quickly approached the heart of Europe. Medieval man's understanding of the 'internal other' was focused on the Jews: it is well known that the terrible history of pogroms is a tradition commencing in the later middle ages, and several of the – still surviving – racist fantasies about the Jews can be traced back to the Middle Ages. Other 'internal' others include homosexuals, heretics, mad people, and lepers. It was, so to speak, an open list.

The fourth category is my own: what I propose to call the 'social other' cannot be defined geographically, temporally, ethnically or sexually. Instead, the social other is defined in relation to a particular social position, namely the one occupied by the courtly and the clerical elite of (most of) the middle ages. The social other is first of all the peasant, the worker, but also hard working traders and salesmen, who are characterised by surviving by earning money from their own work, would fall into this category of the *vileins* which may be translated into terms like 'brutes' or simply the non-noble.[2]

## Chrétien de Troyes and the Chivalric Novel

The material I wish to briefly discuss in this context is, as mentioned above, samples from the work of Chrétien de Troyes. We know almost nothing about this man except that he wrote in a northern old French dialect and that he wrote his five chivalric novels or romances, a genre he virtually invented, and a few poems from about 1160 to 1181. At first sight these texts may appear to be light-hearted tales in adventurous settings, with knights and virgins who act as nobly as they speak. The elegant rhymed verses seem perfectly suited to

---

[2]    According to Georges Duby, medieval ideology or mentality is constituted by a tripartite division of society: The chanting (clergy), the fighting (aristocracy) and the working layers of society. See Duby 1996.

function as entertainment, relaxation and hedonistic escapism for the courtly listeners to whom the texts were directed.[3] But a closer look will show that Chrétien, probably by a conscious effort, manages to introduce some of the violent and dichotomist elements of the medieval identity construction in his fictional texts.

I would like to begin my discussion by pointing to one of the puzzling but perhaps significant examples from Chrétien's hand, from the Epilogue of his romance *Cligès* (ca. 1170). *Cligès* is, in several ways, a rather exceptional romance in Chrétien's oeuvre. The Arthurian themes – *Cligès* is Chrétien's version of the Tristan and Isolde material – are almost absent, and structurally it differs in relation to the other romances. Furthermore, contrary to what he usually did, Chrétien produced an epilogue to the romance. Chrétien is famous for his sophisticated prologues, opening up a number of interesting concepts of structure, reading, and irony in his texts, while the finishing verses serve the practical purpose of simply closing the romances.[4]

After having concluded the main plot of the romance, the marriage of Fenice and Cligès, Chrétien, or rather his narrator, stresses the further meaning and importance of the story. First we have the famous conclusion, where Cligès is finally able to combine Fenice the lover and Fenice the lady or wife; in a sense the perfect solution of the Tristan and Iseult conflict. We would suppose, having the rest of Chrétien's work in mind, that the romance would end here, but it does not. Instead, the epilogue continues:

> Et chascun jor lor amors crut,
> Onques cil de li ne mescrut,
> Ne querela de nule chose;
> N'onques ne fu tenue anclose,
> Si com ont puis esté tenues
> Celes qu'aprés li sont venues;
> Einz puis n'i ot empereor
> N'eüst de sa fame peor
> Qu'ele nel deüst decevoir,

---

3     This is more or less the interpretation made by Erich Auerbach (1946) in his chapter on Chrétien in *Mimesis*, definitely one of the weaker parts of Auerbach's work.

4     For a discussion of the poetics of Chrétien, partly focused on the prologues, see Jørgen Bruhn: "Between Fiction and Deferral – *Erec et Enide*", Bruun and Fleischer (eds.): *The Cultural Heritage of Medieval Rituals*. Amsterdam: Brepols 2009.

Se il oï ramantevoir

Comant Fenice Alis deçut,

Primes par la poison qu'il but,

Et puis par l'autre traïson.

Por ce einsi com an prison

Est gardee an Constantinoble,

Ja n'iert tant haute ne tant noble,

L'empererriz, quex qu'ele soit:

L'empereres point ne s'i croit,

Tant con de celi li remanbre;

Toz jorz la fet garder en chanbre

Plus por peor que por le hasle,

Ne ja avoec li n'avra masle

Qui ne soit chastrez en anfance.

De ce n'est crienme ne dotance

Qu'Amors les lit an son lïen.

Ci fenist l'uevre Crestïen.[5]

Each day their love grew stronger. He never doubted her in any way or ever quarrelled with her over anything; she was never kept confined as many empresses since her have been. For since her days every emperor has been fearful of being deceived by his wife when he remembered how Fenice deceived Alis, first with the potion he drank, then later by that other ruse. Therefore every empress, whoever she is and regardless of her riches and nobility, is kept like a prisoner in Constantinople, for the emperor does not trust her when he recalls the story of Fenice. He keeps her confined each day to her chamber, more from fear than because he does not want her skin to darken, and allows no male to be with her unless he is a eunuch from childhood, since there is no fear or question that Love's snares will trap such men. Here ends Chrétien's work (*Cligès*, Kibler: 205).

The epilogue mimics the end of the medieval exemplum genre as it openly declares the meaning of the romance. The meaning of the text is, apparently, to explain the habit in Constantinople of imprisoning the emperors' wives. Consequently, the closing of the romance seems to criticize the un-chivalric, not to say tyrannical habit of the Byzantine Empire and thus stigmatizing the 'geographical (Eastern) other'. But is this to be read as a serious state-

---

5    See Chrétien de Troyes: *Cligès* in *Oeuvres complètes* (ed. Poirion), edition de Pléiade, Gallimard, Paris 1994, v. 6747-6768.

ment? It might be nothing but a joke concerning the exotic and utterly fictional habit of a 'barbaric' custom no longer in use. It could also be read as a hidden critique of any attempt, in East or in the West, to hold women captive against their will, and this reading would imply that if a man behaves like Alis, he *deserves* to be deceived. The passage might, however, contrary to what has just been said, also be read as a topos expressing misogynistic medieval thoughts on the nature of women (being deceiving and treacherous by nature), an oft-repeated, if not uncontested element in popular fabliaux and clerical writings. And finally: the mention of the eunuchs? Is it just a dab of colour on the description, or was it meant to impose some kind of castration anxiety on the male readers?[6]

I offer this fragment as one example amongst several in the work of Chrétien, where the other plays a more or less significant role. Chrétien refrains from being openly antagonistic towards any of the groups that become the target of his ironic descriptions, which has made it difficult to pinpoint with any accuracy Chrétien's 'own' ideological position.

## Meeting the other in *Yvain*

In the following I shall focus on *Yvain*, also known as the *Knight of the Lion*, probably written shortly after *Cligès* in the last third of the twelfth century. This chivalric romance is, like *Cligès,* set in the days of the mythical King Arthur, that is, about 600 years before Chrétien writes his text. It describes the young, ambitious and impatient knight-to-be (juvene) Yvain. After many violent and exotic adventures including a nervous breakdown, a sexual massage bringing the 'dead' Yvain back to life, living with a hermit in the woods, Yvain, who has by then become the Knight of the Lion, finally grows up to assume the responsibilities of a mature knight (chevalier). Pursuing the question of identity as based on meeting the other, it is significant that the romance produces several scenes and narrative structures that are clearly centred on the question of identity and the other.

On the surface, *Yvain* deals with conventional chivalric questions: a young bachelor warrior is on the look-out for adventures that may qualify him both in the eyes of the Arthurian community he is part of, and in the eyes of suitable

---

6    In my *Lovely Violence. Chrétien de Troyes' Critical Romances*, 2010, I pursue the discussion of gender and chivalric love in *Cligès* further.

(that is: wealthy) women. The aim is to be knighted possibly as a result of the joint recognition of both the Arthurian community *and* finding a woman who may marry him. Consequently, the romance may be understood as a kind of Bildungs-story; Yvain must learn that in order to be a true knight, superficial adventures or circumstantial violent behaviour must be avoided, and instead a responsible, Christian approach to his role as a knight must be pursued. It appears, however, as if Chrétien has deliberately complicated what could have been a relatively straight-forward plot.[7]

In other words, in the personal 'Bildung' of Yvain, Chrétien offers two possible ontological positions that Yvain – and the readers or listeners – must either negate or follow – namely a subhuman and a superhuman agenda. The *superhuman* possibility would mean that Yvain was to follow the exemplary life, living by himself in the woods like the hermit whom Yvain meets during his prolonged personal breakdown. The hermit seems to represent an ideal, elevated beyond the base human needs: he lives primitively in the woods and represents a life informed by the medieval *imitatio Christi* ideal, which was also crucial to several of the monastic movements of the time: namely to live a simple, even poor, anti-materialistic life, totally devoted to the praise of God. The young Yvain searches immaturely for his own identity by actively *pursuing* adventures instead of simply meeting the necessary and ethically demanding challenges partly introduced to him during the sojourn with the hermit.

In the following I want to discuss the novel's construction of the *subhuman* position that may have bearings on the discussion of identity and mentality in a wider European context. Earlier in the text we find another essential meeting in the progress of Yvain. The hermit-episode leads Yvain to find his own way of becoming a responsible, mature knight. Partly hidden in this seemingly successful individuation process ruled by love and chivalric norms, we meet the subhuman choice. The subhuman represents the negative, problematic and destructive otherness, and it seems to be constructed in direct opposition to the Hermit's utopian negation of all base and bodily needs which are instead transformed into religious transcendence. The subhuman opportunity is represented in an adventure that befell Yvain's cousin, Calogrenant who in a subsequent reflection of Yvain *pursues* adventures. On this quest he meets

---

7    In Bruhn 2010 I discuss *Yvain* from a somewhat different point of view, considering the representation of violence as a partly concealed, partly critizied element in the text. My inspiration to construct a sub-human reading of *Yvain* comes partly from Eugene Vance: *From Topic to Tale. Logic and Narrativity in the Middle Ages*, 1987.

an indefinable creature that is so to speak beyond the conventional categories of the chivalric world. The creature that guards wild bulls on a meadow has a

Si vi qu'il ot grosse la teste,

Plus que roncins la teste

Chevox mechiez et front pelé,

S'ot pres de deus espanz de lé

Oroilles mossues et granz

Autiex com a uns olifanz,

Les sorcix granz et le vis plat,

Ialz de çuete, et nes de chat,

Boche fandue come lous,

Dans de sengler aguz et rous.[8]

Head was larger than a nag's or other beast's. His hair was unkempt and his bare forehead was more than two spans wide; his ears were as hairy and as huge as an elephant's; his eyebrows heavy and his face flat. He had the eyes of an owl and the nose of a cat, jowls split like a wolf's, with the sharp reddish teeth of a boar (*Yvain*, Kibler: 227).

The creature wears clothing consisting of "freshly skinned" pelts. Questioned directly whether he is good or bad, he answers surprisingly (and not directly to the point) by saying: "I am a man". What kind of man is disclosed earlier in a passage, I left out above: "A peasant who resembled a Moor, ugly and hideous in the extreme – such an ugly creature that he cannot be described in words – was seated on a stump, with a great club in his hand." (*Yvain,* Kibler: 227; "Uns vileins, qui resanbloit Mor,/ Leiz et hideus a desmesure,/ Einsi tres leide creature/ Qu'an ne porroit dire de boche/ Assis s'estoit so rune çoche,/ Une grant maçue en sa main").[9]

This marvellous and strange figure first of all incarnates the 'social other' in the aristocratic social system. The peasant, or *vileins* in Old French, was defined by being neither clerical, nor aristocratic, and as such was a kind of unwanted, but highly necessary (as working force) part of medieval mental and social categorisations. This particular *vileins* has another trait, though, which is probably no coincidence: he is directly compared to a Moor (Old French: 'mor'), one of several medieval pejorative descriptions of Muslims – who is one of the threat-

---

8 See Chrétien de Troyes: *Yvain* in *Oeuvres complètes* 1994, v. 293-302.

9 See Chrétien de Troyes, *Yvain* in *Oeuvres complètes* 1994, v. 286-291.

ening 'geographical others' of the medieval imaginary. But the peasant is also very clearly 'animalised' and thus transformed into a subhuman category.

The adventures of Yvain's cousin Calogrenant is meant to be a critique of chivalric violence, but the subhuman Moor has a deeper symbolic message, too: on a deeper level he, or 'it', symbolizes the role of the 'other' of the courtly culture, which strongly opposes itself to both peasants, the exotic but also dangerous Muslims – and even animals. Under one heading these three examples of others may be understood as the threat of the primitive, natural aspect of human life (which is not surprising since chivalric culture is defined by an attempt to civilize the primitive aspects of violent masculinity).[10] In Freudian terms Calogrenant (or is it the author Chrétien?) thus seems to meet his own unconscious fears in symbolic form when facing this unknown beastly figure.

This scene may work as an example of a prevalent trend in medieval literature and thinking, and therefore it should also make us aware that texts like these are not only entertaining escapism. *Yvain* seems to function on several levels at the same time, partly divided into different socially defined receptive positions (see the introductory chapter in Bruhn, 2010). The historical context is of course significant; Chrétien, who probably lived on the patronage goodwill of one or more of the wealthy courts of Europe, wrote his texts in the early consolidating phase of European aristocracy, a class which was partly founded on chivalric codes appeased with Christian ideals. But this is of course also the time of the crusades the long period where 'Europeans', i.e. Christians, from Norway to Italy, could agree upon one thing, if on nothing else: to travel towards southeast, via Constantinople to Jerusalem, on what was not yet in the Middle Ages called crusades but instead 'armed pilgrimage' (for two opposing views on the crusades, see Runciman 1951 and Riley-Smith 1991). Dreams of worldly material goods blended with profound religious conviction in these pilgrim-travels that in 1204 ended up destroying the *Christian* city Constantinople. 'The other' of medieval European culture was encountered in these pilgrimages, and if geopolitical or ideological dogmas demanded it, even fellow Christians could be 'the other'.

My brief discussion of medieval questions of identity and the other has attempted to exemplify the banal fact that identity does not create itself; an identity, be it a personal, cultural or national identity, is construed as an imaginary or imagined entity or community that per definition needs to create borders beyond which the others reside. The borders may be temporal or

---

[10]   Lucidly discussed in the work of the cultural historian R. W. Kaeuper (1999).

geographical, social or ethnic, religious or biological, and are of course fluid, moving, almost impossible to establish as firm facts – just like media borders or genre borders.

The 'other' functions as a trope by which the 'same' can construe a narrative with friends and enemies, an acceptable prehistory and, often, an optimistic future. To meet the others in such constructions results in either positive encounters where knowledge, goods and gods are exchanged; but there will also be negative situations, where the nature, history and intentions of the other are consciously or unconsciously perverted and misconstrued. In Chrétien's text the open meetings and the exchanges inform what may be called the explicit surface of the text, whereas a darker construction of the dangerous other lies under the surface, in almost imperceptible signs of the text.

Finally, a more general question arises that I have already mentioned above: is it possible to glimpse the contours of a more general form of exclusion and inclusion? In other words, is the medieval process of understanding and misunderstanding 'the other', which I have exemplified briefly by way of Chrétien de Troyes' chivalric novel, typical? According to R. I. Moore, it is. Moore, whose work I referred to above, does not limit himself to describing the medieval background of what he considers to be the persecuting nature of contemporary European societies, he also tries to define the mechanism as such. Moore combines ideas of the French sociologists and historians Émile Durkheim and Michel Foucault and concludes that all societies exclude parts of their population in order to create an identity. Moreover, he states that societies have a tendency to create threats by way of discursive constructions which veil unconscious and often impenetrable power relations.

As a result, Moore provides a classical definition of the society of persecution. The exclusion and persecution of those groups that are defined, in a given moment, as 'the other', express a desire to hide the real social and ideological mechanisms ruling a given society. Consequently, medieval persecutions of the 'other' were not, as has been proposed, the result of popular fear or anger: *vox populi* was just an excuse for the church and the aristocracy to use these scapegoated others for their own purposes. Is Moore too conspiracy-prone? Does he paint a too gloomy picture of both the Middle Ages and our own epoch? He might be. But Moore's, and other scholars' attempt to rethink the medieval cultural and political landscapes in order to approach new understandings of our own epoch may inspire us to see that Europe, in the 21st century, still suffers from the effects of long standing excluding mechanisms, where ethnic, sexual or religious otherness are put to use in order to divert our attention from socially defined, historical conflicts.

# Bibliography

Auerbach, E. (2003 [1946]): *Mimesis*. Princeton: Princeton University Press.

Bennett, J. M. and C. W. Hollister (2006): *Medieval Europe. A Short History*. Boston: McGraw-Hill.

Bouchard, C. B. (1998): *Strong of Body, Brave & Noble. Chivalry and Society in Medieval France*. Ithaca: Cornell University Press.

Bruhn, J. (2010): *Lovely Violence. Chrétien de Troyes' Critical Romances*. Cambridge: Cambridge Scholars Publishing.

Bruhn, J. (2009): "Between Fiction and Deferral – *Erec et Enide*". In: Bruun and Fleischer (eds.): *The Cultural Heritage of Medieval Rituals*. Amsterdam: Brepols.

Camille, M. (1989): *The Gothic Idol. Ideology and Image-making in Medieval Art*. Cambridge: Cambridge University Press.

Cantor, N. F. (1991): *Inventing the Middle Ages. The Lives, Works, and Ideas of the Great Medievalists of the Twentieth Century*. New York: Quill.

Cardini, F. (1990): "The Warrior and the Knight". In: *Medieval Callings* ed. by Jacques Le Goff. Chicago: Chicago University Press.

Chrétien de Troyes (1991): *Arthurian Romances*, ed. and trans. by William W. Kibler except *Erec and Enide*, trans. by Carleton W. Carroll. London: Penguin Books.

Chrétien de Troyes (1994): *Oeuvres complètes* (ed. Poirion). Paris: Gallimard.

Duby, Georges (1996): "À propos de l'amour dit courtois", "Que sait-on de l'amour en France au xiieme siècle? and "*Les trois ordres ou l'imaginaire du féodalisme*. In: Georges Duby: *Féodalité*. Paris: Quarto Gallimard.

Eco, Umberto (1986): "Dreaming the Middle Ages". In: *Travels in Hyperreality*, transl. by W. Weaver. NY: Harcourt Brace.

Hartling, S.: "L'Autorité dissimulée – l'autorité manifeste. L'écriture de la violence chez Yasmina Khadra" doctoral thesis. Linnæus University Press 2012.

Heer, F. (1991 [1961]): *The Medieval World: Europe 1100-1300*. England: Weidenfeld.

Jordan, W. C. (2002): "'Europe' in the Middle Ages". In: Anthony Pagden (ed.): *The Idea of Europe. From Antiquity to the European Union*. Cambridge and New York: Woodrow Wilson Press and Cambridge University Press.

Keen, M. (1984): *Chivalry*. USA: Yale University Press.

Moore, R. I. (1987): *The Formation of a Persecuting Society: Power and Deviance in Western Europe, 950-1250*. Oxford: Oxford University Press.

Nirenberg, D. (1996): *Communities of Violence: Persecution of Minorities in the Middle Ages*. Princeton: Princeton University Press.

Nykrog, P. (1996): *Chrétien de Troyes. Romancier discutable*, chapter 1 ("Chrétien chez les médiévistes"). Paris: Droz.

Riley-Smith, J (1990): *The Crusades, a Short History*. London: Athlone.

Runciman, S. (1988 [1951]): *A History of the Crusades*. Cambridge and New York: Cambridge University Press.

Southern, R. W. (1953): *The Making of the Middle Ages*. London: Hutchinson's University Library.

Topsfield, L. T. (1981): *Chrétien de Troyes: a Study of the Arthurian Romances*. Cambridge: Cambridge University Press.

Vance, E. (1987): *From Topic to Tale. Logic and Narrativity in the Middle Ages*. Minnesota: Minnesota University Press.

# Pilgrims' Progress: Leaving the Old World for the New World, with Robert Cushman[1]

*Øyunn Hestetun*

But now we are all in all places strangers and pilgrims, travellers and sojourners, most properly, having no dwelling but in this earthen tabernacle … (Robert Cushman 1963: 89).

The "strangers and pilgrims, travellers and sojourners" of the above epigraph were a group of English Puritan separatists who left Europe for the New World in 1620 and laid the foundation of the Plymouth Plantation. They are commonly known as the *Mayflower* Pilgrims, in reference to the name of the vessel that brought them across the Atlantic and to their religious dissident status. The epigraph is taken from a short piece entitled "Reasons and Considerations Touching the Lawfulness of Removing out of England into the Parts of America," signed with the initials R. C. The author has been identified as Robert Cushman, and his piece appeared in a small volume generally referred to as *Mourt's Relation*, published in London in 1622.[2] When it comes to the notion of "Europe's interior others" – understood in terms of positioning and legitimacy in relation to religious, social, and political structures of power – Robert Cushman and his fellow Pilgrims represent an interesting case in point. As will be argued below, Cushman's "Reasons and Considerations" – a text largely forgotten today – raises a number of questions regarding religious intolerance and discourses of othering at home and abroad in early modern Europe. Although Cushman and his fellow separatists represented a perse-

---

[1]  The title alludes to John Bunyan's *The Pilgrim's Progress from This World to That Which Is to Come*, which was published in 1678. A converted Baptist, Bunyan was – like the *Mayflower* Pilgrims – a Puritan separatist, and he wrote his Christian allegory whilst imprisoned for his lay preaching.

[2]  The title page of the original 1622 printing carries the longer title, descriptive of its contents: *A Relation or Iournall of the beginning and proceedings of the English Plantation setled at Plimoth in New England, by certaine English Aduenturers both Merchants and others. With their difficult passage, their safe ariuall, their ioyfull building of, and comfortable planting themselues in the now well defended Towne of New Plimoth* (Heath, ed. 1963: xxvii).

cuted religious minority at home, his tract, which is primarily addressed to an audience at home, presents nothing less than an apology for British colonial expansion and an endorsement of settlement in foreign parts. In order to grasp the significance of Cushman's remarks on the venture he was part of, however, it is well worth first to inquire into the circumstances that may have led this group of religious dissenters to decide to leave Europe.

## Religious Intolerance and Colonial Expansionism

In looking back at European history over the last few centuries, one will find that religious zeal and intolerance – which could be considered two sides of the same coin – have repeatedly given rise to conflict at the national as well as the international levels. Oppression and persecution have time and again been legitimized by Holy Scripture, and religion has served as motivation and driving force of mechanisms of othering by which religious dissidents have been relegated to the position of "interior others." During the early modern period Europe underwent changes that served to consolidate not only the state, but also the church, be it Catholic or Reformed, leading to a greater degree of religious conformity. The Protestant Reformation had brought an upsurge of dissident sectarian movements, and, as Benjamin J. Kaplan observes, the circumstances under which dissenters lived were "ranging from comfortable and secure to furtive and dangerous" (Kaplan 2004: 497). Kaplan notes that the general climate of intolerance is reflected in the term heretic, derived from the Greek *hairesis*, which means "choice." Considered to have made the "wrong" choice, heretics tended to be looked upon as rebels or blasphemers, and, accordingly, "intolerance was raised to the status of an essential mark of true piety" (Kaplan 2004: 491). In the early modern period the general understanding of religious tolerance was, in other words, radically different from today. As Kaplan explains: "Defined as respect for the right of all humans to religious freedom, it [tolerance] is a modern phenomenon born of the Enlightenment" (Kaplan 2004: 501-52). As separatist dissenters, the *Mayflower* Pilgrims held the status of heretics, and religious intolerance was the primary reason why they left for the New World in 1620, seeking a place where they could practice their religion without persecution while remaining English subjects.

Early seventeenth-century Europe was also impacted by the colonizing adventures undertaken in the wake of the Age of Exploration. This was a time when England along with other European nations expanded their territories by establishing colonies abroad, thereby laying the foundation for a colonial empire that would reach its peak in the late nineteenth century. The first permanent English colony on the American continent was established in 1607 and named Jamestown, located in today's Virginia. The first colony that provided asylum and protection for a group of "Europe's others," however, was the second permanent English colony, located further up the coast in an area that had become known as New England. This is where the *Mayflower* Pilgrims set foot on Plymouth Rock in 1620 and founded the Plymouth Plantation, which remained a separate colony until 1692, when it was merged under a new charter with the nearby Massachusetts Bay colony, originally established in 1630.

It is important to keep in mind that the European colonies in the New World, although geographically located on a distant continent, were legally as well as for all practical purposes considered as parts of the mother country. Hence Jamestown, the Plymouth Plantation, and other English colonies remained within the sovereign state of the Kingdom of England, and from 1707 the Kingdom of Great Britain, until the 13 colonies declared their independence in 1776. Accordingly, the English crown, which opened up for settlement by issuing royal charters, would retain jurisdiction in the colonies. Hence local governments enjoyed only limited powers, and were legally and formally subsumed under the power of the crown.[3] Typically, the joint stock companies that financed and furnished the adventures in the interest of monetary gain collected their revenue in the home country, and the settlers, although transported to distant locations, remained English subjects. As John Demos puts it, "most residents of the British colonies in America continued to think of themselves as transplanted Englishmen, as carriers of *the* culture to a distant land. Theirs was indeed a 'New World,' but it was new in a territorial sense alone" (Demos 1972: 1). This was the case until well into the eighteenth century, when the American Revolution brought an end to British rule.

---

[3]  The Plymouth Pilgrims did not have their own Crown charter, which means that they were largely dependent on the London merchants and adventurers who invested in the project (see e.g. Bangs 2009: 588-95, 647-49). Dawson notes: "… the parties that had joined in the New Plymouth venture … first defined their relations by agreement and only later derived a patent from the Corporation for New England" (Dawson 1998: 125).

## Radical Puritanism, Separatism, and the Religious "Other"

The Church of England had undergone decisive changes after it was separated from the Roman Catholic Church in 1534, when King Henry VIII replaced the pope as head of the church. Even as Reformed Protestantism was adopted by the established Church, some felt that reforms had not been far-reaching enough. As noted by John Coffey and Paul C. M. Lim, Puritan was a new term that came into use in the 1560s to designate certain people both within and outside the church, mainly as "an insult launched at nonconformist clergy" (Coffey and Lim 2008: 1). With time, however, Puritanism has come to designate the form of Reformed Protestantism embraced by the Church of England, which was "aligned with the continental Calvinist churches rather than with the Lutherans" (Coffey and Lim 2008: 2). They further explain:

> Puritanism is the name we give to a distinctive and particularly intense variety of early modern Reformed Protestantism which originated within the unique context of the Church of England but spilled out beyond it, branching off into divergent dissenting streams, and overflowing into other lands and foreign churches (Coffey and Lim 2008: 1-2).

Whereas most Puritans advocated the purification of the Church from within, others chose to break with the established church altogether and became separatists. It is primarily these sectarian communities, which emerged especially in the East Midlands in the latter part of the sixteenth centuries, that could be said to represent Europe's "interior others." To the more radical Puritans, the extent to which the English Church had been "purified" did not suffice. Their followers were persecuted on the basis of their religious conviction, and lay preachers in particular risked imprisonment for spreading the word of their faith.[4] These were people who pursued the ideal of evangelical simplicity and the cultivation of personal sanctity. To sum up some of their grievances against the conservatism of the established church, they wanted no priest or clergy to act as mediator between the individual soul and God, and they resented all forms of ritual, ceremony, or other types of outward display. Instead, they cultivated the plain sermon and the direct communion with God.

The *Mayflower* Pilgrims were among the radical Puritans who formed separatist congregations, which means that they were among the dissenters that

---

[4]   Bangs notes that Robert Cushman was imprisoned in Canterbury as "non-conformist lay-man ... 'for certain reasons'" (Bangs 2009: 47).

suffered the more severe consequences of religious intolerance, especially after the passing of The Act Against Puritans in 1593, which stipulated mandatory church attendance and forbade religious congregations outside the established church (see e.g. Bangs 2009: 11-12). In his historical account *Of Plymouth Plantation* William Bradford, elected governor of the colony a few months after its foundation, describes the conditions members of the Scrooby congregation endured before seeking refuge in the Netherlands:[5]

> But after these things they could not long continue in any peaceable condition, but were hunted and persecuted on every side, so as their former afflictions were but as flea-bitings in comparison of these which now came upon them. For some were taken and clapped up in prison, others had their houses beset and watched night and day, and hardly escaped their hands; and the most were fain to flee and leave their houses and habitations, and the means of their livelihood (Bradford 1981: 9).

A group of Scrooby separatists in the end decided to leave their home country; having first fled to Amsterdam in 1607, they moved on to Leiden in 1608. Bradford further explains their motivation for migration:

> Yet seeing themselves thus molested, and that there was no hope of their continuance there, by a joint consent they resolved to go into the Low Countries, where they heard was freedom of religion for all men; as also how sundry from London and other parts of the land had been exiled and persecuted for the same cause, and were gone thither, and lived at Amsterdam and in other places of the land. So after they had continued together about a year, and kept their meetings every Sabbath in one place or other, exercising the worship of God amongst themselves, notwithstanding all the diligence and malice of their adversaries, they seeing they could no longer continue in that condition, they resolved to get over into Holland as they could. Which was in the year 1607 and 1608 ... (Bradford 1981: 10).

In Leiden the separatists enjoyed religious freedom, although precarious, because of growing political and religious unrest. As Jeremy Dupertuis Bangs puts it, "the Netherlands was no longer safe" (2009: 573). An added concern was that they saw the young ones leave their closely knit community to seek employment, and many among them started to fear that they would be

---

5    Bradford provides an account of their background in England, their sojourn in Holland, and the early years of the Plymouth colony. Written between 1630 and 1661, the manuscript was first published in 1856.

assimilated into the local population and no longer retain their English culture and identity. Consequently, they began to seek means of relocating (see e.g. Bangs 2009: 569-75). Inspired by Captain John Smith's 1616 account of his travels up the New England coast and similar tracts, they started seeking opportunities for migration to the New World, at first by negotiating with the Virginia Company that stood behind the Jamestown settlement. In the end they obtained a contract with some London merchants and adventurers willing to invest in the venture for the passage across the Atlantic (see e.g. Bangs 2009: 590-95; Fender 1983: 35-36). Paradoxically, then, this particular group of England's "interior others" first sought refuge within Europe, in another European nation, only to return to England little more than a decade later. However, they chose not to return to their place of origin, but instead to a distant outpost, in which the authorities of the law and the church would not be in a position to keep a close eye on their religious practices.

Robert Cushman, who had joined the Leiden community in 1609, acted as one of their agents in negotiating the contract for passage to the New World.[6] He was not himself one of the *Mayflower* Pilgrims, although he was supposed to have been part of this first contingent of migrants. But the *Speedwell*, the sister ship of the *Mayflower*, had to return to port for repairs, and he stayed behind with those who were detained or chose to return to Leiden. About a year later he crossed the Atlantic with a new flock of migrants and spent about a month with the colonists in the Plymouth Plantation in November and December of 1621.[7] It was on his return to London in early 1622 that the short tract attributed to him was published as part of *Mourt's Relation*. As Stephen Fender points out, it was probably first and foremost intended "to inform the backers of their success, and to encourage new recruits" (Fender 1983: 36). Hence, the entire publication, including Cushman's contribution, could be considered a promotional script, encouraging others – prospective investors and settlers alike – to try their luck in the New World.

---

[6]   For Cushman's part in arranging the venture, see e.g. Bradford 1981: chapters 5-8; Bangs 2009: 582-604; Lovejoy 1990: 233-34.

[7]   See e.g. Bradford 1981: 101-05; Bangs 2009: 647; Lovejoy 1990. Bradford includes a note about Cushman's death in 1625 (Bradford 1981: 101-05; 200).

## Cushman's "Reasons and Considerations": Apology, Promotion, and Calling

Under the title of "Reasons and Considerations Touching the Lawfulness of Removing out of England into the Parts of America," Cushman presents his views on the legal and religious implications of their venture. The opening sections of Cushman's piece, which consider the legal aspects of settling in foreign parts, to a large extent take the form of an apology for colonization and a promotional tract for settlement. Acknowledging that there are those who speak against English settlements on colonized land, he defines his task as a defense of their undertaking. Accordingly, he presents his rationale for "the going into, and inhabiting of, foreign desert places," declaring that, as far as he knows, his is "the first attempt that hath been made ... to defend those enterprises" (Cushman 1963: 88). To the extent that the text is also motivated by the aim of attracting new settlers, it also reads as a promotional tract. Despite this obvious intent, however, Cushman's text is markedly different from the typical promotional script, written by explorers like Captain John Smith who was instrumental in the founding of the Jamestown colony (see e.g. Fender 1983: 8-31), while another text included in *Mourt's Relation* – a letter attributed to Edward Winslow – fits this overall pattern. Designed to attract prospective settlers, this genre of writing normally took the form of travelogue or report, and tended to abound in catalogues enumerating in detail the wonders of the foreign lands.

Instead of providing topographical description, however, Cushman sets himself the task of delivering a convincing argument to legally justify the venture he was part of. Notably, the first of two passages annotated with the word "Object" in the margin of the text – indicating that the writer will state the aim of his discussion – reads: "And so here falleth in our question, how a man that is here born and bred, and hath lived some years, may remove himself into another country" (Cushman 1963: 90). Apparently echoing frequent objections to settlement in the colonies, Cushman also presents a second "Object" by posing the question: "But some will say, what right have I to go live in the heathens' country?" (Cushman 1963: 91). When he chooses to open his legal defense by stating that the land in question "is proper to the king of England," it should be read as a gesture of recognition that it was only because they were English citizens that the Leiden separatists, like other settlers, had been granted legal permission to establish a colony in the first place.[8]

By relocating to the outskirts of the empire, the Pilgrims not only secured the possibility of preaching and practicing their religion amongst themselves without the threat of persecution. In their new abode they also found a way to spread the gospel to the indigenous population, representing Europe's "external others." Closely related to the judicial side of the matter, then, is the fact that the Pilgrims considered themselves to be on a holy mission, which at the time would be deemed a legitimate civilizing enterprise. For obvious reasons, given that *Mourt's Relation* was published in London, Cushman never directly addresses the separatist quarrel with the Church of England that Bradford describes in his history of the colony. As Dwight B. Heath remarks: "In such an effort to excite more prospective settlers, it would have been sound public relations to minimize the degree of identification between the plantation and the 'Saints,' who were popularly scorned as heretics and criminals" (Heath, "Editor's Introduction" 1963: xv). He only alludes to the conflict when arguing that the zeal that has gone into "the bitter contention that hath been about religion" could be transformed into something good if it were "turned against the rude barbarism of the heathens." The implication is that their religious calling authorizes their enterprise, as spreading the knowledge of the Gospel to the infidels on foreign shores would lead to "exceeding great joy and gladness" (Cushman 1963: 95). Especially those among them who are not bound by duties at home, and "live as outcasts, nobodies, eye-sores" would be able to find a new calling by which they could fulfill God's purpose of being of "service to others and his own glory" and take part in the project of bringing "salvation [to] the sons of Adam in that New World" (Cushman 1963: 90-91). Although they could "daily pray for the conversion of the heathens" while at home, their mission work would obviously be rendered more effective by direct contact with the prospective converts. Besides, it would be more expedient for the missionary Pilgrims to travel to foreign lands than it would be to have "the heathens" come to England, since, as he argues, "our land is full; to them we may go, their land is empty," and he adds: "their land is spacious and void,

---

[8]    As mentioned above, the Plymouth colonists did not have charter of their own, but as Fender points out, the king "would not refuse them permission for unmolested passage" (Fender 1983: 36). It should also be noted that during the early years of the colony, as Bangs states, "the land was all still mortgaged to the investment company known as the adventurers" (Bangs 2009: 648).

and there are few and do but run over the grass, as do also the foxes and wild beasts" (Cushman 1963: 91).

An obvious question in the light of statements such as these is to what extent the Pilgrim settlers recognized the rights and privileges of the indigenous other. In spite of Cushman's use of terms like "empty" and "void" in the passages cited above, it is unlikely that the implication is that the land is conceived as *terra nulla*, especially as Cushman directly addresses the question of sovereignty and the legal rights that entitle the settlers to occupy the land. It would be difficult to prove Cushman's claim, but he explicitly states that the local leader Massasoit, titled "imperial governor," "hath acknowledged the King's Majesty of England to be his master and commander," and that he has done so even "in writing" (Cushman 1963: 92). He makes a point of insisting that their "warring" with the indigenous population is "after another manner, namely by friendly usage, love, peace, honest and just carriages, good counsel, etc." (Cushman 1963: 92). The local Indian leader – now referred to as "the emperor" – allows the presence of the English settlers and their taking possession of the land that they need. The reason for this peaceful situation, he argues, is that the Indian leader recognizes the settlers as "the servants of James, King of England" who owns title to the land (Cushman 1963: 92-93). Besides, because the settlers have behaved in a manner that is "just, honest, kind, and peaceable," the Indian leader, he writes, "loves our company."[9] Summing up, Cushman spells out a three-step rationale for their migration and taking possession of the land:

> It being then, first, a vast and empty chaos; secondly, acknowledged the right of our sovereign king; thirdly, by a peaceable composition in part possessed of divers of his loving subjects, I see not who can doubt or call in question the lawfulness of inhabiting or dwelling there ... (Cushman 1963: 93).

The legal foundation of the colonizing venture as laid out in this passage represents a case in point for the kind of attitudes regarding territorial expansionism that were predominant in Europe at the time. In the light of history, it is apparent that some of the attitudes and ideological implications embedded in the construction of Europe's "topographical other," for instance as based on the dichotomy of civilization versus wilderness and savagery, fall into the category of colonizing or orientalizing discourse.

---

[9]   However, as Emory Eliot, among others, points out, the peace was short-lived, and armed conflict became a real threat already in the mid-1620s (Eliot 2002: 11).

The same applies to Europe's construction of its "human other." There is no denying that the image that Cushman renders of the indigenous other, as exemplified in some of the statements cited above, is somewhat troubling. Interestingly, Karen Ordahl Kupperman notes in her study of cultural encounters and exchange between English settlers and the American indigenous population in early colonial times, that, on the basis of various contemporary accounts:

> … one could "prove" that the English admired the Indians, that they had contempt for the Indians, that the Indians were childlike, that they were savage, that they were noble, that the English treated the Indians well, that they treated the Indians badly, and so on (Kupperman 2000: 10).

Cushman's text conforms to the attitudes and structural patterns that Kupperman finds in these early writings when she says that the English take the role of "supplicants rather than conquerors," and the Americans are not portrayed as passive victims, but as active participants in cultural debate. Nonetheless, as she observes, "even the most sympathetic writers easily moved into chilling denigration or worse" (Kupperman 2000: 14; 15). If the contemporary construction of the exotic other tended to be contradictory rather than consistent, it is no wonder that some of the ambiguity and conflicting ideas can also be traced in Cushman's text. Drawing on an implied opposition between civilization and wilderness, and referring to the precepts of "the ancient patriarchs," Cushman insists that the natives are "not industrious" and that they are lacking in "art, science, skills or faculty to use either the land or the commodities of it." To his mind, it is therefore reasonable that those who possess such abilities and talents are justified in taking control: "… so it is lawful now to take a land which none useth, and make use of it" (Cushman 1963: 91-92). Still, Cushman emphasizes that when it comes to the legal relationship between them, the settlers and the American Indians share the common aim that they may all "live in peace in that land" (Cushman 1963: 92).

In spite of the attitudes expressed in statements such as these, however, it is worth noticing that the "poor blind infidels," as Cushman calls them (Cushman 1963: 93), are considered human souls to be brought to salvation rather than less-than-human others. For the Pilgrims also entertain another and higher aim, of a spiritual nature, namely that the indigenous population not only "yield subjection to an earthly prince, but that as voluntaries they may be persuaded at length to embrace the Prince of Peace, Christ Jesus, and rest in peace with him forever" (Cushman 1963: 92).[10] Hence, motivated by their commitment to their religious calling, Europe's "interior others" take on the role of Europe's missionaries to the "external others" on the outskirts of empire. Interestingly, it almost appears as though a discourse of othering has left its traces on the parts that focus on legal matters and the Kingdom of England, whereas a more egalitarian discourse, according to which all humans are considered to be on equal terms, is employed when Cushman turns to religious matters and the kingdom of God. Regardless, as settlers in foreign territories the Pilgrims served as instruments in the colonial enterprise, and although they may have looked upon the indigenous population as equals in the eyes of God, their missionary endeavor must nonetheless be considered as part and parcel of an imperialist civilizing scheme.

## Cushman's "Reasons and Considerations": Religious Sermon

While Cushman applies his persuasive powers in defending the legal aspects of the colonizing enterprise and the settlers' relationship to the indigenous population, he also reflects on the religious significance for the Pilgrims themselves of their venture in the New World, and expresses his ideals for their religious community and their future in their new abode. These ideals are most clearly spelled out in a sermon he delivered during his short sojourn in the colony, commonly referred to as "The Sin and Danger of Self-Love," in which he, as Bangs puts it, "urged the colonists to work together for the common good rather than to concentrate on individualistic profit-taking" (Bangs 2009: 648). Published on his return to London in 1622 under the title of *A Sermon Preached at Plimmoth in New-England December 9, 1621*, this is considered the first printing of a sermon preached on New England soil.[11] But religious ideals and moral precepts are expressed even in his "Reasons and Considerations," for instance when he admonishes his readers to heed how "a man must not respect only to

---

10  Bangs points to a contradiction between creed and practice that Cushman does not dwell upon: "The Calvinist doctrine of predestination made it questionable whether missionary activity could be either effective or commendable" (Bangs 2009: 650).

11  The title page of the original 1622 printing provides the additional information: "In an assemblie of his Maiesties faithfull Subjects, there inhabiting. Wherein is shewed the danger of selfe-loue, and the sweetnesse of true Friendship." The sermon was reprinted in 1846 under the title of *The Sin and Danger of Self-Love: Described, in a Sermon Preached at Plimmoth, in New-England, 1621.*

live, and do good to himself," but should also see to it that he would "live to do most good to others" (Cushman 1963: 90). Hence, this early text could be considered a prime example of the kind of literature that was to develop in the New England colonies, which according to Richard Slotkin typically consisted of "theological argument and polemic, in sermon form" (Slotkin 1996: 65).

On close examination it becomes evident that Cushman's "Reasons and Considerations" comes close to the sermon form not only in its ideational content. It also relies on tropes and structural elements borrowed from the generic conventions of the sermon, to the extent that Heath, for instance, in his "Editor's Introduction" describes the text as "a thinly veiled promotional tract organized like a sermon, which cites Scripture to justify the plantation and to persuade others to follow" (Heath 1963: xi).[12] Perry Miller, in *The New England Mind: The Seventeenth Century*, provides an overview of the characteristic features of the Puritan sermon. Generally referred to as the "plain style" the basic framework of this variety of the sermon consists of "doctrine, reasons, and uses," and the text "is mechanically and rigidly divided into sections and subheads, and appears on the printed page more like a lawyer's brief than a work of art" (Miller 1970: 332). It would typically begin with scriptural citation and exposition, which would serve as an "opening" of the text by "rewording of the texts into doctrinal statements," whereby its contents would be made accessible to the listeners (Miller 1970: 344). Next it would turn to "reason" and "proof," complemented with "uses or applications," all provided in "numbered sequence" (Miller 1970: 333). Several features of this template of the prototypical Puritan sermon can be detected in Cushman's "Reasons and Considerations." After a few opening paragraphs marked "The Preamble" and "Cautions," the main body of the texts consists of a series of paragraphs that are marked in the margins by key terms – "Object," "Answ.," and "Reas." – which echo the "doctrine, reasons, and uses" of the sermon structure, often accompanied by numbers, and supplemented with brief summaries of the argument and Biblical correspondences.

While the opening section, designated as "The Preamble" in the margin of the text, serves to state Cushman's aim of defending the venture of "going into and inhabiting of foreign desert places" (Cushman 1963: 88), the next section, marked "Cautions" and accompanied by references to both the Old and the New Testament, provides the Scriptural basis for his deliberations.

---

[12]    Fender deems that Cushman's contribution is "certainly addressed to the 'saints' still dawdling in the old country," and that it takes "the form of a sermon" (Fender 1983: 40).

In keeping with the structural model of the Puritan sermon's "plain style" of "doctrine, reasons, and uses," Cushman instructs his readers how their venture should be interpreted:

> ... whereas God of old did call and summon our fathers by predictions, dreams, visions, and certain illuminations to go from their countries, places, and habitations, to reside and dwell here or there, and to wander up and down from city to city, and land to land, according to his will and pleasure, now there is no such calling to be expected for any matter whatsoever, neither must any so much as imagine that there will now be any such thing. God did once so train up his people, but now he doth not, but speaks in another manner ... (Cushman 1963: 89).

Insisting that God no longer directly intervenes in worldly affairs by charging the elect with the task of carrying out his divine design, Cushman admonishes his audience to heed "the ordinary examples and precepts of the Scriptures, reasonably and rightly understood and applied" (Cushman 1963: 89). Implicit in Cushman's insistence is the doctrine that the Old Testament covenant of works is revoked and replaced by the New Testament covenant of grace. In theological terms, what he cautions against is that the present venture be interpreted in terms of providential history based on Christian typology. Simply put, as Deborah L. Madsen explains, typology refers to a religious practice involving "the reading of history as a pattern of promises and fulfillments," with the consequence that "typology assumes the power to confer a quasi-divine legitimacy upon human political decisions ..." (Madsen 1996: 38; see also 9 and 41). In due course, this religious practice became, however, the rule rather than the exception in early New England.

Consequently, for readers who are familiar with other and far better known texts from the same period, Cushman's refusal to regard their venture in terms of typology and providential history may come as a surprise. John Winthrop's lay sermon "A Modell of Christian Charity" has gained almost paradigmatic status as an expression of Puritan thought concerning their status in the New World. According to tradition, the sermon was delivered aboard the ship *Arbella* before the migrants landed in New England to found the Massachusetts Bay colony in the nearby Salem in 1630, only eight years after the publication of Cushman's text.[13] The group that Winthrop led consisted of non-separatist

---

[13]  Interestingly, Dawson argues that Winthrop's sermon was not composed at sea, as tradition would have it, but that it was meant for England (see Dawson 1998: 131-36).

Puritans, and based on the message he delivered in his sermon it is evident that unlike Cushman, Winthrop considers their undertaking as an instance of providential history. Accordingly, he interprets their passage to foreign lands in terms of Christian typology, by which he and his fellow elect are defined as God's chosen people, the Israelites of their time. Winthrop states: "Thus stands the cause betweene God and us. We are entered into Covenant with Him for this worke. ... The Lord will be our God, and delight to dwell among us, as his oune people, and will command a blessing upon us in all our wayes" (Winthrop 1838: 46-47). However, their covenant with God dictates that in return for the privileged position of being God's chosen people, the elect should dedicate themselves to the task of serving God and carrying out God's design in the world. The mission at hand is to establish a model community on earth, a New Jerusalem, which should be understood not only as a privilege, but also as a calling and responsibility, as evidenced in Winthrop's admonition to his listeners: "For wee must consider that wee shall be as a citty upon a hill. The eies of all people are uppon us ..." (Winthrop 1838: 47). That is to say, they have embarked on a holy errand into the wilderness, and they had better accomplish their task, lest the wrath of God fall upon them.

This notion of divine election and divine mission – which later provided the religious foundation of the secular ideology of American exceptionalism and manifest destiny[14] – is generally assumed to have been shared by all Puritans who sought refuge in the New World. But Cushman is unmistakably of a different opinion. It is almost as if he were addressing readers who might think along the same lines as Winthrop does about a decade later when he insists that the time of "extraordinary revelations" is of the past:

> Neither is there any land or possession now, like unto the possession which the Jews had in Canaan, being legally holy and appropriated unto a holy people .... but now there is no land of that sanctimony, no land so appropriated, ... much less any that can be said to be given of God to any nation as was Canaan ... (Cushman 1963: 89).

Instead of proclaiming himself and his fellow Pilgrims the chosen people of God, destined and appointed to establish God's kingdom on earth, he states that at this time and place in history, "we are all in all places strangers and

---

14    The term was coined by John L. O'Sullivan in an 1845 newspaper editorial arguing for the annexation of Texas, expressing a religious-nationalist justification for territorial expansion in the latter half of the nineteenth century (see Pratt 1927).

pilgrims, travellers and sojourners, most properly, having no dwelling but in this earthen tabernacle …" (Cushman 1963: 89). As opposed to Winthrop, it is worth noticing, as Madsen observes in *Allegory in America*, that Cushman represents one of the "voices of dissent" that "presents natural, civil, and religious reasons for migration in place of providential coercion" (Madsen 1996: 40; 44). In *American Exceptionalism* Madsen makes the additional comment that, "Separatists argued that the biblical promises of the Old and New Testaments can only, at this stage in the world's history, be fulfilled on a purely spiritual plane; the Bible can no longer be used to predict the future of human history" (Madsen 1998: 17). Evidently, then, Cushman voices the separatist stance, while Winthrop voices the non-separatist position, which would have a more enduring impact on the course of American history.

## Religious Investment: An "Other" in this World, an Elect in the World to Come

While Cushman resists the inclination to envision their settlement in the New World as a "city upon a hill" or a New Jerusalem, he is pleased by what he finds in the Plymouth Plantation about a year after its foundation, as he writes: "But we have here great peace, plenty of the Gospel, and many sweet delights, and variety of comforts" (Cushman 1963: 93-94). Nonetheless, Cushman's high hopes for religious fulfillment are invested elsewhere. The Pilgrims' progress does not end in this world, but only in the hereafter, for, as Cushman submits: "… our dwelling is but a wandering, and our abiding but as a fleeting, and in a word our home is nowhere, but in the heavens, in that house not made with hands, whose maker and builder is God, and to which all ascend that love the coming of our Lord Jesus" (Cushman 1963: 89-90). In this world Cushman and his fellow dissenters remain "strangers and pilgrims, travellers and sojourners" (Cushman 1963: 89). The epithets that Cushman has chosen in this passage are noteworthy, since, as Jeremy Bangs points out, it is the first documented use in writing of the word pilgrim by a member of the group that would later be known by that designation (Bangs 2009: 615). Cushman's final appeal is also noteworthy, as he adheres to the model of the sermon by ending his piece with "a suit to all men … whether they live there or here," asking that they keep their peace "both with God and men, that when the day of account shall come, they may come forth as good and fruitful servants, and freely be received, and enter into the joy of their Master" (Cushman 1963: 96).

It is fair to conclude that Cushman goes a long way in his "Reasons and Considerations" in endorsing European empire building by defending his and his fellow Pilgrims' venture in the New World. Ironically, then, the Pilgrims became participants in a European expansionist enterprise as a direct result of their own banishment from their home due to religious intolerance. As explained above, it could even be argued that Cushman himself engages in religious intolerance, as it is possible to find traces in his script of a discourse of othering directed at the indigenous population. Nonetheless, he is clear in recognizing that in the eyes of God the "heathens" – also referred to as "the sons of Adam in that New World" (Cushman 1963: 91) – were human souls, not less-than-human others.  Consequently, in the grand scheme of God's plan of redemption, the proper "home" even for the "exterior others" would be "nowhere, but in the heavens" (Cushman 1963: 90), provided that the Pilgrims fulfill their calling of spreading the word of God in foreign parts. Understandably, Cushman avoids direct mention of their disagreement with the Church of England and legal authorities at home. Nonetheless, the Pilgrims' prime motivation for seeking a new abode in the New World was that it provided an opportunity to escape religious intolerance, even though they remained heretics and thereby retained their status as outcasts and outlaws. The Pilgrims may have held the position of Europe's "interior others" in this world, whether it be on the one or the other side of the Atlantic. But they were firm in their belief that in their future home – in God's heaven – they would enjoy the privileged status of the elect.

## Bibliography

Bangs, Jeremy Dupertuis (2009): *Strangers and Pilgrims, Travellers and Sojourners: Leiden and the Foundations of Plymouth Plantation*. Plymouth, Mass.: General Society of Mayflower Descendants.

Bradford, William (1981 [1856]): *Of Plymouth Plantation 1620-1647*. Modern Library College edition. New York: Random House.

Coffey, John and Paul C. H. Lim (2008): "Introduction." In: Coffey, John and Paul C. H. Lim (eds.): *The Cambridge Companion to Puritanism*. Cambridge: Cambridge University Press, 1-15.

Cushman, Robert (1963 [1622]): "Reasons and Considerations Touching the Lawfulness of Removing out of England into the Parts of America." In: Heath, Dwight B. (ed.): *A Journal of the Pilgrims at Plymouth: Mourt's Relation: A Relation or Journal of the English*

*Plantation Settled at Plymouth in New England, by Certain English Adventurers Both Merchants and Others*. New York: Corinth Books, 88-96.

Cushman, Robert (1846 [1622]): *The Sin and Danger of Self-Love: Described, in a Sermon Preached at Plimmoth, in New-England, 1621*. Boston: Charles Ewer. Google Books.

Dawson, Hugh J. (1998): "'Christian Charitie' as Colonial Discourse: Rereading Winthrop's Sermon in Its English Context." *Early American Literature,* 33 (2), 117-48.

Demos, John (1972): "Introduction." In: Demos, John (ed.): *Remarkable Providences 1600-1760*. New York: George Braziller, 1-22.

Eliot, Emory (2002): *The Cambridge Introduction to Early American Literature*. Cambridge: Cambridge University Press.

Fender, Stephen (1983): *American Literature in Context, 1: 1620-1830*. London: Methuen.

Heath, Dwight B. (1963): "Editor's Introduction." In: *A Journal of the Pilgrims at Plymouth: Mourt's Relation: A Relation or Journal of the English Plantation Settled at Plymouth in New England, by Certain English Adventurers Both Merchants and Others*. New York: Corinth Books, vii–xvii.

Heath, Dwight B. (ed.) (1963 [1622]): *A Journal of the Pilgrims at Plymouth: Mourt's Relation: A Relation or Journal of the English Plantation Settled at Plymouth in New England, by Certain English Adventurers Both Merchants and Others*. New York: Corinth Books.

Kaplan, Benjamin J. (2004): "Coexistence, Conflict, and the Practice of Toleration." In: Hsia, R. Po-chia (ed.): *A Companion to the Reformation World*. Oxford: Blackwell, 486-505.

Kupperman, Karen Ordahl (2000): *Indians and English: Facing Off in Early America*. Ithaca: Cornell University Press.

Lovejoy, David S. (1990): "Plain Englishmen at Plymouth." *New England Quarterly,* 63 (2) (June), 232-48.

Madsen, Deborah L. (1996): *Allegory in America: From Puritanism to Postmodernism*. Basingstoke: Macmillan.

Madsen, Deborah L. (1998): *American Exceptionalism*. Edinburgh: Edinburgh University Press.

Miller, Perry. (1970 [1939]): *The New England Mind: The Seventeenth Century*. Boston: Beacon Press.

Pratt, Julius W. (1927): "The Origin of 'Manifest Destiny.'" *The American Historical Review,* 32 (4) (July), 795-98.

Slotkin, Richard (1996 [1973]): *Regeneration Through Violence: The Mythology of the American Frontier, 1600-1860*. New York: Harper Perennial-Harper Collins.

Winthrop, John (1838 [1630]): "A Modell of Christian Charity." In: *Collections of the Massachusetts Historical Society*, 3rd series 7: 31-48. Boston: Hanover Historical Texts Project, August 1996, web, 12 April 2012.

# Resistance to History: Heinrich von Kleist's War Poem *Germania an ihre Kinder*

*Michael Grote*

From a German studies' perspective, the issue of "Europe and Its Interior Other(s)" might remind one of what has been called the *Sonderweg* in German history: The development of the cultural nation (*Kulturnation*) from the Kleinstaaterei in the Holy Roman Empire to the foundation of an empire in the late nineteenth century, and the rise and fall of the Third Reich as a grotesque answer to its role as a "delayed nation" in Europe (cf. Plessner 1959). In the history of mind, Germany's difficult relationship with the idea of Europe has its roots here, in the "saddle period" between 1750 and 1850 (cf. Koselleck 1972: 14). As Reinhard Koselleck has shown, the fundamental transition from early modern times to modernity takes place in the period of the French Revolution, the Napoleonic Wars and industrialisation. This had strong consequences for the conception of time: A new consciousness of historicity was emerging, and the static, timeless concepts of philosophy, politics and culture were dynamised and related to the concept of historical change.

The literature of Heinrich von Kleist has often been seen as an important representative for this historical shift. At the same time as the German classics Goethe and Schiller contributed with their writings to a cosmopolitical European self-consciousness, Kleist endured an unsuccessful struggle for recognition, creating one of the most provocative and confusing works of German literature, inacceptable for many readers because of its representations of violence and its general nationalist and militant tone.[1] Even today it is a moot point how the writings of Heinrich von Kleist are to be regarded in the history of German literature. On the one hand, Kleist crossed borders between

---

[1] The reception of Kleist as an anti-European has stressed his personal opposition to Goethe, who was known for his humanistic universalism, aiming at a balance of the extremes (cf. Mommsen 1974). But in fact, the actual conflict between Kleist and Goethe, which besides the personal disappointment and jealousy on Kleist's behalf can be seen as founded in Kleist's anticlassical modernity and critical thought against the spirit of his time, was quite temporary. Like Schiller, Goethe was not only an antagonist, but also a role model for Kleist's work, in which we find a wide range of intertextual references to the literary heritage of the classics (cf. Benthien 2009: 222).

historical times and social classes due to his intermediate position between his aristocratic background and his interest for the values of Enlightenment and the civil state, and he anticipated fundamental aspects of the aesthetics of modernism in his literature as well as in his life. On the other hand, he has been read as a pioneer for a crude nationalism in Germany due to his political engagement against the Napoleonic occupation of Europe, especially because of his propaganda poems and political writings, where he developed and glorified a concept of a total war as a guerilla strategy in the wars of liberation from French hegemony.[2]

Even though the earlier works of Kleist had a specific political dimension as well,[3] his literary production never achieved such a political conviction and aesthetic unambiguity as in the writings from 1808/09. Particularly the ode *Germania an ihre Kinder* ("Germania to Her Children", 1809) has become notorious for its violent theme, its aggressive nationalist, anti-French tone and its one-sided, propagandistic nature. These aspects contributed to the popularity of the poem in the growing nationalist propaganda in Germany, from the Wars of Liberation up to the totalitarian cultural politics in the Third Reich.[4] This reception has a strong influence on our perception of Kleist today, and paradoxically this applies especially to those writings that were designed explicitly for the historical moment, as Kleist wrote about his drama *Die Herr-*

---

[2]   The ambivalent status of Kleist's writings in the history of German literature is not least a consequence of a well calculated poetical attitude, which Kleist himself, according to friends of his, characterised with the sentence: "In mir ist nichts beständig, als die Unbeständigkeit." This statement, that Kleist is reputed to have expressed towards a member of the family von Schlieben, is presented in Eduard von Bülow's biography from 1848 (cf. Sembdner 1996: 102, no 108).

[3]   Wolf Kittler has shown the concrete political aspects of the piece *Der zerbrochene Krug* (Kittler 1987: 138).

[4]   Especially in the beginning of the twentieth century, the nationalism in Germany discovered a simplified Kleist, and particularly the nationalist poems and plays became popular. Having said that, Kleist's radical modernist language praxis left the conservative and nationalist reception reluctant, and it is significant that the nazi-reception of his literature did not focus on the anti-classical, modernist character of his work, but tried to create a new "classic of the nationalsocialist Germany" (George Minde-Pouet 1935, cit. DKV 3: 1003). After the fall of the Third Reich with its selective reading of Kleist's work and the creation of an early witness for the Nazi-ideologies of total war and for the foundation myths of an ancient Germania, the reception of Kleist's works remained hesitant. Only after a fundamental rereading, particularly of the drama *Die Herrmannsschlacht*, a new reception of Kleist was made possible. As a result of this process, Kleist is one of the most played dramatists in Germany today.

*mannsschlacht,* "as this play more than any other is written for the moment, and I almost wish to withdraw it, if the circumstances, as may well be, do not allow it to be performed now".⁵ This calls for an exploration of the historical context in which the poem emerged.

## The cult of the German nation and the "war at all costs"

While King Frederick William III of Prussia and his advisors pursued a course of neutrality in the Napoleonic Wars, Kleist was a strict opponent of this policy, which he interpreted as a sign of weakness and, according to his aristocratic corporative attitude of mind, as lacking in honour.⁶ Prussia's short attempt at military resistance against the Napoleonic dominance was defeated in Jena and

---

⁵   Kleist, H. v.: Letter to Heinrich Joseph von Collin, 22 February 1809 (transl. M. G.). ("indem dies Stück mehr, als irgend ein anderes, für den Augenblick berechnet war, und ich fast wünschen muß, es ganz und gar wieder zurückzunehmen, wenn die Verhältnisse, wie leicht möglich ist, nicht gestatten sollten, es im Laufe dieser Zeit aufzuführen", DKV 4: 429.)

⁶   In December 1805, when the Napoleonic pressure on Prussia increased, Kleist complains to his friend Otto August Rühle von Lilienstern about the passivity of Frederick William's policy: "Warum hat der König nicht gleich, bei Gelegenheit des Durchbruchs der Franzosen durch das Fränkische, seine Stände zusammenberufen, warum ihnen nicht, in einer rühren-den Rede (der bloße Schmerz hätte ihn rührend gemacht) seine Lage eröffnet? Wenn er es bloß ihrem eignen Ehrgefühl anheim gestellt hätte, ob sie von einem gemißhandelten Könige regiert sein wollen, oder nicht, würde sich nicht etwas von Nationalgeist bei ihnen geregt haben. Und wenn sich diese Regung gezeigt hätte, wäre dies nicht die Gelegenheit gewesen, ihnen zu erklären, daß es hier gar nicht auf einen gemeinen Krieg ankomme. Es gelte Sein, oder Nichtsein; und wenn er seine Armee nicht um 300000 Mann vermehren könne, so bliebe ihm nichts übrig, als bloß ehrenvoll zu sterben. Meinst du nicht, daß eine solche Erschaffung hätte zu Stande kommen können? Wenn er alle seine goldnen und silbernen Geschirre hätte prägen lassen, seine Kammerherrn und seine Pferde abgeschafft hätte, seine ganze Familie ihm darin gefolgt wäre, und er, nach diesem Beispiel, gefragt hätte, was die Nation zu thun willends sei." (DKV 4: 351f.) How personal the question of honour was for Kleist, is also reflected in his repeated challenges to duels, as for example in a letter to Friedrich von Raumer, who in Kleist's view was the person mainly responsible for the failure of his newspaper project "Die Abendblätter," with the words: "Ew. Hochwohlgebohren fühlen von selbst, daß ich, zu so vielen Verletzungen meiner Ehre, die ich erdulden muß, vor Sr. Exzellenz nicht noch als ein Lügner erscheinen kann; und indem ich Denenselben anzeige, daß ich im Fall einer zweideutigen oder unbefriedigenden Antwort, Dieselben um diejenige Satisfaction bitten werde, die ein Mann von Ehre in solchen Fällen fordern kann, habe ich die Ehre zu sein, Ew. Hochwohlgebohren gehorsamster H. v. Kleist." (Kleist, H. v.: Letter to Friedrich von Raumer, 22 February 1811, in: DKV 4: 474.)

Auerstedt, and on 27 October 1806 Napoleon and his troops marched into the capital of Prussia, Berlin, while the king and his family fled to Königsberg.[7] In the Treaties of Tilsit in 1807, Prussia lost about half of its territory, was forced to pay a large indemnity and had to accept French occupation of its territory. Napoleon was at the height of his power, and in the following years nearly the whole of continental Europe was under French control.

The breakdown of the Prussian state became the occasion for a series of constitutional, administrative, social, and economic reforms in the kingdom of Prussia, known as the Stein-Hardenberg Reforms. From today's point of view these reforms appear as a first step towards the unification and foundation of the German Empire in 1871. Kleist was an eager supporter of the reforms, while King Frederick William implemented them only reluctantly. While Prussia's political situation improved in the following years, the discontent with the French domination increased in the circles of the reformers. Politicians like Karl August von Hardenberg, Freiherr vom Stein and Wilhelm von Humboldt, military officers like August Graf Neidhardt von Gneisenau and Gerhard von Scharnhorst, journalists and poets like Ernst Moritz Arndt, Johann Gottlieb Fichte, Theodor Körner and Heinrich von Kleist, published position papers, articles and poems, that agitated more or less openly for Prussia's, or indeed "Germany's," independence from France. At this point in time the concept of *Germany* described a fiction more than a political reality. But precisely this fictionality was a reason for the appeal of the term within the patriotic discourse and opened for a more or less mythological projection. Here the poets obtained a specific new assignment, that had its source in a fundamental achievement of the French revolution: the authority of the word and the acquisition of majorities by persuasion (cf. Schulz 1993: 60f.). The poets' new mission was, in opposition to the historical reality of "patchwork rug," and "Kleinstaaterei," to *invent* "Germany," and "the Germans."[8]

The qualities of the "Germans" were among others found in texts from pietism, whose secularisation lead, as Gerhard Schulz has shown, to the ste-

---

[7]    The Fourth Coalition was formed by Prussia together with Russia, later joined by Saxony, Sweden, and the United Kingdom. The Prussian ultimatum from 26 August 1806, demanding that French troops should retreat to the French side of the Rhine, was answered by Napoleon with an attack on the Prussian capital Berlin, and the Prussian troops collapsed in the battle of Jena and Auerstedt.

[8]    For antecedents in the discourse about the "Vaterland" in the 18th century cf. Blitz, Hans-Martin: *Aus Liebe zum Vaterland. Die deutsche Nation im 18. Jahrhundert*. Hamburg: Hamburger Edition 2000.

reotypical German attributes of naïvety, humbleness, honesty (cf. Schulz 1993: 62f.). This can clearly be seen in the poem "Deutscher Trost" by Ernst Moritz Arndt from 1813:

> Deutsches Herz, verzage nicht,
> Tu, was Dein Gewissen spricht,
> Dieser Strahl des Himmelslichts,
> Tue recht und fürchte nichts.
>
> Baue nicht auf bunten Schein,
> Lug und Trug ist dir zu fein,
> Schlecht gerät dir List und Kunst,
> Feinheit wird dir eitel Dunst.
>
> Doch die Treue ehrenfest
> Und die Liebe, die nicht läßt,
> Einfalt, Demut, Redlichkeit
> Stehn dir wohl, o Sohn vom Teut
> (Arndt 1912: 132).[9]

The contrasting concept of the enemy soon follows:

> Laß den Welschen Meuchelei,
> Du sei redlich, fromm und frei;
> Laß den Welschen Sklavenzier,
> Schlichte Treue sei mit dir
> (Arndt 1912: 133).[10]

According to the stereotype, the French had cultivated the "make-believe" mode, that is inauthenticity, irony, illusion. At the same time, the "German"

---

[9]  "German heart, do not despair, / Do what your conscience tells you, / This beam of Heaven's light, / Do the right thing and do not be afraid of anything. // Do not rely on colourful illusions, / Lies and deception are to genteel for you, / You do not succeed with cunning and artfulness, / Your finery turns into vain fumes. // But honour founded loyalty, / And love, that will not let go, / Naïvety, humbleness, honesty, / Becomes you well, o son of Teut." Transl. M. G.

[10]  "Leave the backstabbing to the French / Be honest, devout and pure / Leave the slavish decorations to the French / Plain fidelity be with you." Transl. M. G.

acquires a specific aura of premodernity. The picture of the German that was invented here had absolutely no roots in reality, and, as Gerhard Schulz has shown, it was specifically inept for the coming 19th century of industrial revolution and expanding capitalism (Schulz 1993: 64).

However, the Pietist background of the new German patriotism, whose songs not uncommonly were sung to the melodies of popular chorals, had to be blended with another driving force in order to develop the specific radicality of nationalism in Prussia in the years of the Napoleonic hegemony. Ironically it was the French Revolution that provided the reformers with a new pattern: The modern revolutionary slogan, "freedom or death," implied a tendency to radicalism, to a combination of enthusiasm and unyieldingness that at the same time had a strong mass-mobilizing effect. The parole of a "human inhumanity," that Jacobins like Danton, Robespierre or St. Just in the Reign of Terror had cultivated for the political discourse, was taken up by the campaigners when launching patriotism in Prussia, and Kleist too, as Hans-Jürgen Schings has shown, was deeply effected by this specific heritage of the French Revolution (cf. Schings 2008/09).

Prussian military reformers like Scharnhorst and Gneisenau discovered the strategic significance of patriotism in a time when the conventional European professional troops were defeated by the new national people's army under the command of Napoleon. Therefore, France was not only an enemy, but also a paragon of nation building for the Prussian politicians. Nationalisation of the army was one of the first demands of the reformers, and in this profound reorientation the poets played a key role in the eyes of Prussian officials, as Wolf Kittler in his book about *The Birth of the Partisan from the Spirit of Poetry* has shown convincingly:

> The experiences of the last years had shown that the army that sprung out the French Revolution could only be defeated if the self interest, as Novalis called it, or fear and hope, as Fichte later called it, were abolished. Therefore, the poets, throughout time specialists in the matter of love, turned out to serve the realignment of the state and the reorganisation of the army just fine. The soldier of the future would no longer be motivated by physical or monetary constraints, but by his soul (Kittler 1987: 141, transl. M. G.).

The fact that the cult of the nation in Prussia, in difference to the development in France, arose from a defeat, contributed to the radicalisation of Prussian patriotism just as much as the fact that the "Germany" figuring in the national fantasies remained a fiction.

In a situation of military inferiority and political powerlessness, any possibility that could stop the advances of Napoleon "the invincible"[11] was of high interest to the Prussians. In this perspective, the general national uprising in Spain, after Napoleon had appointed his brother Joseph king of Spain in 1808, was observed with detailed attention in Prussia. The Spanish resistance remained an unsolved problem for Napoleon and demanded a large number of his troops, who were confronted with a highly motivated enemy whose conduct of war was until this point in time unknown even for the French people's army. In his *Theorie des Partisanen*, Carl Schmitt has described in detail, how the Spanish guerrilla with its partisan warfare became a role model for the Prussian reformers (cf. Schmitt 1975: 12-14; Kittler 1987: 218ff). In opposition to the 18th century's "legal war," with its clear distinctions between war and peace, soldier and civilian, enemy and criminal, the guerrilla fought an irregular war, which subverted the traditional distinctions. The partisan warfare has no regards for the differences between regular troops and civilian population, between war zone and hinterland, it aims towards a total war, preferably conducted at night, a war in which women and children become warriors and enemies are regarded as bandits who have to be exterminated. In this "absolute war", as Kleist's contemporary Carl von Clausewitz named it, the honour of the battlefield counts for nothing, but survival or death is the only valid distinction. In the drama *Die Herrmannsschlacht* ("The Battle of Herrmann") Kleist depicts a new military strategy that calls for resistance "by any means": agreements do not have to be kept, foreign and own properties loose their value, lost territory is to be devastated, the whole population is considered as combatants, the enemy is regarded as an animal. It is, as Clausewitz stated, "a war of all against all. Not that the king makes war against another king, not one army against another, but one people against another, and king and army are included in the people" (cit. Kittler 1987: 242, transl. M. G.).[12]

---

[11] In a poem after Napoleon's first defeat against Austrian troops in the battle of Aspern, 21/22 May 1809, Kleist characterised the victorious Archduke Charles, Duke of Teschen, as "Überwinder des Unüberwindlichen" (cf. DKV 3: 440).

[12] "ein Krieg aller gegen alle. Nicht der König bekriegt den König, nicht eine Armee die andere, sondern ein Volk das andere, und im Volke sind König und Heer enthalten." In this context the following passage is of interest as well: "Lassen wir es darauf ankommen, Grausamkeit mit Grausamkeit zu bezahlen, Gewalttat mit Gewalttat zu erwidern! Es wird uns ein leichtes sein, den Feind zu überbieten und ihn in die Schranken der Mäßigung und Menschlichkeit zurückzuführen" (cit. Kittler 1987: 238).

Not until two years after Kleist's death, in 1813, the *Landsturm* was established as a last array of forces for the defence of Prussia against the Napoleonic invasion that "justified the use of all means" in warfare.[13] In 1809, when Kleist wrote most of his political statements and poems, Frederick William III refused to follow the arguments of the political reformers, and decided not to join the Austrian campaign, which lead to the Fifth Coalition against France.[14] In the Austrian Empire the Spanish popular revolt was considered to be a model for a national uprising even in the highest political circles, and Kleist, depressed by the passivity of his king, wrote at least two hymnic poems to the Austrian minister of war and commander-in-chief, Archduke Charles, Duke of Teschen. In one of these poems, written "Als der Krieg im März 1809 auszubrechen zögerte," the absoluteness of the Kleistian concept of war is expressed with all desirable explicitness:

---

[13] "§ 7. Ist der Fall des Aufgebots eingetreten; so ist der Kampf, wozu der Landsturm berufen wird, ein Kampf der Nothwehr, der alle Mittel heiligt. Die schneidigsten sind die vorzüglichsten, denn sie beenden die gerechte Sache am siegreichsten und schnellsten. § 8. Es ist daher die Bestimmung des Landsturms, dem Feinde den Einbruch, wie den Rückzug zu versperren, ihn beständig ausser Athem zu halten; seine Munition, Lebensmittel, Couriere und Rekruten aufzufangen; seine Hospitäler aufzuheben; nächtliche Ueberfälle auszuführen, kurz, ihn zu beunruhigen, zu peinigen, schlaflos zu machen, einzeln und in Trupps zu vernichten, wo es nur möglich ist. Dränge selbst der Feind vorwärts, und wäre 50 Meilen weit; so bringt es ihm geringen Vortheil, wenn der Strich, den er einnimmt, keine Breite hat, wenn er nicht mehr wagen darf kleine Detaschements zum Fouragiren und Recognosciren auszusenden, ohne die Gewissheit, dass sie ihm erschlagen werden, und wenn er nur in Masse und auf gebahnten Wegen vordringen kann, wie das Beispiel von Spanien und Russland lehrt. [...] § 39. Eigen für den Landsturm verfertigte Uniformen oder Trachten werden nicht verstattet, weil sie den Landstürmer kenntlich machen, und der Verfolgung des Feindes leichter Preis geben können. [...] § 43. Die Waffen sind: alle Art von Flinten mit oder ohne Bajonett, Spiesse, Piken, Heugabeln, Morgensterne, Säbeln, Beile, gerade gezogene Sensen, Eisen etc. [...]" (Verordnung über den Landsturm vom 21. April 1813. In: Frauenholz 1941: 161-171, here 162, 166). As Dierk Walter has pointed out, the "Landsturmedikt" marked a specific caesura in the history of war in Prussia: "Dieses aus der Rückschau fast unwahrscheinlich anmutende Dokument, das sich selbst aus der einmaligen historischen Konstellation des beginnenden Befreiungskampfes gegen die europäische Supermacht Frankreich und selbst eingedenk einer dominant propagandistischen Zielsetzung nicht völlig erklärt, war der demonstrative Höhepunkt einer dramatischen Wandlung des Kriegsbildes in Preußen vom Kabinettskrieg im Stile des 18. Jahrhunderts hin zum Volkskrieg des 19. Jahrhunderts" (Walter 2003: 297).

[14] Prussia remained a neutral state under French occupation and was even forced to join the Napoleonian army in a campaign against Russia in 1812.

Nicht der Sieg ists, den der Deutsche fodert,
Hülflos, wie er schon am Abgrund steht;
Wenn der Kampf nur fackelgleich entlodert,
Wert der Leiche die zu Grabe geht.

Mag er dann in finstre Nacht auch sinken
Von dem Gipfel, halb bereits erklimmt,
Herr! Die Träne wird noch Dank dir blinken,
Wenn dein Schwert dafür nur Rache nimmt
(DKV 3: 435f.).[15]

These stanzas clearly show what Kleist and his contemporaries had in mind when they talked about a "holy war":[16] In a political blueprint, probably written after the Austrian defeat in Wagram 5/6 July 1809, Kleist stressed that a war for "Austria's redemption"

> weder für den Glanz noch für die Unabhängigkeit, noch selbst für das Dasein ihres Thrones geführt werde, welches, so wie die Sache liegt, lauter niedere und untergeordnete Zwecke sind, sondern für Gott, Freiheit, Gesetz und Sittlichkeit, für die Besserung einer höchst gesunkenen und entarteten Generation, kurz für Güter, die über jede Schätzung erhaben sind, und die um jeden Preis, gleichviel welchen, gegen den Feind, der sie angreift, verteidigt werden müssen – und deren Verteid[ig]ung einen heiligen Krieg, oder einen Krieg für die Menschheit konstituiert (DKV 3: 498).[17]

The aim of war for Kleist is abstract ideas like "God," "freedom," "law," and "morality." It is a war "at all costs" that has no need for a justification. In his

---

15  "It is not the victory the German demands, / Helplessly standing at the abyss; / If only the battle flares up like torches, / Worth the corpse carried to the grave. // May he then sink into the dark night / From the pinnacle, half already ascended, / Lord! Even the tear will gleam in your gratitude, / If only your sword wreaks vengeance on it." Transl. M. G.

16  The "holy war" is a common topos in the patriotic discourse in the wars of liberation, see examples of Theodor Körner and Zacharias Werner in Schulz (1993: 67).

17  "would be carried out neither for the glory nor for the independence nor for the mere existence of their throne, all of which are, as matters stand, inferior and subordinate purposes, but for God, freedom, law and morality, to the reform of a highly fallen and decadent generation, briefly for values that are above every estimation, and that at any cost, no matter which, have to be defended against the enemy who attacks them – and whose defence constitutes a holy war, or a war for mankind." Transl. M. G.

*Catechism of the Germans*, drawn up on the pattern of an anti-Napoleonic tract which was first published in Spain in 1808 and spread in Austria in 1809 (cf. DKV 3: 1073), Kleist gives a fictive dialogue between a father and his son:

> *Fr.* Du liebst dein Vaterland, nicht wahr, mein Sohn?
> *Antw.* Ja, mein Vater; das tu ich.
> *Fr.* Warum liebst du es?
> *Antw.* Weil es mein Vaterland ist (DKV 3: 480).[18]

Tautological argumentations substitute an actual justification for patriotism. In the last chapter of the *Catechism*, Kleist returns to the question of the aims of war.

> *Fr.* Gleichwohl ist, wenn der Zweck des Kriegs nicht erreicht wird, das Blut vieler tausend Menschen nutzlos geflossen, die Städte verwüstet und das Land verheert worden.
> *Antw.* Wenn gleich, mein Vater.
> *Fr.* Was; wenn gleich! – Also auch, wenn Alles unterginge, und kein Mensch, Weiber und Kinder mit eingerechnet, am Leben bliebe, würdest du den Kampf noch billigen?
> *Antw.* Allerdings, mein Vater.
> *Fr.* Warum?
> *Antw.* Weil es Gott lieb ist, wenn Menschen, ihrer Freiheit wegen, sterben.
> *Fr.* Was aber ist ihm ein Greuel?
> *Antw.* Wenn Sklaven leben (DKV 3: 491).[19]

With the obvious lack of motivation and the absolute nature of his concept of a total and "holy" war, Kleist surpassed even the most radical of his contemporaries. And the same applies for the most notorious of his political poems, the ode *Germania an ihre Kinder*. In a letter to Heinrich Joseph von Collin the 20 April 1809, containing a copy of the Germania-ode alongside other patriotic poems, Kleist wrote about his songs:

---

[18] "*Question:* You love your country, do you not, my son? / *Answer:* Yes, my father, I do. / *Q.:* Why do you love it? / *A.:* Because it is my country." Transl. M. G.

[19] "*Q.:* Nonetheless, if the aim of the war is not to be achieved, the blood of many thousands of humans is shed, cities and towns are ruined and the land is devastated. *A.:* So what, my father. *Q.:* What, so what! – So even if all would perish, and no human being, women and children included, would survive, you still would approve of the battle? *A.:* Indeed, my father. *Q.:* Why? *A.:* Because it is dear to God, if men die for their freedom. *Q.:* And what does he loathe? *A.:* When slaves live." Transl. M. G.

Ich auch finde, man muß sich mit seinem ganzen Gewicht, so schwer oder leicht es sein mag, in die Waage der Zeit werfen; Sie werden inliegend mein Scherflein dazu finden [...]; ich wollte, ich hätte eine Stimme von Erz, und könnte sie, vom Harz herab, den Deutschen absingen (DKV 4: 431).[20]

Kleist's wish to "throw himself onto the scales of time" is based on an optimism both in regard to the prospects of a "German" war and to the effects of poetry. One month later, on 25 May 1809, Kleist wrote in a letter to Joseph von Buol:

Nun zweifle ich keinen Augenblick mehr daß der König v. Preußen und mit ihm das ganze Norddeutschland losbricht, und so ein Krieg entsteht, wie er der großen Sache, die es gilt, würdig ist (DKV 4: 434).[21]

But as the Austrian army on 5 and 6 July 1809 was defeated in the battle of Wagram, this hope for a conversion of the Austrian into a German war became obsolete.

## The rhetorical impact of *Germania an ihre Kinder*

Germania an ihre Kinder
Eine Ode

§ 1
Die des Maines Regionen,
Die der Elbe heitre Aun,
Die der Donau Strand bewohnen,
Die das Odertal bebaun,
Aus des Rheines Laubensitzen,
Von dem duftgen Mittelmeer,
Von der Riesenberge Spitzen,
Von der Ost und Nordsee her!

---

[20] "I think too that one has to throw oneself onto the scales of time, even if it might be hard; enclosed you will find my mite [...]; I wish I had a voice of ore, and could sing them, from the Harz, down to the Germans." Transl. M. G.

[21] "Now I do not for a moment doubt that the king of Prussia and the whole northern Germany with him will break forth, and a war arise, that merits the great matter in hand." Transl. M. G.

Chor

Horchet! – Durch die Nacht, ihr Brüder,
Welch ein Donnerruf hernieder?
Stehst du auf, Germania?
Ist der Tag der Rache da?

§ 2

Deutsche, mutger Völkerreigen,
Meine Söhne, die, geküßt,
In den Schoß mir kletternd steigen,
Die mein Mutterarm umschließt,
Meines Busens Schutz und Schirmer,
Unbesiegtes Marsenblut,
Enkel der Kohortenstürmer,
Römerüberwinderbrut!

Chor

Zu den Waffen! Zu den Waffen!
Was die Hände blindlings raffen!
Mit der Keule, mit dem Stab,
Strömt ins Tal der Schlacht hinab!

§ 3

Wie der Schnee aus Felsenrissen:
Wie, auf ewger Alpen Höhn,
Unter Frühlings heißen Küssen,
Siedend auf die Gletscher gehn:
Katarakten stürzen nieder,
Wald und Fels folgt ihrer Bahn,
Das Gebirg hallt donnernd wider,
Fluren sind ein Ozean!

Chor

So verlaßt, voran der Kaiser,
Eure Hütten, eure Häuser;
Schäumt, ein uferloses Meer,
Über diese Franken her!

§ 4

Alle Plätze, Trift' und Stätten,
Färbt mit ihren Knochen weiß;
Welchen Rab und Fuchs verschmähten,
Gebet ihn den Fischen preis;
Dämmt den Rhein mit ihren Leichen;
Laßt, gestäuft von ihrem Bein,
Schäumend um die Pfalz ihn weichen,
Und ihn dann die Grenze sein!

Chor

Eine Lustjagd, wie wenn Schützen
Auf die Spur dem Wolfe sitzen!
Schlagt ihn tot! Das Weltgericht
Fragt euch nach den Gründen nicht!

§ 5

Nicht die Flur ists, die zertreten,
Unter ihren Rossen sinkt,
Nicht der Mond, der, in den Städten,
Aus den öden Fenstern blinkt,
Nicht das Weib, das, mit Gewimmer,
Ihrem Todeskuß erliegt,
Und zum Lohn, beim Morgenschimmer,
Auf den Schutt der Vorstadt fliegt!

Chor

Euren Schlachtraub laßt euch schenken!
Wenige, die sein gedenken.
Höhrem, als der Erde Gut,
Schwillt die Seele, flammt das Blut!

§ 6

Gott und seine Stellvertreter,
Und dein Nam, o Vaterland,
Freiheit, Stolz der bessern Väter,
Sprache, du, dein Zauberband,
Wissenschaft, du himmelferne,
Die dem deutschen Genius winkt,

Und der Pfad ins Reich der Sterne,
Welchen still sein Fittich schwingt!

Chor
Eine Pyramide bauen
Laßt uns, in des Himmels Auen,
Krönen mit dem Gipfelstein:
Oder unser Grabmal sein!

The exact time of origin of *Germania an ihre Kinder* is not known, but it is probable that Kleist wrote the poem shortly after Austria's uprising against the French, 9 April 1809.[22] It is published in several different versions[23] – which goes to show the importance Kleist attached to the rhetorical efficacy of the text as a means of agitation. *Germania an ihre Kinder* contains an appeal for liberation of a mere geographically defined German territory, located between the North Sea, the Mediterranean, and the rivers Rhine to the west, and Oder to the east. In an antiphony between the allegorical "Germania" and her children, who answer her appeal in chorus, Kleist develops a scene of a German insurrection against the French occupants. Germania calls her peoples to arms, to fall into a campaign of destruction against their enemies.

Formally and substantially the poem is a contrafacture of Friedrich Schiller's ode *An die Freude* ("To Joy"), which serves as a pattern for Kleist's poem both as to its figures and stanza-construction. Schiller's poem is an ovation to the classical ideal of a society of equal human beings, who are united through joy and friendship:

Freude, schöner Götterfunken,
Tochter aus Elisium, [...]
Alle Menschen werden Brüder,

---

[22]  I quote the poem from "Manuscript a" in DKV 3: 426-432 [left pages]. According to a marginal note by Ludwig Tieck on a manuscript of Kleist's, the poem was written already in 1808, but this was relativised by a later statement of Tieck's (cf. BKA 3: 78, comment to H2); a letter to Heinrich Joseph von Collin that probably followed a manuscript including the poems *An Franz den Ersten*, *Kriegslied der Deutschen* and *Germania an ihre Kinder* is dated 20 April 1809 (DKV 4: 998) – it is presumable that all the poems were written in April 1809, at least Kleist authorised the publication of *Germania an ihre Kinder* in this letter (cf. DKV 4: 431).

[23]  To the complex tradition of the text see DKV 3: 997-1010 and BKA 3: 77-125.

Wo dein sanfter Flügel weilt
(Schiller 1992: 248).[24]

This is the cosmopolitan humanistic European thought, an anthem not only to joy, but, though written already in 1785, also to the universalism of the achievements of the French Revolution. It is not a coincidence that Schiller's poem, celebrating the brotherhood and unity of all mankind, in 1993 was adopted as the European Union's Anthem. In comparison to Kleist's usurpation, particularly the vision of a world led by humanity and mercy in Schiller's poem is of interest:

Groll und Rache sei vergessen,
Unserm Todfeind sei verziehn,
Keine Träne soll ihn pressen,
Keine Reue nage ihn.

Chor.
Unser Schuldbuch sei vernichtet!
Ausgesöhnt die ganze Welt!
Brüder – überm Sternenzelt
Richtet Gott, wie wir gerichtet
(Schiller 1992: 250).[25]

The agitatorial tone of uncompromising nationalistic hostility in Kleist's ode *Germania an ihre Kinder* stands in a sharp contrast to the humanistic conception we find in Schiller's poem. Unlike Schiller's universalism, Kleist's poem begins with a catalogue of the different regions from which Germania's children come. In this, Kleist is constructing an imaginary Germany – as said before, in 1809 the real Germany was far away from its constitution as a state or a nation. But yet more interesting than the geographical references is the *grammatical* construction in this first stanza:

---

[24] "Joy, beautiful spark of the gods, / Daughter of Elysium, [...] / All human beings become brothers / Wherever your gentle wing is." Transl. M. G.

[25] "Anger and vengeance be forgotten, / Our archenemy be forgiven. / No tear shall press him, / No remorse shall gnaw on him. // Chorus / Our debt be wiped out! / The entire world reconciled! / Brothers – over the starry vault of heaven / God judges, as we have judged." Transl. M. G.

Die des Maines Regionen,

Die der Elbe heitre Aun,

Die der Donau Strand bewohnen[26]

This is even for a German native speaker not easy to understand. The syntax is close to incomprehensible,[27] its complexity forces the reader to follow the poem's own rules already from the beginning with its marching rhythm.

After this unfocused and a bit confusing start, the choir sets the focus of the poem:

Horchet! – Durch die Nacht, ihr Brüder,

Welch ein Donnerruf hernieder?

Stehst du auf, Germania?

Ist der Tag der Rache da?[28]

In 1809 it is totally clear which political situation this refers to: the revenge for the Napoleonic occupation of the German countries. In the next stanza the Germans are described as "Unbesiegtes Marsenblut, / Enkel der Kohorten-stürmer, / Römerüberwinderbrut!"[29] – a reminiscence of the German narrative of Arminius' victory over the Roman legions in the Teutoburger Wald, about which Kleist had written his play *Die Herrmannsschlacht*. The answer of the choir, calling to arms, is given in the spirit of partisan warfare – as outlined before, a vexed issue in the reformer circles in Prussia. The arms of Germania's children are "clubs" and "bars," according to the concept of the partisan, who arms himself more or less spontaneously with the devices that are accessible in everyday life, against an enemy not worthy of an honourable death:[30]

---

[26]   "Those who live in the regions of the river Main, / In the light meadows of the Elbe, / On the beaches of the Donau." transl. M. G.

[27]   The fusion of the relative and demonstrative pronouns, the combination of several relative clauses and the anastrophe of the inverted genitives lead to a condensed mode of expression.

[28]   "Listen, through the night, brothers / How the thunder roars down? / Are you rising, Germania? / Has the day of vengeance come?" transl. M. G.

[29]   "Unconquered blood of the Marsen, / Grandchildren of the cohortstormers, / Breed of those who defeated the Romans", transl. M. G.

[30]   The preference for extermination instead of subjection is the consequence of this choice. For the historical implications of this "discourse of extermination" cf. Seeba 2007: 60.

Zu den Waffen! Zu den Waffen!

Was die Hände blindlings raffen!

Mit der Keule, mit dem Stab,

Strömt ins Tal der Schlacht hinab![31]

Whilst in Schiller's ode the perspective was directed upwards, to heaven and the reiterative motifs of "stars" and "suns," the view is directed downwards in Kleist's depiction of war; with the idyllic figure of the "cataract," following the rigorously alternating trochaic metre, it trails the Germans down to the valley of the battle.

So verlaßt, voran der Kaiser,

Eure Hütten, eure Häuser;

Schäumt, ein uferloses Meer,

Über diese Franken her![32]

The Germans appear here as a natural force, claiming its natural right – and as readers today we cannot escape the rememberance of the ideology of German natural superiority and its climax in racism and genocide in the Third Reich. And indeed, what is described in Kleist's writings from 1808/09, is the concept of a total war, with its complete mobilisation of available resources and population, as it was invented by the *levée en masse* in the French revolutionary wars and by the absolute warfare in the Napoleonic wars. In the last verses of *Germania an ihre Kinder* this concept is expressed in clarity:

Eine Pyramide bauen

Laßt uns, in des Himmels Auen,

Krönen mit dem Gipfelstein:

Oder unser Grabmal sein![33]

These verses state an absolute alternative between freedom or death, which corresponds with the reasons for war given in the fifth and sixth stanza. Neither the devastation of territories nor the civil victims of war are considered sufficient

---

[31]  "To arms! To arms! / Everything that hands blindly grab! / With the club, with the bar, / Surge down to the valley of the battle!" Transl. M. G.

[32]  "Leave now, the emperor ahead, / your cottages, your houses; / foam, a boundless see, / over these Franks!" Transl. M. G.

[33]  "Let us build a pyramid / In the meadows of heaven / And crown it with a summitstone / Or let it be our gravemonument." Transl. M. G.

causes for war: "worldy goods" are only obstacles in the scorched earth-warfare strategy of the partisan, as Herrmann outlines in *Die Herrmannschlacht*:

> Kurz, wollt Ihr, wie ich schon einmal Euch sagte,
> Zusammenraffen Weib und Kind,
> Und auf der Weser rechtes Ufer bringen,
> Geschirre, goldn' und silberne, die Ihr
> Besitzet, schmelzen, Perlen und Juwelen
> Verkaufen oder sie verpfänden,
> Verheeren Eure Fluren, Eure Herden
> Erschlagen, Eure Plätze niederbrennen,
> So bin ich Euer Mann –
> (DKV 2: 461).[34]

Instead, Herrmann claims the abstract value of "freedom" as the objective of war, and also in *Germania an ihre Kinder* the motivation for war remains equally vague, explained by "Gott" and "Vaterland" as well as freedom, language, and knowledge.

From today's moralistic point of view, Kleist's propagandist insistence on a total war appears both extreme and disgusting. Though, as outlined before, Kleist was far from alone in taking on this kind of aggressive anti-French rhetoric. The poet Theodor Körner, the romantic theorist and philosopher Adam Müller, the famous painter Caspar David Friedrich – there were a lot of intellectuals who during the French occupation sympathised with or indeed wrote anti-Napoleonic propaganda-poetry. What is unusual about Kleist's writing is not the topic in itself, but *how* the topic is presented. It is the specific expressiveness of violence that has brought the attention to Kleist's war poems. Particularly the fourth stanza of *Germania an ihre Kinder* has become notorious in this context:

> Alle Plätze, Trift' und Stätten,
> Färbt mit ihren Knochen weiß;

---

[34] "In short, as I have already asked you once before, / If you will just gather together your women and children, / And bring them to the right bank of the Weser, / Melt all the gold and silver dishes / You possess, take your pearls and jewels / And sell them off or pawn them, / Lay waste to your lands, slaughter / Your cattle, set fire to your camps, / Then I'm your man –" (Kleist / MagShamhráin 2008: 18).

Welchen Rab und Fuchs verschmähten,

Gebet ihn den Fischen preis;

Dämmt den Rhein mit ihren Leichen;

Laßt, gestäuft von ihrem Bein,

Schäumend um die Pfalz ihn weichen,

Und ihn dann die Grenze sein![35]

This monstrous picture of war bears with it a special irony not only in its hyperbolic figures, but also in the intertextual reference to Schiller's contemporary hit *An die Freude*. The exceptional aspect of Kleist's poem lies not as much in its propagandist function as in its inappropriateness, in the way it exaggerates its own intention, regarding the total immoderateness and the obvious fascination for its own rhetorical figures of violence and cruelty. It is here, in its rhetoric, not in its "message," the poem is fascinating: in its antimoralist attitude, in the fury of a rampant subjectivity, that has lost faith in the rationality of moralistic and reasonable derivation of arguments:

Eine Lustjagd, wie wenn Schützen

Auf die Spur dem Wolfe sitzen!

Schlagt ihn tot! Das Weltgericht

Fragt euch nach den Gründen nicht![36]

The animalization of the enemy, not unusual for the patriot discourse of the time (Schulz 1993: 70), licences a dispensation from rules of warfare and suspension from any humanitarian, or other, considerations.

## The rhetorical nature of Kleist's political mindset

The majority of the scholarly literature after 1945 has concluded with the estimation that *Germania an ihre Kinder* is the climax of an, at least from a

---

[35] "All the sites and roads and places / Colour them white with their bones; / Those who were shunned by raven and fox / Feed the fish with them; / Dam the Rhine with their corpses; / Let him, restrained of their bones, / Evade foaming around the palatinate / And there be the new border." Transl. M. G. In the Wars of the French Revolution the Palatinate was dissolved, and from 1792 until 1815 its left bank territories were occupied by France.

[36] "A chase, as when hunters / Follow the traces of the wolf! / Swat him! The Last Judgement / Won't ask you for your reasons!" Transl. M. G.

moralistic point of view, "wrong" track in Kleist's literary production, an abhorrent line that begins with the play *Die Herrmannsschlacht* in 1808 and ends with the French defeat of the Austrian army in the battle of Wagram in 1809. Especially after the experience of the Third Reich and its ideological exploitation particularly of the patriotic writings of Kleist's, their unscrupulous onesidedness and violent chauvinism could appear as "poetical insipidness,"[37] and until today *Germania an ihre Kinder* has been characterised as "disgusting,"[38] as "rants of hate, hard to tolerate,"[39] that show "scaring parallels to nationalsocialistic fantasies of the Twilight of the Gods"[40]. Even though Kleist's propagandist writings from 1809 came about in a situation where the Prussian state was threatened, and can not be mistaken as legitimising an aggressive and expansive war policy, yet the historical resemblances to the rhetoric of Nazi-Germany propaganda remain disturbing, and all readings from today's perspective will have in mind the propagandist use of Kleist's poems in the Third Reich. The fact that they could be instrumentalised as propaganda for total warfare and for the policy of extermination has therefore been related to the one-dimensional nature and the "forced unambiguity" of Kleist's war poems.[41] However, the critical view on Kleist's writings from 1808/09 has become more sophisticated over the last decades. A spectacular theatre production by Claus Peymann in 1982, in which the play was seen as an exemplary model for a liberation war, especially contributed to a rehabilitation of Kleist's war piece *Die Herrmannsschlacht* (cf. Peymann / Kreutzer 1984). In 1986, Wolf Kittler in his study about "Heinrich von Kleist and the Strategy of the War of Liberation" described Kleist's writings from 1809 as in line with his earlier literary production.[42] And even if Kittler's lectures have a tendency to paro-

---

[37]  "poetische[] Geschmacklosigkeiten" (cf. Grab / Friesel 1970: 56).

[38]  "abstoßend" (cf. Schulz 1993: 71).

[39]  "schwer erträgliche Hetztiraden" (cf. Blamberger 2011: 362).

[40]  "erschreckende Parallelen zu nationalsozialistischen Götterdämmerungsphantasien" (cf. Klaus Müller-Salget in DKV 3: 1003).

[41]  "forcierte Eindeutigkeit" (cf. Müller-Salget 2002: 258).

[42]  "Die Pamphlete und Kriegslieder, die Kleist im Frühjahr und Sommer 1809 verfaßte, bedürfen keines Kommentars. Sie sprechen die Ideen der 'Herrmannsschlacht' im Klartext aus. Und das einzige Rätsel, das sie stellen, ist die Frage, wie es möglich war, das dichterische Werk ihres Verfassers so weit von diesen propagandistischen Texten abzuspalten, daß man die eindeutig wehrpolitische Tendenz seiner Dramen und Novellen übersehen konnte. Denn Kleist bleibt sich auch in diesen Texten treu. Er vertritt in militärischer Hinsicht eine radikale Theorie des Partisanen, und er bezieht im Hinblick auf das Staatsrecht eine aristokratisch-ständische Position" (Kittler 1987: 254).

chial reductions (cf. Stephens 1999: 38f.), reading literary texts nearly as plain historical sources for military affairs, they have at least shown the importance of the contemporary political discourse for Kleist's works.

The moralist criticism of Kleist's patriotic writings on the one hand and Kittler's discourse analysis on the other share their strong interest for the author's intentions, and over the last years various pragmatic functions of Kleist's writings have come into the focus of attention. But even if Kleist had specific political purposes with his publications, this fact cannot serve as proof of actual meanings and political implications of poems like *Germania an ihre Kinder*.[43] As a rule, literature is not an extension of the intentions of its author, and the writings of Kleist's, even in their most decisive manifestations, cannot be reduced to simple messages. We find a prominent example of this in *Die Herrmannsschlacht*, which can be seen as a piece of propaganda just as well as a piece *on* propaganda (cf. Blamberger 2011: 374f.). Beyond that, Kleist's intentions, seen from today's perspective, seem to be quite variable. As Gerhard Schulz has pointed out, the political situation in Dresden in the years after 1806 was a maze of crossing loyalties,[44] and the single poet's individual positioning in it far from predictable. Kleist's personal inconsistency and his often expressed indifference about his own situation contribute to the impression of obscurity of his political attitudes. The harsh attacks against Napoleon, who in the *Catechism* from 1809 was apostrophised as "the beginning of all that which is evil and the end of all that which is good,"[45] contrast with Kleist's attempt, only six years earlier, to join Napoleon's army in order to take part in the invasion of England in 1803, "to die the beautiful death of the battles."[46]

---

43  Walter Hettche has pointed out "daß hier eine noch zu definierende 'Germania' zu einer ebenfalls noch nicht näher bestimmten Gruppe von 'Kindern' spricht – und nicht, wie man angesichts einiger oberflächlicher Deutungen vermuten könnte, Kleist selbst" (Hettche 1986: 165). Already in 1979 Rudolf Berg demonstrated that in the political writings one would find "eher eine Taktik zur Mobilisierung Unschlüssiger denn ein politisches Credo Kleists" (Berg 1979: 204).

44  "Gewirr von Loyalitäten" (Schulz 2007: 318).

45  In his *Katechismus der Deutschen* from 1809, Kleist calls Napoleon "einen verabscheuungs-würdigen Menschen", "Anfang alles Bösen und das Ende alles Guten" "einen, der Hölle entstiegenen, Vatermördergeist" – cf. Kleist, H. v.: Der Katechismus der Deutschen [1809] (DKV 3: 479-491, here 484f.). Cf. also Grathoff 1994 and Hamacher 2009: 215.

46  "den schönen Tod der Schlachten zu sterben", cf. Kleist, H. v.: Letter to Ulrike von Kleist, 26 October 1803 (DKV 4: 321). One year earlier, Kleist wrote several letters from Swit-zerland in which he expressed his strong aversion against Napoleon and the French, see below, footnote 54.

But later as well, only months after the – for Prussia – humiliating Treaties of Tilsit, Kleist did not hesitate to aim at a publication of the *Code Napoléon* in the purpose of establishing himself as a publisher, as we can read in a letter to his sister Ulrike from 25 October 1807:

> Es ist nicht unmöglich, daß wir den Codex Napoleon zum Verlag bekommen, und daß unsere Buchhandlung überhaupt von der französischen Regierung erwählt wird, ihre Publicationen in Deutschland zu verbreiten; wodurch, wie du leicht denken kannst, die Assiette des ganzen Instituts mit einem Male gegründet wäre. Du wirst nicht voreilig sein, politische Folgerungen aus diesem Schritte zu ziehen, über dessen eigentliche Bedeutung ich mich hier nicht weitläufiger auslassen kann (DKV 4: 391).[47]

The rhetorical nature of Kleist's political mindset appears not only in his letters, but also in those writings that he had considered for publication, as we can see in a text that Kleist had drafted shortly before the battle of Aspern, 21/22 May 1809 (cf. Weiß 1984: 325-329), and that often has been read as some sort of cosmopolitan counterbalance in contrast to the one-sided chauvinism of *Germania an ihre Kinder*.[48] In *Was gilt es in diesem Kriege?*, after a long list of questions concerning the reasons for the war against Napoleon, Kleist outlines the utopia of a community,

> deren ausgelassenster und ungeheuerster Gedanke noch, von Dichtern und Weisen, auf Flügeln der Einbildung erschwungen, Unterwerfung unter eine Weltregierung ist, die, in freier Wahl, von der Gesamtheit aller Brüdernationen, gesetzt wäre (DKV 3: 478).[49]

The rhetoricity of this cosmopolitan projection is obvious, and neither of the traditional stereotypes of the "German" and the "French" are missing:

---

[47] "It is not impossible that we can get the commission for publishing the Codex Napoleon, and that our bookshop will be chosen by the French government to distribute their publications in Germany; whereby, as you easily will understand, the position of the whole company at once would be established. Be not too hasty and draw political consequences following this step, whose proper meaning I cannot explain extensively now." Transl. M. G.

[48] Cf. Richard Samuel, cit. DKV 3: 1068; Hettche 1986: 170; but also Hettche concedes that the imagination of a "Weltregierung" ("world government") in the situation of 1809 "selbst ein Teil der Agitation ist und mit der Realität nicht allzuviel gemein hat".

[49] "whose most sprightly and tremendous thought, invented on the wings of poet's and wise men's imagination, is the subjection under a government of the world, that would be appointed by the entirety of all brother nations in free elections", transl. M. G.

Eine Gemeinschaft gilt es, deren Wahrhaftigkeit und Offenherzigkeit, gegen Freund und Feind gleich unerschütterlich geübt, bei dem Witz der Nachbarn zum Sprichwort geworden ist (DKV 3: 478).[50]

The members of this universal community are defined as "truthful" and "frank," and it is not by chance their authenticity reminds of Arndts "Sohn vom Teut." In his rhetorical mode of surpassing, Kleist is not shy of using the most daring images:

Eine Gemeinschaft mithin gilt es, die dem ganzen Menschengeschlecht angehört; die die Wilden der Südsee noch, wenn sie sie kennten, zu beschützen herbeiströmen würden; eine Gemeinschaft, deren Dasein keine deutsche Brust überleben, und die nur mit Blut, vor dem die Sonne verdunkelt, zu Grabe gebracht werden soll (DKV 3: 479).[51]

The grotesque imagination of a German community to whose protection "the savages of the south seas" would come in flocks, is only exceeded by the final paradoxical vision of a collective doom, in which the coming community will not survive its own birth. This idea of an existence in extinction has been a continuous motive in Kleist's letters right up to his own spectacular suicide, "joyous and inexpressibly cheerful," as he wrote in his last letter (Kleist / Constantine 1997: 427).[52] The cosmopolitan tone of *Was gilt es in diesem Kriege?* can hardly be brought in accord with the harsh aristocratical attitude that the author shows in other writings.[53] It rather fits the indetermination

---

[50] 'The concern now is a community whose veracity and sincerity, equally unaffected executed unto friend and foe, in our neighbours' wit has become a saying.' Transl. M. G.

[51] "Therefore the concern now is a community that belongs to the whole of mankind; to whose protection the savages of the south seas would come in flocks if they only were acquainted with it; a community whose existence no German breast shall survive, and that only with blood, that darkens the sun, shall be carried to the grave." Transl. M. G.

[52] Kleist, H. v.: Letter to Ulrike von Kleist, 21 November 1811: "Ich kann nicht sterben, ohne mich, zufrieden und heiter, wie ich bin, mit der ganzen Welt, und somit auch, vor allen Anderen, meine theuerste Ulrike, mit dir versöhnt zu haben [...]; wirklich, du hast an mir gethan, ich sage nicht, was in Kräften einer Schwester, sondern in Kräften eines Menschen stand, um mich zu retten: die Wahrheit ist, daß mir auf Erden nicht zu helfen war. Und nun lebe wohl; möge dir der Himmel einen Tod schenken, nur halb an Freude und unaussprechlicher Heiterkeit, dem meinigen gleich: das ist der herzlichste und innigste Wunsch, den ich für dich aufzubringen weiß" (DKV 4: 513).

[53] Cf. f.e. the ending of *Die Herrmannsschlacht*, where the election of a German king is reserved to "der gesamten Fürsten Rat" ("the council of all the princes"), DKV 2: 552.

and the willingness of Kleist to join varying alliances, if they only served his personal purposes.

But even though Kleist in several letters stressed that he "did not have a political opinion"[54] and "even in thoughts would not interfere in the disagreements of the world,"[55] one should still not underestimate the political dedication of the writings from 1808/09 and how they relate to the reality of the times. Whilst the details of domestic policy might not have been of first priority for Kleist, foreign affairs were of high interest for the Prussian poet. Through its more abstract character, foreign policy is less binding, more tenta-

---

[54]   Assertions like this can not be taken as representative for Kleist's political mindset, they are of a rhetorical character, as their context shows. The quoted passage is taken from a letter Kleist wrote from Bern to his sister Ulrike 12 January 1802: "Die Güter sind jetzt im Durchschnitt alle im Preise ein wenig gesunken, weil mancher, seiner politischen Meinungen wegen, entweder verdrängt wird, oder freiwillig weicht. Ich selbst aber, der ich gar keine politische Meinung habe, brauche nichts zu fürchten und zu fliehen." This lack of political opinions obviously means *public* opinions, as Kleist's next letter to his sister, only one month later, tells another story: "Es hatte allen Anschein, daß die Schweiz sowie Zisalpinien, französisch werden wird, und mich ekelt vor dem bloßen Gedanken. – So leicht indessen wird es dem Allerwelts-Konsul mit der Schweiz nicht gelingen. Zwar tut er sein Mögliches, dieses arme Land durch innere Unruhen immer schwach zu erhalten, und jetzt in diesem Augenblicke noch ist Zürich im Aufstande; indessen gewiß, wenn er sich deutlich erklärt, vereinigt sich alles gegen den allgemeinen Wolf" (Letter to Ulrike, Thun, 19 February 1802, DKV 4: 299). And another month later, Kleist writes: "Es ist fast so gut wie ausgemacht, daß dies unglückliche Land auf irgend eine Art ein Opfer der französischen Brutalität wird, und ich weiß aus sichern Händen, daß die Schweizer Regierung, die bisher immer noch laviert hat, auf dem Punkte ist, sich ganz unzweideutig gegen die Franzosen zu erklären. Die Erbitterung der Schweizer gegen diese Affen der Vernunft ist so groß, daß jede andere Leidenschaft weicht, und daß die heftigsten Köpfe der Parteien durch den Würfel entscheiden lassen, wer sich in die Meinung des andern fügen soll, bloß um, wie schmollende Eheleute, sich gegen den Dieb zu wehren, der einbricht. Ein Krieg also steht wahrscheinlicher Weise diesem Lande schon in diesem Sommer bevor [...]" (Letter to Ulrike, Thun, 18 March 1802, DKV 4: 302).

[55]   Kleist in a letter to Christoph Martin Wieland, 10 March 1807 after his arrest and imprisonment in France accused of espionage: "Erschrecken Sie nicht, es muß ein Mißverstä<nd>nis dieser Sache zugrunde liegen, denn auch nicht in Gedanken, wie Sie sich leicht überzeugen werden, mischt ich mich in den Streit der Welt. Unsre Order lautet auch auf weiter nichts, als Gefangenschaft bis zum Frieden, und wenn wir unsre Gefängnisse nur mit Zimmern verwechseln dürfen, wie wir auszuwirken hoffen, so sind wir völlig zufrieden. Die ganze Veränderung mindestens, die *ich* dadurch erleide, besteht darin, daß ich nunmehr in Joux, statt in Dresden oder Weimar dichte; und wenn es nur *gute Verse* sind, was gilt das Übrige?'" (DKV 4: 371f)

tive and therefore allows a higher degree of ideological positioning, especially at times when war was estimated as a legitimate "continuation of policy by other means", as Kleist's contemporary von Clausewitz stated in his book *On War* (Clausewitz 1832-34: 210). In a way, foreign affairs had a higher *aesthetic* value than domestic policy to Kleist, they were more suitable for dramatisation, as we can see in most of his plays. Kleist's interest for politics is not least motivated by the search for subject matters for his literature.

Kleist's political writings from 1809 have been regarded as a more or less homogenous unit, that could be connected to a particular period in the author's life – right up to the practice of the editors of his works, who as a rule subsume these publications under the common label "Politische Schriften von 1809". But the fact that Kleist's writings in this period in many respects follow his "intention to throw myself, mediately or immediately, into the stream of incidents"[56] and to "write nothing but works that fall into the middle of time"[57] should not lead to the assumption that they actually represent a coherent unit of sense. Even in instant proximity to Kleist's *Germania an ihre Kinder* we find writings of a very different nature, as for example *Das letzte Lied* (DKV 3: 438f.).[58] Because of its contradictory representation of the horrors of war and its obvious mistrust in the power of poetry, the poem has for a long time been considered as having been written after the Austrian defeat against Napoleon at the battle of Wagram in July 1809. But it was in reality written in April 1809, thus in the same month as *Germania an ihre Kinder*.[59] The fact that two such contradictory poems were written practically simultaneously, is a strong argument against the assumption that the texts in any way are mere representations of certain historical events. Even if the first losses of the Austrian troops might have depressed Kleist, it seems speculative to reduce the highly complex poetical construction of *Das letzte Lied* to a reflex on short-

---

[56]   Kleist, H. v.: Letter to Ulrike von Kleist, 17 July 1809: "Ich gieng aus D[resden] weg, wie du weißt, in der Absicht, mich mittelbar oder unmittelbar, in den Strom der Begebenheiten hinein zu werfen" (DKV 4: 437).

[57]   Kleist, H. v.: Letter to Karl von Stein zum Altenstein, 1 January 1809: "Und wenn der Tag uns nur völlig erscheint, von welchem Sie uns die Morgenröthe heraufführen, so will ich lauter Werke schreiben, die in die Mitte der Zeit hineinfallen" (DKV 4: 427).

[58]   DKV 3: 438f. For a detailed reading of the poem cf. Hettche 1986: 182-191.

[59]   The earlier dating of the poem is based on two dated manuscripts of the poem (cf. Weiss 1984: 310-313).

term political events and subsequently a personal crisis of the author.[60] On the contrary, the inconsistency of the political orientation in Kleist's writings can only be explained by their rhetoricity. Even in his most unambigous poems, Kleist's focus lies on literariness, not on a realistic propagandistic function.[61]

In this context it is of interest that the reasons for war given in *Germania an ihre Kinder* are absolutely not of such a nature that would best serve the immediate aim of mobilisation to war. The abandonment of worldly goods to the advantage of abstract values like freedom, fatherland and god, not to mention the German language and knowledge, would have been difficult to place in the "Germany" of 1809. And also Kleist's drastic and hyperbolic representations of war are not as compelling to participation in the war as the idealisations and glorifications of the warrior in contemporary propaganda poems like those of Körner or Arndt. The politicisation of sacral forms,[62] from Germania's resurrection ("Stehst du auf, Germania?") to the proclamation of a "holy war" in Kleist's political writings, appears equally overdone to the reader as the exaggerated, rhetorically styled descriptions of war. The whole construc-

---

[60]  Weiss' meticulous reconstruction of the historical background of *Das letzte Lied* (Weiss 1984: 306-313) therefore occasionally falls back on modal adverbs and conjunctives, when it speculates about the references of the words in the poem. The limited significance of the conjecture becomes evident, when for instance the poetical picture of war as a flow that tears away the older states is regarded as a representation of Napoleon's early successes in the battles of Regensburg between 19 and 23 April 1809 (Weiss 1984: 311). For an analysis of the rhetorical structure of *Das letzte Lied* cf. Hettche 1986: 182-188. Yet Hettche's conclusion, "daß in einer Zeit voller Widersprüche die Hervorbringungen der Kunst notwendig auch widerspruchsvoll sein müssen", reduces the writings to a representation of history as well (Hettche 1986: 189).

[61]  As seen before, the patriotic writings in the time of the Napoleonic expansion in Europe have a double function: On the one hand the harsh opposition against 'the French' was a reaction to a real experience of military defeat and occupation. On the other hand, the distorted pictures of "die Welschen" had a retroactive effect on the process of the German nationbuilding. The concept of *negative integration* that Otto von Bismarck came to use sixty years later for the consolidation of the first German Empire had its outset here (cf. Wehler 1973: 96). In the situation of 1809, at a time when the commonalities of the different "German" countries to the most of their peoples were not clear, in this respect "the French" were a welcome common enemy. And as it is clear to the contemporary reader that "the Germans" in *Germania an ihre Kinder* is a utopian construction, the picture of "the French" gains a more constructive, if not fictional character as well.

[62]  Hettche 1986: 214, to the contamination of Christian propagation and political plea and its transformation into a national religious proclamation in *Germania an ihre Kinder* cf. also Detering 2009: 178f.

tion can not be read as anything but a literary text, i.e. a text that reacts to and within a given literary tradition and that has to be read in its literary context, and not exclusively is a source for historical or biographical information. As Gerhard Schulz has stated, *Germania an ihre Kinder* has not entered the repertoire of the German singing societies[63] – and this gives evidence for the fact that Kleist's poetical language was not suitable for propagandist purposes. Ironically Schulz points out that the extraordinary description of the Germans as Germania's sons, who, kissed, crawl into her lap, rather would qualify the author for psychoanalysis than the poem for inspiration of an embattled crowd of people.[64] Furthermore, composita like the "Römerüberwinderbrut" have an almost comical effect – not to mention the fact that the Germans themselves appear as a "breed" in the poem, in their fury no longer distinguishable from their enemies, who in *Die Herrmannsschlacht* were described as "the whole breed, that has felted itself into Germania's body like a swarm of insects."[65] This casualness in the distribution of metaphors, seeing the Germans and their enemies as "breeds" demonstrates an attitude more occupied by rhetoric than by its actual purport in respect to real-life politics.[66]

In a significant scene, Kleist's friend Friedrich Christoph Dahlmann, later known as leader of the "Göttingen Seven,"[67] shows how Kleist's image of himself as a politically well-informed contemporary taking part in the political discourse of his time is carried away by the all-embracing make-believe, even into and beyond the reality of the battlefields. Kleist and Dahlmann, eager campaigners for a Prussian support of the Austrian army's war against

---

[63] Cf. Schulz 1993: 71.
[64] Cf. Schulz 1993: 72.
[65] "Die ganze Brut, die in den Leib Germaniens / Sich eingefilzt, wie ein Insektenschwarm" (DKV 2: 514).
[66] However, concerning the intentions of Kleist's, it cannot be denied that he obviously had hopes for a practical influence of *Germania an ihre Kinder*, as a comparison of the different versions of the poem confirms. As Walter Hettche has shown, the earliest and the latest wording of the ode feature a significant difference: Whilst the earliest version stresses the unimportance of worldly goods, the last version inverts the argumentation into its opposite, possibly with the intention to strengthen the practical propagandist appeal of the poem (cf. Hettche 1986: 175 f.). Considering the impression of the whole poem, this attempt shows above all Kleist's fundamental misjudgement of the efficacy of poetry.
[67] The "Göttingen Seven" protested in 1837 against the abolition of the constitution of the Kingdom of Hanover by Ernest Augustus and were relieved of their posts at the university as a consequence. Furthermore, Dahlmann and the Brothers Grimm were expelled from the country.

Napoleon, travelled as "Schlachtenbummler" to the battlefield of Aspern, where the French army had suffered its first defeat by Austrian troops on 21/22 May 1809. After a conversation with a local, Kleist and Dahlmann were suspected of being spies, and ran into trouble:

> Zwei Tage nach der Schlacht von Aspern erlebten wir, die das Schlachtfeld zu betrachten kamen, einen sonderbaren Auftritt. Beim Hin- und Herwandern standen wir der Lobau gegenüber, und ich fragte, auf einen schmalen Arm der Donau zeigend, einen Bauern, der Kugeln sammelte, ob die Franzosen hier eine Brücke gebaut oder die Furt, die nicht tief schien, durchwatet hätten? Der ehrliche Mann verstand das so, als ob ich zu den Franzosen auf der Lobau hinüber wolle, und machte gleich seine Anzeige. Als aber auf den Lärm von zwei Spionen sich eine große Schar von Soldaten schimpfend um uns sammelte, da war es ein halb trauriger, halb komischer Anblick, wie Kleist seine franzosenfeindlichen Gedichte aus der Tasche zog und dadurch Wunder zu wirken glaubte. Allein selbst bei den Offizieren tat das keine andere Wirkung, als daß die einen zur Schmach eines ehrenvollen Namens Kleisten fragten, ob er dem Magdeburger Kleist verwandt sei, die andern aber, welche einzelnes in den Gedichten lasen, dem Verfasser Vorwürfe machten, daß er sich in Politik und überhaupt in Dinge mische, die einen guten Untertanen gar nichts angingen. Die Sache selbst war ungefährlich und ward durch den Feldmarschall Grafen Hiller, in dessen Hauptquartier zu Neustädtl [Neusiedl] wir geführt wurden, unmittelbar mit großer Freundlichkeit beendigt.[68]

The "half sad, half comical sight" of Kleist's attempt to convince the soldiers that he was not a spy through his patriotic poems is significant for his total

---

[68]    Friedrich Christoph Dahlmann, *Autobiographie* (1849), cit. Sembdner 1996: 297f., no. 316 ("Two days after the battle of Aspern we, who came to view the battlefield, experienced a peculiar scene. Walking around, we were standing across from the Lobau, and I, pointing at a narrow arm of the Donau, asked a peasant, who was gathering bullets, if the French had built a bridge here or if they had waded through the ford, that didn't seem deep? The honest man took it, that I wished to get over to the French on the Lobau, and made at once a complaint. Because of the clamour over two spies a large flock of scolding soldiers gatheredaround us, and it was a half sad, half comical sight how Kleist abstracted his francophobe poems out of his pocket, expecting them to work miracles. But the only effects this had, even amongst the officers, was that some, humiliating the honourful name, asked Kleist if he was related to the Kleist from Magdeburg, others, who read in the poems, blamed the author for interfering with politics and generally things that did not concern a good commoner at all. The matter itself was harmless, and the Field Marshal Graf Hiller, to whose headquarters at Neustädtl [Neusiedl] we were led, ended it immediately and with great kindness." Transl. M. G.)

misjudgement of the effect of literature in actual politics. The soldiers' question of Kleist's relations to the "Magdeburger Kleist," the commander of the garrison in Magdeburg Franz Casimir von Kleist, who in 1806 controversially surrendered the town to the French without a fight, must have been wounding for Kleist,[69] but even more humiliating was the patronising treatment as a civilian, who was supposed to refrain from military affairs and debates that were none of his concern. For Kleist, who dreamt of a reconstitution of the Holy Roman Empire of the German Nation by a total mobilisation of all Germans under the command of the Austrian Emperor Franz I, "Wiederhersteller und provisorischer Regent der Deutschen,"[70] this must have been a blatant demonstration of the unrealistic nature of his poetical attempts, a renewed confirmation of the failure of his personal project.

## Germania and Penthesilea, heroines of performativity

As the analysis has shown, Kleist's political writings can not be judged as an "error" or sidetrack in his works, suggesting that he sacrificed his literary aspirations for the requirements of current propaganda during the times of the Napoleonic expansion in Europe. Poems like *Germania an ihre Kinder* with its exaggerated, hyperbolic representations of war and the fury of uncompromising nationalism seem to be driven by a fascination for its own rhetorical figures rather than by propagandist regards. The dynamic of the poem is driven by an absolutisation of metaphors (cf. Blamberger 2011: 341) that we know from other writings of Kleist's, particularly from the drama *Penthesilea*, finished one year before *Germania an ihre Kinder* (DKV 2: 143-256). Penthesilea's blundering violence resembles Germania's call for a "blindfold" fury. Even though the obvious connection with historical reality in *Germania an ihre Kinder* makes a striking difference to the ancient, or at least historically remote, locations of other fictional writings of Kleist's, the references to "actuality" and "reality" are equally subjected to the processes of rhetorical fictionalisation, whether they be the idea of the "Germans" or the "French." Through a perspective that no

---

[69] Franz Casimir von Kleist was a distant relative of Heinrich von Kleist's, the great-grandson of the brother of Kleist's Great-great-grandfather. The surrender of Magdeburg despite the military superiority of the defenders was controversial, and Franz Casimir was posthumously sentenced to death penalty by an inquiry panel, that was appointed by king Frederick William III in 1807.

[70] Kleist, H. v.: Über die Rettung von Österreich [1809] (DKV 3: 500f.).

longer distinguishes between the real and the seeming,[71] reality becomes partly fictionalised – right up to the poet's celebration of his own suicide.

Yet the pragmatic aspect of *Germania an ihre Kinder* is undeniable. Evidently Kleist urged his publisher to quick publication of his patriotic poems and tried to optimise the impact of them, and even if he did not succeed in this, it is obvious that Kleist in 1808/09 gave his writing and texts a new function. They are no longer merely *about* reality, but they are part of and an intervention in reality. This pragmatic turn also manifests itself in the often critiqued call for regardless, unhesitating, *unconsidered* manslaughter in *Germania an ihre Kinder* that explicitly denies the necessity of reasoning in times of war: "Schlagt ihn tot! Das Weltgericht / Fragt euch nach den Gründen nicht!" Besides the moralist scandal of this call for unreflective action, it should not be overlooked that this concept obviously is informed by Kleist's poetics, which he already in 1805 had outlined in an article "On the Gradual Production of Thoughts whilst Speaking" (*Über die allmähliche Verfertigung der Gedanken beim Reden*, DKV 3: 534-540). Here Kleist developed a model of a performative poetics deeply sceptical of any possibility of free thought and the cognoscibility of the world. "Denn nicht *wir* wissen, es ist allererst ein gewisser *Zustand* unsrer, welcher weiß,"[72] reads Kleist's essay: Thinking appears as a function of its own mediality, not a requirement, but a product of action.

In an article in his *Berliner Abendblätter* in 1810, *Von der Überlegung. Eine Paradoxe* ("Reflection. A paradox"), Kleist outlined his performative concept in detail. In principle, the text is the fictional speech of a father, to be delivered to his son, if he at some point "might assign himself to become a soldier":

> Die Überlegung, wisse, findet ihren Zeitpunkt weit schicklicher *nach*, als *vor* der Tat. Wenn sie vorher, oder in dem Augenblick der Entscheidung selbst, ins Spiel tritt: so scheint sie nur die zum Handeln nötige Kraft, die aus dem herrlichen Gefühl quillt, zu verwirren, zu hemmen und zu unterdrücken; dagegen sich nachher, wenn die Handlung abgetan ist, der Gebrauch von ihr machen läßt, zu welchem sie dem Menschen eigentlich gegeben

---

[71]  In a letter to Karl Freiherr von Stein zum Altenstein, 13 May 1805, Kleist reflected this aspect explicitly in the often quoted words: "Denn es kommt überall nicht auf den Gegenstand, sondern auf das Auge an, das ihn betrachtet, und unter den Sinnen eines Denkers wird alles zum Stoff" (DKV 4: 339).

[72]  DKV 3: 540. "For it is not *we* who know things but pre-eminently a certain *condition* of ours which knows" (Kleist / Constantine 1997: 408).

ist, nämlich sich dessen, was in dem Verfahren fehlerhaft und gebrechlich war, bewußt zu werden, und das Gefühl für andere künftige Fälle zu regulieren (DKV 3: 554).[73]

Reason appears in this perspective merely as a disturbing factor in action. Even the consciousness one acquires through experience will hardly be applicable on "other occasions in the future," because then again action will precede reflection. When it comes to the "regulation of feelings" that Kleist invokes here, the prospects are not too good, as we can often see in the stories and plays of Kleist, from the excesses of violence in *Penthesilea* to the German fury in *Germania an ihre Kinder*.

In the following, Kleist develops an approach to a performative aesthetics through a comparison between human acting and a wrestling match:

Das Leben selbst ist ein Kampf mit dem Schicksal; und es verhält sich auch mit dem Handeln wie mit dem Ringen. Der Athlet kann, in dem Augenblick, da er seinen Gegner umfaßt hält, schlechthin nach keiner anderen Rücksicht, als nach bloßen augenblicklichen Eingebungen verfahren; und derjenige, der berechnen wollte, welche Muskeln er anstrengen, und welche Glieder er in Bewegung setzen soll, um zu überwinden, würde unfehlbar den Kürzeren ziehen, und unterliegen. [...] Wer das Leben nicht, wie ein solcher Ringer, umfaßt hält, und tausendgliedrig, nach allen Windungen des Kampfs, nach allen Widerständen, Drücken, Ausweichungen und Reaktionen, empfindet und spürt: der wird, was er will, in keinem Gespräch, durchsetzen; vielweniger in einer Schlacht (DKV 3: 554f.).[74]

---

[73] 'The proper time for reflection, let me tell you, is not *before* you act, but *after*. If reflection plays a part beforehand or at the very moment of decision it seems only to confuse, inhibit and repress the power we cannot act without and which has its splendid source in the feelings; whereas after, when the deed is done, our powers of reflection may serve the purpose they were actually given us for, namely to bring us to consciousness of what was wrong or unsound in how we acted and to regulate the feelings for other occasions in the future" (Kleist / Constantine 1997: 410).

[74] "Life itself is a struggle with Fate; and in our actions it is much as it is in a wrestling match. The wrestler, having hold of his opponent, cannot possibly at that moment proceed otherwise than according to the promptings of the moment; and a man who tried to calculate which muscles he should employ and which limbs he should set in motion in order to win would inevitably be disadvantaged and defeated. [...] A man must, like that wrestler, take hold of life and feel and sense with a thousand limbs how his opponent twists and turns, resists him, comes at him, evades him and reacts: or he will never get his way in a conversation, much less in at battle" (Kleist / Constantine 1997: 410).

The conception of time in this simile is revealing: Here, aesthetic practice appears as a proceeding "according to the promptings of the moment", that subverts the continuity of reasonable and predictable considerations. In this Kleist follows the early romanticist discourse of *suddenness* (cf. Bohrer 1981), though radicalising it by a regression to physical basics. This concept of an embodied mind has its roots in a performative concept of thought. As Günter Blamberger has shown, creativity is to Kleist "not at all a calculable process in the sense of a transformation of knowledge and plans in practical acting, but a modus of experience in acting itself".[75] And it is just this performative aspect that opens the romantic conception of aesthetics for a basic critique of language and media.[76] Whilst the romantic "ironical overdetermination," by which the signs set aside their actual meanings and become manifestations of the infinite (Frank 1989: 366), directs the view away from the materiality of the letters, Kleist's performative aesthetics focus on the concrete and physical practice of communication. It is important to understand this poetological background in romanticist reflection of language in order to estimate what Kleist's writing actually deals with. The descriptions of wrestling matches, conversations and battles serve as models for literature itself.

As indicated before, the tragedy of *Penthesilea* from 1808, by Goethe rejected as "unplayable" (Lamport 1990: 161), can be seen as a role model for Kleist's poetics of performativity. And it is no coincidence that we find a strong concurrence between the war poem *Germania an ihre Kinder* and *Penthesilea*, both regarding the rhetorical dynamics in the representation of violence and the topic of "acting before thinking" – in the case of Germania as a matter of honour and patriotism, in the case of Penthesilea as a matter of eroticism. The storyline of the play takes place in the battlefield at the gates of Troy. The war between the Amazones and the Greeks is developing into a conflict between the Greek prince Achilles and the queen of the Amazones, Penthesilea. In the last act the Greek hero meets Penthesilea, with whom he has fallen in love, but in a sudden furious and unconsidered attack the Amazon queen kills the

---

[75]  "Kreativität ist bei Kleist keineswegs ein kalkulierbarer Prozess im Sinne einer Transformation von Wissen und Plänen in praktisches Handeln, sondern Modus der Erfahrung im Handeln selbst" (Blamberger 2011: 494).

[76]  Even if the self-reflection of the early romantic irony, by moving the focus from the represented to the reception, bears witness to a consciousness of a limit of language (Japp 1983: 185), it yet adhered to the principle of representation in literature. Poetry was for authors like Novalis and Schlegel still a "copy of the mind" and conveyed "a true picture of life", cf. (Novalis 1968: 655, no. 580; Schlegel 1963: 198, no. 21).

unarmed Achilles. The terrifying showdown between Achilles and Penthesilea, who, together with her dogs, tears her lover to pieces, is caused by a characteristic misunderstanding. As Penthesilea awakes from her fury, realising what she has done, she says:

> So war es ein Versehen. Küsse, Bisse,
> Das reimt sich, und wer recht von Herzen liebt,
> Kann schon das Eine für das Andre greifen
> (DKV 2: 254).[77]

The scepticism about the capability of language to individual expression and its suitability as a medium of insight that Kleist had declared already in the beginning of the decade,[78] becomes a driving moment of action in the drama *Penthesilea*. Achilles' death does not make sense, it is caused by nothing but a horrible confusion of words. When one year later violence and language, as in *Germania an ihre Kinder*, suddenly chime together in Kleist's writings, this is not a consequence of a mere suspension of the subject's alienation from language and history on behalf of the author's patriotic commitment.[79] On the contrary, the alienation is radicalised by a transfer of literature into life practice ever since the play *Die Herrmannsschlacht*. From this point of view Kleist's propagandist activity becomes prominent as an artificial, rather than an actual political practice. It is aesthetics, not history that moved Kleist to his harsh engagement for the war against Napoleon.

---

[77] "So it was a mistake. Kisses, bites, / That rhymes, and when we love straight from the heart, / It's easy to do one when we mean the other." Transl. M. G.

[78] Kleist elaborated on the insufficiency of words as a medium of understanding in a letter to his sister Ulrike, 5 February 1801: "Ach, Du weißt nicht, wie es in meinem Innersten aussieht. Aber es interessirt Dich doch? – O gewiß! Und gern möchte ich Dir Alles mittheilen, wenn es möglich wäre. Aber es ist nicht möglich, u wenn es auch kein weiteres Hinderniß gäbe, als dieses, daß es uns an einem Mittel zur Mittheilung fehlt. Selbst das einzige, das wir besitzen, die Sprache taugt nicht dazu, sie kann die Seele nicht mahlen u was sie uns giebt sind nur zerrissene Bruchstücke. Daher habe ich jedesmal eine Empfindung, wie ein Grauen, wenn ich jemandem mein Innerstes aufdecken soll; nicht eben weil es sich vor der Blöße scheut, aber weil ich ihm nicht *Alles* zeigen kann, nicht *kann*, u daher fürchten muß, aus den Bruchstücken falsch verstanden zu werden" (DKV 4: 196).

[79] Cf. Stephens 1999: 40: "Gewalt und Sprache harmonieren in Kleists patriotischen Schriften auf eine Art und Weise miteinander, die keine Entfremdung des Sprechenden von diesem sonst so widerspenstigen Medium kennt, weil Kleists niemals abgeschlossener, kritischer Dialog mit den Wertsetzungen der Aufklärung eine Zeitlang schlichtweg suspendiert wird."

# Bibliography

Kleist, H. v. (1987): *Sämtliche Werke und Briefe in vier Bänden*, ed. by Ilse-Marie Barth, Klaus Müller-Salget, Stefan Ormanns, Hinrich C. Seeba, vol. 2: *Dramen 1808-1811*, ed. by Ilse-Marie Barth and Hinrich C. Seeba, ass. by Hans Rudolf Barth. Frankfurt a. M.: Deutscher Klassiker Verlag 1987 (= DKV 2).

Kleist, H. v. (1990): *Sämtliche Werke und Briefe in vier Bänden*, ed. by Ilse-Marie Barth, Klaus Müller-Salget, Stefan Ormanns, Hinrich C. Seeba, vol. 3: *Erzählungen, Anekdoten, Gedichte, Schriften*, ed. by Klaus Müller-Salget. Frankfurt a. M.: Deutscher Klassiker Verlag 1990 (= DKV 3).

Kleist, H. v. (1997): *Sämtliche Werke und Briefe in vier Bänden*, ed. by Ilse-Marie Barth, Klaus Müller-Salget, Stefan Ormanns and Hinrich C. Seeba, vol. 4: *Briefe von und an Heinrich von Kleist 1793-1811*, ed. by Klaus Müller-Salget and Stefan Ormanns. Frankfurt a. M.: Deutscher Klassiker Verlag 1997 (= DKV 4).

Kleist, H. v.: *Sämtliche Werke. Brandenburger Ausgabe*, ed. by Roland Reuß and Peter Staengle, vol. 3: *Sämtliche Gedichte*. Frankfurt a. M.: Stroemfeld/Roter Stern 2005 (= BKA 3).

Kleist, H. v. and D. Constantine (1997): *Selected writings*, ed. and transl. by David Constantine. London: J. M. Dent.

Kleist, H. v. and R. MagShamhráin (2008): *The Battle of Herrmann. A Drama*, transl. by Rachel MagShamhráin. Würzburg: Verlag Königshausen & Neumann.

Arndt, E. M. (1912): *Arndts Werke. Auswahl in zwölf Teilen. Erster Teil. Gedichte*, ed. by August von Leffson. Berlin, Leipzig, Wien, Stuttgart: Deutsches Verlagshaus Bong & Co. n.d.

Benthien, C. (2009): "Schiller." In: Breuer, I. (ed.): *Kleist-Handbuch. Leben – Werk – Wirkung*. Stuttgart, Weimar: Verlag J. B. Metzler, 219-227.

Berg, R. (1979): "Intention und Rezeption von Kleists politischen Schriften des Jahres 1809." In: Kanzog, K. (ed.): *Text und Kontext. Quellen und Aufsätze zur Rezeptionsgeschichte der Werke Heinrich von Kleists*. Berlin: E. Schmidt, 193-253.

Blamberger, G. (2011): *Heinrich von Kleist. Biographie*. Frankfurt a. M.: Fischer.

Bohrer, K. H. (1981): *Plötzlichkeit. Zum Augenblick des ästhetischen Scheins*. Frankfurt a. M.: Suhrkamp Verlag.

Clausewitz, C. v. (1832-1834): *Vom Kriege*. Hinterlassenes Werk des Generals Carl von Clausewitz, vol. 1-3. Berlin: Ferdinand Dümmler.

Detering, H. (2009): "Lyrik." In: Breuer, I. (ed.): *Kleist-Handbuch. Leben – Werk – Wirkung*. Stuttgart, Weimar: Verlag J. B. Metzler, 175-180.

Frank, M. (1989): *Einführung in die frühromantische Ästhetik. Vorlesungen*. Frankfurt a. M.: Suhrkamp Verlag.

Frauenholz, E. v. (1941): *Das Heerwesen des XIX. Jahrhunderts*. München: Verlag C. H. Beck (= *Entwicklungsgeschichte des deutschen Heerwesens*, ed. by E. v. Frauenholz, vol. 5).

Grab, W. and U. Friesel (1970): *Noch ist Deutschland nicht verloren. Eine historisch-politische Analyse unterdrückter Lyrik von der Französischen Revolution bis zur Reichsgründung*. München: Carl Hanser Verlag.

Grathoff, D. (1994): "Heinrich von Kleist und Napoleon Bonaparte, der Furor Teutonicus und die ferne Revolution". In: Neumann, G. (ed.): *Heinrich von Kleist. Kriegsfall – Rechtsfall – Sündenfall*. Freiburg i. Br.: Rombach Verlag, 31-59.

Hamacher, B. (2009): "Goethe". In: Breuer, I. (ed.): *Kleist-Handbuch. Leben – Werk – Wirkung*. Stuttgart, Weimar: Verlag J.B. Metzler, 214-219.

Hettche, W. (1986): *Heinrich von Kleists Lyrik*. Frankfurt a.M., Bern, New York: Peter Lang.

Japp, U. (1983): *Theorie der Ironie*. Frankfurt a. M.: Klostermann.

Kittler, W. (1987): *Die Geburt des Partisanen aus dem Geist der Poesie. Heinrich von Kleist und die Strategie der Befreiungskriege*. Freiburg: Verlag Rombach.

Koselleck, R. (1972): "Über die Theoriebedürftigkeit der Geschichtswissenschaft." In: Conze, W. (ed.): *Theorie der Geschichtswissenschaft und Praxis des Geschichtsunterrichts*. Stuttgart: Klett, 10-28.

Lamport, F. J. (1990): *German Classical Drama: Theatre, Humanity and Nation, 1750-1870*. Cambridge: Cambridge University Press.

Mommsen, K. (1974): *Kleists Kampf mit Goethe*. Heidelberg: Lothar Stiehm Verlag.

Müller-Salget, K. (2002): *Heinrich von Kleist*. Stuttgart: Reclam.

Novalis (1968): *Schriften. Die Werke Friedrich von Hardenbergs*, ed. by Paul Kluckhohn and Richard Samuel (2. ext. ed.), vol. III: *Das philosophische Werk II*, ed. by Richard Samuel in ass. with Hans-Joachim Mähl and Gerhard Schulz. Stuttgart: Kohlhammer.

Peymann, C. and Kreutzer, H. J. (1984): "Streitgespräch über Kleists 'Herrmannsschlacht'." In: *Kleist-Jahrbuch*, 77-97.

Plessner, H. (1959): *Die verspätete Nation. Über die politische Verführbarkeit bürgerlichen Geistes*. Stuttgart: Kohlhammer (1. ed. 1935 with the title "Das Schicksal deutschen Geistes im Ausgang seiner bürgerlichen Epoche").

Schiller, F. (1992): *Werke und Briefe in zwölf Bänden*, ed. by Otto Dann et al., vol. 1: Gedichte, ed. by Georg Kurscheidt. Frankfurt a. M.: Deutscher Klassiker Verlag.

Schings, H.-J. (2008/09): "Über einige Grausamkeiten bei Heinrich von Kleist." In: *Kleist-Jahrbuch*, 115-137.

Schlegel, F. (1963): *Kritische Friedrich-Schlegel-Ausgabe*, ed. by. E. Behler et al., vol. XVIII: *Philosophische Lehrjahre. 1796-1828*, part one, ed. by Ernst Behler, München, Paderborn, Wien, Zürich: Thomas-Verlag.

Schmitt, C. (1963 [1975]): *Theorie des Partisanen. Zwischenbemerkung zum Begriff des Politischen*. Berlin: Duncker & Humblodt.

Schulz, G. (1993): "Von der Verfassung der Deutschen. Kleist und der literarische Patriotismus nach 1808." In: *Kleist-Jahrbuch*, 56-74.

Schulz, G. (2007): *Kleist. Eine Biographie*. München: Verlag C. H. Beck.

Seeba, H. C. (2007): "Die Filzlaus im Leib Germaniens. Kleists 'Herrmannsschlacht' als Programm ethnischer Säuberung." In: Martin Maurach (ed.): *Kleist im Nationalsozialismus* [= *Beiträge zur Kleist-Forschung* 2005, vol. 19, ed. by Lothar Jordan]. Würzburg: Königshausen & Neumann, 45-60.

Sembdner, H., ed. (1996): *Heinrich von Kleists Lebensspuren. Dokumente und Berichte der Zeitgenossen*. München: Hanser.

Stephens, A. (1999): *Kleist – Sprache und Gewalt*. Freiburg: Rombach Verlag.

Walter, D. (2003): *Preußische Heeresreformen 1807-1870. Militärische Innovation und der Mythos von der "Roonschen Reform"*. Paderborn, München, Wien, Zürich: Schöningh (= *Krieg in der Geschichte*, vol. 16).

Weiß, H. F. (1984): *Funde und Studien zu Heinrich von Kleist*. Tübingen: Max Niemeyer Verlag.

Wehler, H.-U. (1973): *Das Deutsche Kaiserreich 1871-1918*. Göttingen: Vandenhoeck & Ruprecht.

# Part 2:
# Europe and the Jews

# Inventing Tolerance in Europe and Utopia: Inclusion and Exclusion

*Torgeir Skorgen*

Even though 'tolerance' today is considered an almost indisputably positive concept, it is important to remember that in European history, tolerance was rather the exception to the rule. Those who encouraged and promoted tolerance would put themselves into a rhetorically and politically rather difficult situation, and could scarcely count on any recognition in their own lifetime. In most cases they would be lucky to survive. For centuries, ideas of interreligious tolerance were considered an heresy in Europe and could be punished by torture and even death. Throughout most of the history of Europe, the concept of interreligious tolerance, in the sense of recognising other individual's or group's rights to freedom of conscience within certain limits, has been considered controversial. Moreover, as a cultural invention, it must be considered rather unlikely. The spokesmen for interreligious tolerance therefore had to deal with tolerance as a deficiency condition. The majority's lack of will or ability to recognise diverse political or religious concepts and spiritual movements within the same borders has in most cases caused reflection and new concepts of tolerance. To some spokesmen, like the philosophers Baruch de Spinoza and Moses Mendelssohn, a broader sense of tolerance among the dominant cultural group has been a precondition for their own possibility to live and publish as thinkers and writers. At the same time, both of them had to fight for recognition within their own minority, a struggle, which in Spinoza's case ended up with his expulsion from the Jewish community of Amsterdam. Others, like John Locke, Pierre Bayle, Voltaire or Henrik Wergeland, struggled for their right to challenge established truths, traditions and concepts within their own cultural group. Following these tracks, we may discover a history of philosophy of tolerance, which also implicated a concept of the intolerable and hence by extension also the construction of the outcasts from Europeanness and European tolerance, like for instance the Muslims, the Jews, the Gypsies (Romani people), tramps, and sexual minority groups. In this paper I will focus on the construction of a European, and basically Christian, history of philosophy of tolerance, and its parallel, although unspoken, exclusionary attitude towards its Jewish outsiders. The main focus in this introduction will be on the conceptual revolution of the Renaissance humanists in Italy,

England, and Holland as well as the European Enlightenment. In the second part, I will moreover focus on some anticipatory projections of interreligious tolerance in utopian fiction, and also look at the encounters between anti-Judaism/anti-Semitism, tolerance, and Jewish and universal human rights in Scandinavia up to 1942.

From the 16th century and onwards until the end of the 18th century, the concepts of Europe and Christianity were frequently used as synonymous terms. As a political slogan the concept of 'Europe' emerged in two historical crises: In the 15th century, when it was launched by Pope Pius II as a mobilizing slogan against the Muslim Turks and in the 17th century it was used by Protestant and Catholic states, which felt that their entire existence was threatened by the dominant super power on the continent, namely the France of Louis XIV. In medieval times the distinction between Christians and pagans was the most powerful criteria for making identities on macro level. In the case of the Fathers of the Church, the notion 'nations' mainly referred to the pagan tribes in contrast to the Christians. These kind of axes are referred to by Reinhart Koselleck as 'inside-outside-relations' (cf. Koselleck 1989). On the other hand the concept 'nation' mostly referred to the nobility families, which were privileged by birth and property and defined in contrast to the unprivileged layers of the population. According to Koselleck, these groups were defined by a vertical above-below relation. The concept of 'Europe' was only used on rare occasions, such as the convention of Mantua in 1459, where Pope Pius II called upon the most powerful princes of Christianity in order to mobilize them to a common crusade against the new infidel enemy, the Ottoman Turks. Consequently the convention decided, "by the help of God to dislodge the Turk from Europe" (Christensen 1988: 67). By this slogan the convention confirmed the idea of the European continent as the home of the Christians, even though there were older Church communities in Africa and the Middle East. Last but not least the formula European=Christian marked a slide from an educated cosmographical description level to a current church political level.

In order to distribute the modern ideas of nationality and Europeanness and overcome catastrophes like the religious wars of the 17th centuries, it was necessary to invent new concepts of peaceful co-existence between diverse religious worldviews within the same borders. These new concepts of tolerance rested upon several cultural and historical preconditions, such as the mind revolution which the European Renaissance humanists brought about. In this period the conception of the modern self as a spiritual individual with moral heights and depths was launched – a creation forever striving for its own perfection. This view was famously expressed by Pico della Mirandola at the age of 24 in his speech "On Human Dignity", which was published in 1486. This speech was supposed to be an introduction to his 900 theses on the profound unity of all religions, and to be defended in a debate with humanist scholars from all over Europe. It was Pico's bold ambition to concretize the humanist dream of an encompassing system, which should dissolve the religious antagonism of his time and build on the new axiom of the dignity of man. While the animals and the angels were confined to their fixed places in the cosmological order according to their divine ideas, God left the place of man empty, challenging man to fill it by his own force and give it a content (Mirandola 2012: 14). Pico thereby rejected the traditional concept of man's intermediate position between God and nature. According to Pico, God had chosen man, after creating the world, to be an observer and admirer of his entire creation, including man himself, who therefore needed to be mobile. At his best, man could rise to the glory of the angels by means of philosophy, leading from ethics, via dialectics and philosophy of nature to theology. But in the worst case, he could also sink to the levels of animals and plants. In his 900 theses and his initial speech, Pico referred to Avicenna, Aristotle, and scholasticism. But above all, Pico leans on two axioms by the Arab-al-Andalusian philosopher Ibn Rushd, who had become famous in Europe under his Latinized name Averroës.

The first axiom refers to the division between the active, over-individual intellect on the one hand, which is creative and immortal, and the human, passive intellect on the other hand, which is receiving and mortal. The second axiom refers to the doctrine on the two-fold truth. According to Averroës, philosophy and religion represent two different forms of truth: Philosophy with its dialectics and religion with its rhetorical truth, should both sit at the same table of the divine truth, without contradicting each other. At the time when Pico was studying at the University of Padua, Averroës was recognized as the leading authority, whom all humanist scholars would have to refer to, if they wanted to be taken seriously. But Pico was also leaning on several other Arab, Jewish, Persian, cabbalistic and mystical thinkers in his 900 theses, claiming to find the same divine unity expressed in all religions and confessions. On the basis of this unity, Pico sought to recognize the individual religion's contributions to this highest divine truth. Pico's conception of a higher common religious truth represents an example of such kind of tolerance concepts, which Rainer Forst refers to as a 'reductive unity': attempts to find a lowest common denominator, being essential enough to unite as many religions and spiritual movements as possible, and found a basis of common understanding (Forst 2003: 130ff.).

Given the fact, that the scale for evaluating the individual contributions of the different religions, turned out to be a Christian-Platonic doctrine of unity, Pico's doctrine also had an exclusionary aspect. In this position, Pico placed the Jews and their religion, which by his opinion attempted to vilify Christianity, while at the same time denying the Christian elements in their own religion. Compared to the anti-Judaic excesses of his time, Pico was relatively progressive in his recognition of cabbalistic or other Jewish sources. For his aspirations to recognize the religion of the magicians, however, he received a Papal correction. At this time, Pope Innocent VIII was concerned with blowing on the embers of the thousands of witch fires, flaming up all over Europe, and when Pico did not immediately give in, he was excommunicated and banned into exile. Hence, nobody would challenge the truth and salvation monopoly of the Catholic Church and claim radical arguments of tolerance without severe risk. An exception from the rule would be the liberal Netherlands, where Erasmus von Rotterdam appeared as the leading Christian thinker of Europe, later on referred to as the 16th century's Voltaire. Erasmus also became a friend of the English writer, lawyer and bishop Thomas More, whom he met as a student in Oxford. At the time, More was studying jurisprudence, while Erasmus was studying theology, both of them being more interested in Greek philosophy and literature. And both of them were also strongly inspired by Pico's optimistic view on the dignity of man, and, consequently, by the possibility to disseminate religious pluralism and tolerance. Thomas More even translated Pico's biography into English. In his famous satire *The Praise of Folly*, Erasmus pleaded with the Catholic conception of heresy. The Greek title *Moriae enkomion* hinted both at the latinised version of Thomas More's name, Morus, and the Greek word moros, which means foolish. But the real folly, Erasmus claimed to find in the numerous heresy trials of scholasticism (cf. Erasmus 2012: 9f.). The charges of heresy were often based on nothing but arbitrary antics and inessentials, or so called 'adioafora'. In reality the charges might as well be motivated by folly or abuse of power. Erasmus himself only avoided such allegations by applying 'Folly' himself, reprimanding religious hypocrisy and division. Instead, Erasmus tried to find a neutral point of view in the theological and military impulses and appeal to common understanding and unity based on what he considered the main core in the lessons of Christ: neighbourly love. His second reason refers to the principle of human freedom of conscience, and thereby also human dignity, targeting "love from a pure heart, a clear conscience, and an uncorrupted faith" (cf. Forst 2003: 141). However, also Erasmus' conception of tolerance turns out to have an exclusionary other category, to which he confined all groups and religions, which seemed to contradict his Christian unity. And also in this case, the Jews were pointed out as the most prominent outsiders by Erasmus and his reductive unity of tolerance. To Erasmus, the Jews pose a threat as a treacherous, greedy, bold and insubordinate people (cf. Forst 2003: 143). Hence also Erasmus' *The Praise of Folly* expresses the dilemma of tolerance in terms of a reductive unity: If it insists too much on a dogmatic core, it risks alienating the religions and the spiritual movements it seeks to reconcile or unite. And conversely: if it offers a core, which is too diluted, it will not have any predictive power with regard to the religious segments it seeks to reconcile.

Another solution model was anticipated in Thomas More's Utopian-essayistic novel *Utopia* from 1516. In the chapter on the religion of the Utopians, More approaches the quest for religious pluralism and tolerance in a much more radical way within the fictional framework of an imagined undiscovered island, than he could have allowed himself in real life. Hence Utopian literature was invented in the 16th century, on the threshold of modernity as an experimental genre, dealing with the following basic question: Which organization of power and society is most suitable in order to secure and further the lives and the welfare of its citizens and protect them from violence, famine or the devastating forces of nature? By projecting imaginary ideal communities on allegedly undiscovered islands, such as Francis Bacon's *New Atlantis* or Thomas More's *Utopia*, the Utopian genre aimed at questioning the obliquities, injustices, and inhuman conditions of existing societies. Its aim was hence to be a catalyst reflecting critically on the existing organization of culture and society by contrasting them with an invented non-existing harmonious society. This is basically also the function of dystopian literature, although it questions the organization and distortion of the contemporary society by confronting it with the worst thinkable organization and conditions of a fictional society, in other words: with a negative utopia. Hence utopian and dystopian fictional societies may occur next to each other in one and the same novel, such as in Ludvig Holberg's *Niels Klim* or Jonathan Swift's *Gulliver's Travels*, which was first published in 1726. On his fourth journey, the rather unreliable narrator Gulliver finds himself in an ideal community of horses, signified by profound wisdom and ethical standards. This utopian horse state is for instance contrasted by some disgusting human creatures, called the yahoos, as well as by the Lilliput society, where Gulliver finds himself shipwrecked on his first journey. The Lilliputians appear to be torn by a deadly hatred between the high-heeled and the low-heeled parties. In Swift's novel, Gulliver appears both as a narrator with deep sympathies and aversions, and as a stranger, who is received by the Utopian locals with a mixture of sensational curiosity, sympathy, suspiciousness, and even hostility.

This is also the reason why dystopian literature should be considered a subgenre of utopian literature. What they have in common, is their experimental and critical modes, reminding the readers of the best or the worst unrealized possibilities of their own society. The contrastive function of utopian fiction makes the socially produced causes of need, injustice and social disparity more transparent to the citizens themselves. According to Jürgen Habermas, the emergence of a modern utopian literature and reflection was made possible by a certain turn in political philosophy. While Plato and Aristotle were mainly concerned with praxis, in terms of guiding the citizens into righteous insight and action, the Renaissance philosophers were more concerned with technical problems considering the possibility of producing a commonly good life and society by means of a new political and social order, which regulates the social interaction in the best possible way. Hence More's novel *Utopia* holds up a contrast to religious bigotry and social injustice. The citizens of Thomas More's fictional ideal state also benefit from the almost unrestricted freedom of religion and conscience: Some of them worship the sun, others the moon or the planets. But most of them assume the existence of a mysterious, inexplicable, life-giving pantheist divinity, referred to as the 'father of all things'. Some of them assume that he is one God, others that he is several, but they all agree upon the fact, that he is a divine creative force in nature. These are ideas, which Sir Thomas More as a bishop would not have tolerated in his own society, but prosecuted as heresy. This is also one of the reasons why More invents a fictional narrator, called Raphael Hythlodaeus, who advocates these highly controversial points of view in a conversation with the arch bishop of Canterbury. This was also a strategy to overcoming state censorship. But Hythlodaeus does not only appear to be a distant and objective observer and narrator. Like Gulliver, he also makes acquaintance with a number of Utopians, presenting them to a kind of communist version of Christ, who had abolished private ownership among his disciples. This was a radical interpretation of Christ which was later also advocated by the Norwegian 19th Century poet Henrik Wergeland (1808-45) and the English Deists. But first and foremost Hythlodaeus stresses the importance of religious tolerance. This is indeed a surprisingly radical idea in contemporary England and Europe. In this sense, Thomas More's *Utopia* also represents the earliest example of an Utopia of interreligious tolerance, and may also in this respect be viewed as a predecessor of Wergeland and the Norwegian-Danish writer Holberg.

Even though the Utopians seem to agree upon the assumption that there must be some kind of creating Father of the Universe, religious pluralism is not considered a problem which needs to be resolved by any kind of oppression or reductive unity. The founder of the ideal community himself, Utopos, had also considered the possibility that God himself had instituted a kind of religious pluralism to avoid monotonous worship. Offending or denying the religious convictions of others, however, is banned along with blasphemy and atheism in the community of the Utopians, because it is considered an insult to the freedom of religion and human dignity. Accordingly, it is also prohibited to despise or condemn the religious views of their fellow citizens, as in the case of a recently baptised Utopian:

> When he had thus long reasoned the matter they laid hold on him, accused him, and con-
> demned him onto exile, not as a despiser of religion, but as a seditious person and a raiser
> up of dissention among the people. For this is one of the ancientest laws among them, that
> no man shall be blamed for reasoning in the maintenance of his own religion. For King
> Utopos, even at the first beginning hearing that the inhabitants of the land were before
> his coming thither at continual dissention and strife among themselves for their religions,
> perceiving also that this common dissension (whiles every several sect took several parts in
> fighting for their country) was the only occasion of his conquest over them all, as soon as he
> had gotten the victory: first of all he made a decree that it should be lawful for every man to
> favour and follow what religion he would, and that he might do the best he could to bring
> other to his opinion, so that he did it peaceably, gently, quietly, and soberly, without hasty
> and contentious rebuking and inveighing against other. If he could not by fair and gentle
> speech induce them unto his opinion, yet he should use no kind of violence, and refrain
> from displeasant and seditious words. To him that would vehemently and fervently in this
> cause strive and contend was decreed banishment or bondage (More 2008 [1516]: 108 f.).

The solution to the problem of tolerance invented by the Utopians is not to reduce the religious diversity by a lowest common denominator, but to adopt common discursive rules, based upon a concept of man's right to the largest amount of happiness, dignity and freedom of conscience.

The invention of dignity and freedom of conscience also led to a division between church authority on the one hand and individual religious beliefs on the other. These new division lines strongly influenced the evolution of the concept of tolerance in the 17th century by philosophers like Baruch de Spinoza, Pierre Bayle, and John Locke, and in the 18th century by Ludvig Holberg, Voltaire, Gotthold Ephraim Lessing, and Moses Mendelssohn. According to Spinoza, the true core of belief rests on the virtues of justice and love, which distinguishes it from dogmas and philosophical search for truth. In his major philosophical work *Ethics*, Spinoza deduces ethical conduct from an encompassing insight in the nature of God and all such things man needs to know about truth and happiness. Ethics should at the same time be a practical guideline, based upon eternal and axiomatic truths. But religion offers a kind of 'Weltanschauung', which does not presuppose such an extensive philosophical knowledge. To Spinoza, the prophets are personalities who distinguish themselves form ordinary people by ethical conduct and their ability to convince others of the same in a transparent way. In this way, Spinoza did not only tempt to distinguish philosophy from religion, but also to deliberate religion from religious authorities (cf. Bartuschat 1996: 156 ff). Finally, Spinoza appealed to state authorities to delimit the power of the church in order to protect the individual freedom of conscience. In 1656 Spinoza's independent religious view eventually led to his expulsion from the Jewish community of Amsterdam. In his *Tractacus Theologico-Politicus* Spinoza appoints the state authorities the role as peace negotiator between the various religious persuasions and the right to define justice and regulate the manifest religious worship practice, but not to interfere in the freedom of conscience and 'the inner religious worshipping'.

Also the French Enlightenment philosopher Pierre Bayle rejects all kinds of compulsory religion. And in accordance with More, he does not only refer to the word of the Bible, but also to pragmatic reasons. Bayle presupposes a divine 'natural light' of reason, above all metaphysical and theological speculation. And from this rational-divine intuition he deduces moral precepts, which should be immediately axiomatic, above all religious impulses. According to Bayle, all kinds of enforced religion are therefore idle, partly because they lead to hypocrisy, partly because they insult the individual freedom of conscience, as long as there is no final evidence for the one and only true religion. By this model of tolerance, Bayle establishes a solution, which has structural parallels to Mikhail Bakhtin's model of literary polyphony in the novel: When no religious belief could claim the final religious truth, it creates room for a dialogic coexistence between ideologically equal positions. Bayle was one of the first and very few Enlightenment thinkers who did not exclude Jews or Muslims from his concept of tolerance: According to Bayle, Judaism and Islam were less associated with beliefs in miracles, and should therefore be considered more rational religions than Christianity (cf. Israel 2001).

At this time, the first Jews had arrived in Denmark at the invitation from King Christian IV. For this purpose he had founded the city Glückstadt, in order to attract especially Portuguese (Sephardic) Jews and to profit from their financial and administrative skills. However, Glückstadt was a failure, and instead, Copenhagen and Altona became the two major Jewish centres of Denmark-Norway. Based on such pragmatic considerations, the Sephardic Jews were granted a limited religious freedom: They were allowed to gather for praying, but not for reading the Talmud. The Ashkenazi Jews however, were not allowed to practice their religion at all. In 1682, the free town of Fredericia was founded, where the Jews were offered religious freedom and stay without having to pay extra taxes. Far more restrictive was the Norwegian law of Christian V. (Christian V. *Norske Landslov*), proscribing that all Jews who entered the Norwegian state territory without safe-conduct, should pay a fine of 1000 thalers. At Holberg's time, it was also decided that so called beggar Jews ('bettel-jøder') should be denied any access to Denmark.

The majority of the about two million Jews in Holberg's Europe, lived in poverty in their ghettoes in Hamburg, Frankfurt, Rome, Amsterdam, and other cities. As mentioned above, this was due to their exclusion from state offices and from guilds, leaving them to do little else than moneylending and hawking. In general, however, there were big differences between the well-educated Sephardic ('Portuguese') Jews on the one hand, and the Ashkenazi ('German') Jews on the other hand, who mostly lived in Poland, and in German cities like Hamburg and Frankfurt. In Amsterdam however, there were many Sephardic Jews, who had fled from Spain after the "Limpieza de Sangre" in 1492. In the liberal Netherlands, some of these came in contact with Protestant philosophers and writers, like the above mentioned French Huguenot Pierre Bayle, who had been forced to leave their Catholic homelands due to the religious strife after the Reformation. And some of these Protestants not only advocated concepts of tolerance, which included the Jews, but also converted to Judaism. Holberg was strongly influenced by Bayle and 18th century Protestant tolerance thinkers as well as Philosemites: gentiles who showed interest in, respect for, and appreciation of the Jewish people, their historical significance and the positive impacts of Judaism in the non-Jewish world. But according to Holberg's 'moralizing' method, exposing virtues and vices as moral examples to his readers, Holberg also perpetuated some anti-Semitic stereotypes of the Jews as greedy and insubordinate hawkers. In so doing, he sometimes also leans on notoriously anti-Semitic German writers like Johann Andreas Eisenmenger, who was a professor in Hebrew at the university of Heidelberg. In his major work *Entdecktes Judentum* ["Judaism revealed"], Eisenmenger warns against Jewish attempts to vilify Christianity and misguide good Christians to converting into Judaism. During his stay in Amsterdam in 1680-81, Eisenmenger claims to have witnessed three Christians converting into Judaism, and a Jewish Rabbi criticizing Christianity in public. Eisenmenger's work contains 2120 pages of hateful allegations against the European Jews, demonstrating that knowledge is no guarantee against xenophobia. Quite opposite, hatred could make the hater observe his hate object with even greater eagerness and zeal.

As announced in his title, Eisenmenger seeks to reveal the secret conspiracies of the Jews against the Christians, repeating the ancient allegations about the Jews as well poisoners and ritual child murderers.

In the late 18th century, the Enlightenment ideals about a strict division between public state authority and private religious freedom of belief and conscience lead to first attempts to modernize and reform European Judaism from within and to quests for Jewish or civil rights. The so called Haskala movement, which later on inspired the Norwegian poet Henrik Wergeland, aimed at raising the German Jews from their ghetto poverty and open Judaism to European Enlightenment culture, by encouraging them to learn the hegemonic literature languages, such as Greek, Latin, French, English and eventually German. In Germany, the Haskala movement was more or less initiated by the friendship between the dramatist Gotthold Ephraim Lessing, a born Protestant, and the Jewish Enlightenment philosopher Moses Mendelssohn. And in his drama *Nathan the Wise* (*Nathan der Weise*) (1779), Lessing erected a monument for his late friend Mendelssohn. Due to the censorship, the drama was only staged after Lessing's death in 1781.

Instead of projecting the utopian ideal societies to imagined undiscovered Pacific islands, they were now projected to a distant future, or more unusually, to a distant past, as in the case of Lessing's *Nathan*. In this way, space was replaced by time as the preferred horizon of Utopian reflection. Koselleck refers to this shift as a turn from Utopia to Uchronia ("von Utopie zur Uchronie") (Koeselleck 1982). In Novalis' influential essay "The Christianity or Europe", which was written in 1799, the vision of a European aesthetic-religious harmonious Utopia was projected both into a medieval Catholic past and into a future state, where the alienating process of modernity would dissolve itself and make room for a new religious spirituality. In our time, this juxtaposition between Europeanness and medieval Christianity has shown a rather frightening exclusionary potential, since it has been revived and radicalized by the so called anti-jihad movement, which brought fuel to the fire that exploded so tragically in Norway on July 22th 2011. Although Novalis regrets the religious hatred between the Catholic and Lutheran churches in the wake of reformation, he seems to sanction the medieval crusades, stating that "Jerusalem had revenged itself". In Lessing's above-mentioned drama *Nathan der Weise,* however, Jerusalem appears both as a battle-field of interreligious hatred, in terms of medieval crusades, but also as a chronotope of tolerance, manifested in the dialogue between Nathan and the Sultan Saladdin, the Muslim conqueror of Jerusalem. Saladdin is known for having liberated Jerusalem from the Christian crusaders almost without any bloodshed or excesses of revenge. Due to the warfare expenses, the Sultan finds himself in a rather difficult financial situation in Lessing's drama. And to solve this problem, Saladdin is setting up a trap for the rich Jew Nathan. Saladdin calls for Nathan and tests him by challenging him to answer the following question: Which one of the three monotheist religions Judaism, Christianity, or Islam represents the true revelation of God's will? Eventually Nathan earns the sultan's respect and friendship by presenting him the parable of the three rings, where nobody can tell which of them is authentic, and which of them are copies. Leaving the question of the authenticity of each ring open, their owners should behave in such manner, that he or she would earn the love and affection of their neighbours. Accordingly the sultan's question about the monopoly on true revelation among the three related religions could not be answered satisfactorily. In Lessing's drama, this question is turned into a practical Utopia, prescribing man to act in accordance with the shared essence of the three religions, which is the golden rule of charity:

> ... demonstrate the magic virtue vested in his ring
> and help that power to grow with gentleness,
> with heartfelt tolerance, with charity
> and deep submission to the will of God!

Hence the city of Jerusalem appears to be a chronotope, where both interreligious hatred and utopian tolerance take place.

While Novalis' utopian vision of a Catholic Europe seems to sanction the crusades and exclude other religions, writers like Gotthold Ephraim Lessing and Henrik Wergeland created utopian chronotopes of interreligious tolerance. Instead of projecting a state of religious tolerance into some undiscovered spatial realm, their ideas of religious tolerance were staged in time, and not as a permanent state or as the end of history, but as punctual Utopian episodes, sometimes contrasted with a rather dystopian back-drop like for instance the crusades in Lessings *Nathan the Wise* or the officially sanctioned Norwegian hatred and bigotry against the Jews in Wergeland's poem cycles "The Jew" and "The Jewess".

In his lyrical-dramatic cycle *The Jewess* (1844), Henrik Wergeland transforms Lessing's ring parable into a contemporary European context, appealing to both Enlightenment struggle against prejudices and for Christian neighbourly love and universal human dignity and civil rights. According to Wergeland, these rights should also be granted to the Norwegians Jews, who had been prohibited from entering the Norwegian state territory according to the

Norwegian Constitution from 1814, unless they were baptised. In his poem "The Women in the Graveyard" Wergeland depicts two women in mourning, one Lutheran and the other Catholic, searching for a free space, where they can bury their dead children next to each other. Eventually they notice a third woman, who turns out to be a Jewess, mourning over her dead child in an isolated corner of the churchyard. As they speak to her, she shows them a jewel which she is wearing on her forehead, made of three precious stones: a blue sapphire, a green emerald, and a red ruby, explaining their meaning to the two other women. The sapphire is a symbol of the Catholic church, the emerald symbolizes the Protestant church communities, while the red ruby represents "The Jew, with his pain and inner bleeding!". But nobody could claim that one is more valuable than the other two:

> Men hvo skjelner mellem disse
> Ædelstenes Værd tilvisse?
> Se! o se! det Solen gjør!
> Seer I? lige klart de straale.
> Hver med deres Brudds Kulør,
> Himmelbilledet igjen (Wergeland 2008: 7,76).

> (But who could tell for certain the difference
> Between the value of these precious stones?
> Can't you see: only the sun can tell!
> Do you see? Equally they reflect
> The heavenly image
> by the colour of their fracture surface.)

According to Wergeland's view, Catholicism and Protestantism as well as Judaism and Islam represent historically and culturally specific revelations of the one and only divine will. In his philosophical essay "Why Does Humanity Advance so Slowly?", Wergeland points at the striking disproportion between the political progress in Europe on the one hand, and the many unresolved conflicts between Catholics and Protestants on the other hand. Wergeland considers these conflicts a result of rigorous religious dogmatism on both sides and advocates a rational religion, abandoning all priests who tend to abuse their power (Wergeland 2000: 94). In Wergeland's poem "The Women in the Graveyard", the churchyard appears both a tragic place of departure and mourning, and a meeting place, where tolerance and the recognition of human dignity are allowed to take place, at least locally and temporally, in the dramatized dialogue between the three mourning women. In this sense, the church yard also has a Utopian dimension in terms of being a 'good place'; an eu-topos. The notion of Utopia was first used by Thomas More in the above mentioned novel *Utopia* in 1516. He coined the word 'utopia' from the Greek ou-topos meaning 'no place' or 'nowhere'. But this was a pun –the almost identical Greek word eu-topos means a good place. And given the mutual recognition and comforting dialogue between the women, the churchyard eventually appears to be a good place, at least in Wergeland's poem.

The main argument for excluding the Jews from Norway were concerns about the allegedly Jewish plans to outmanoeuvre the Norwegian interests by their financial skills and take control of the silver mine at Kongsberg. In the wake of emerging nationalism, the Jews were accused of not really belonging to the national community, forming a political fifth column, being hateful to their Christian host nations and, due to their fanatic Messianism, only willing to recognize a state run by the Jews themselves (cf. Bergmann 2010: 28). They were also accused of being dirty, smelling, and offering depraved meat to the Christians. The notorious Jew paragraph in the Norwegian constitution was abolished only in 1851, six years after Wergeland's death, due to the campaign he had initiated. This campaign was also supported by non-Jewish writers within Norway and Jewish writers outside the Norwegian borders (cf. Skorgen 2010). In all other countries, except for Spain and Portugal, Jews were allowed to settle down, and live and work on more or less equal conditions. In France, the great revolution of 1789 had granted the French Jews more freedom than they had dreamed of: Namely full civil and political rights, although the Sephardic Jews received their full political rights only in 1790, one year before the Ashkenazi Jews were granted the same. Also in Germany and all parts of Europe which were conquered by Napoleon, the real political emancipation of the Jews was only brought about by Napoleonic legislation. Already in 1806, Napoleon had gathered prominent representatives of the Jewish community in Paris to negotiate and inform him about their adaptation to the civil republican society in matters like marriage, military service, hawking, and religious worship, according to French laicism.

The late 19th century anti-Judaist campaigns both in France and Germany, urging to reverse the modernization and emancipation of the European Jews, must be considered examples of modern anti-Judaism. (Bergmann 2010: 27f.). In conservative nationalist circles, the Jews were held responsible for all depraving influence of modernity, such as Liberalism, Marxism, urbanization and all kinds of political mass-movements (cf. Erb & Bergmann 1989). In 1879, the German publicist Wilhelm Marr launched his concept 'anti-Semitism' as a collective definition of all political movements and groups, advocating a racially pseudo-scientifically based anti-Judaism, opposing the modern Jewish emancipation. Anti-Semitism in its strict sense therefore refers to this modern amalgam of racism, anti-Judaism and political opposition against modern Jewish emancipation.

At the beginning of the 20th century, these anti-Semitic movements were nourished by Germanic blood mystery and pseudo-scientific theories about the 'Nordic race' as an aristocratic stock of permanent resident land owning peasants. The anti-Semitic 'Nordic movement' claimed that the 'Nordic master race' was threatened by the Jewish 'merchant race' and international 'financial Judaism'. Such views were also expressed in the anti-Semitic pamphlet *Jøder og Gojim* [*Jews and Gojim*], first published in 1910 by the Norwegian barrister Eivind Saxlund. Paradoxically he and his kindred spirits at the same time warned against the Jewish-Bolshevik conspiracy for world domination. Saxlund also organized the translation and publication of *The Protocols of the Elders of Zion*, in reality a forgery, fabricated by the secret police in Tsarist Russia in order to compromise the political revolutionaries and reformers. Saxlund and his combat aunts, were inspired by the reactionary German völkisch movement, opposed to all kinds of modern depravation, ascribed to 'Jewish modernity', be it Marxist or Liberalist or cultural modernists.

During his stay in Germany in the spring of 1941, Vidkun Quisling held a speech, stressing the unfamiliarity of the 'Jewish race' from the European 'Aryan race', idealizing the cultural and racial purity of the ancient Vikings. At the same time, Quisling warned against the 'Jewish contamination' through cinema, theatre and literature, run by the international 'financial Judaism' and its 'evil and disturbing power', which had also taken control over the Norwegian press. In particular, Quisling was upset by the activities of the Jewish 'pornographers' Wilhelm Reich, who had been living in Norwegian exile, and Sigmund Freud (cf. Quisling 1941). It should be emphasized that Saxlund and his combat aunts only formed an extreme minority of the Norwegian publicity and that they were countered by numerous Jewish and non-Jewish writers and journalists like Harry Koritzinsky and Pål Gjesdahl. In 1936, The 'Reichsparteitag' of Hitler's NSDAP passed their so called Nuremberg racial laws, prohibiting German Jews from marrying or having intercourse with so called 'Aryan Germans', and excluding Jews from numerous state offices and senior positions as school masters, etc. In order to communicate the spirit of the 'Aryan laws' to children, the 21 year old kindergarten teacher Elvira Bauer wrote and illustrated the anti-Semitic children's book *Trau keinem Fuchs auf grüner Heid und keinem Jud bei seinem Eid! Ein Bilderbuch für Groß und Klein.*

Bauer was a Fanatic admirer of the notorious Nazi publisher and Gauleiter Julius Streicher, owner and editor of the pornographic and anti-Semitic propaganda Newspaper *Der Stürmer*, and Bauer's book was published at Streicher's Stürmer Verlag in Nuremberg. In the book, Streicher himself is depicted as the child friendly saviour of the Aryan 'master race' from the insidious Jews. In reality, Streicher had been dismissed from his position as a public school teacher after participating in Hitler's failed 'beer cellar coup' before making his career as a leading propagandist of the NSDAP. After the war, Streicher was sentenced to death for crimes against humanity by the war crime tribunal, which ironically was held in Nuremberg, and hanged in 1946. With her somewhat unusual children's book, Bauer wanted to explain the basic principle of the Nuremberg racial laws by rhymes, rhythms and drawings, containing for instance the following concern, expressed by an 'Aryan' father to his daughter:

> The father says to his daughter dear:
> 'you cause me great distress, I fear!
> The blood of all of us is pure,
> But for the sake of selfish gain
> For fine dresses and money, too,
> You're always with Sol Rosenfeld, the Jew,
> Thinking to maybe become his wife!
> This means no good.
> I won't have it, d'ye hear?
> A dachshund is never put between the shafts
> Of a wagon where a cow belongs!
> That's just impossible, I say.
> So mark your words for once and all:
> 'Don't trust a fox on the greensward
> And never a Jew on his plighted word!
> (www.calvin.edu).

A common feature of the other above-mentioned anti-Semitic pamphlets however, is their obsession with collecting and reproducing negative citations and points of view about Jews, and this is one reason why they appear to be poor workmanship and tiresome reading. Eisenmenger's cut and paste method formed a common pattern of anti-Semitic writing throughout the 19th and even 20th century, picking and gathering quotations from famous men and women, who in some context had made some negative remarks on the Jews. Today, much of the same bad literary workmanship could be found in many right extremist, so called 'anti-Jihadist' pages, which inundate the Internet. Like Eisenmenger, some of them show a remarkable interest for and twisted knowledge about the people they seem to hate the most: the Muslims, now being conceptualized as Europe's internal others.

## Bibliography

Arendt, H. (2004): *The Origins of Totalitarianism*, Introduction by Samantha Power. New York: Schocken.

Bartuschat, W. (1996): *Baruch de Spinoza*. München: Verlag C. H. Beck.

Bauer, E. (1936): *Trau keinem Fuchs auf grüner Heid und keinem Jud bei seinem Eid! Ein Bilderbuch für groß und Klein*. Nürnberg: Stürmer Verlag. English translation: www.calvin. edu, downloaded 20.11.2012.

Bergmann, W. (2010): *Geschichte des Antisemitismus*. München: Verlag C. H. Beck.

Christensen, S. (1988): "Europa som slagord". In: Hans Boll-Johansen & Michael Harbsmeier (eds.): *Europas opdagelse. Historien om en idé*. København: Christian Ejlers' Forlag.

*Den nye Verdenskeiseren eller Zions lærdes ældste protokoller* (1920). Kristiania: Helge Erichsen Co.s forlag.

Eisenmenger, J. A. (1711): *Entdecktes Judentum*. Königsberg.

Erb, R. & W. Bergmann (1989): *Die Nachtseite der Judenemanzipation: der Widerstand gegen die Integration der Juden in Deutschland 1780-1860*. Berlin: Metropol.

Forester, V. (2001): *Lessing und Mendelssohn: Geschichte einer Freundschaft*. Berlin: Europäische Verlagsanstal.

Forst, R. (2000): "Einleitung". In: Forst, Rainer (ed.): *Toleranz. Philosophische Grundlagen und gesellscahftliche Praxis einer umstrittenen Tugend*. Frankfurt a. M.: Campus Verlag.

Forst, R. (2003): *Toleranz im Konflikt*. Frankfurt a. M.: Suhrkampf Verlag.

Holberg, L. (1742): *Den Jødiske Historie fra Verdens Begyndelse Forstatt til disse Tider*. København.

Israel, J. (2001): *Radical Enlightenment: Philosophy and the Making of Modernity 1650-1750*. Oxford: Oxford University Press.

Koritzinsky, H. (1922): *Jødernes Historie i Norge: Henrik Wergelands kamp for jødesaken*. Kristiania.

Koselleck, R. (1982): "Die Verzeitlichung der Utopie." In: W. Vosskamp (ed.): *Utopieforschung. Interdisziplinäre Studien zur neuzeitlichen Utopie*. Stuttgart: J. B. Metzler, bd. 3, s. 3 ff.

Koselleck, R. (1989): "Zur historisch-politischen Semantik asymmetrischer Gegenbegriffe." In: *Vergangene Zukunft. Zur Semantik geschichtlicher Zeiten*. Frankfurt a. M.: Suhrkampf.

Lessing, G. E. (1791): *Nathan der Weise. Ein dramatisches Gedicht in fünf Aufzügen*. Hamburg.

Menocal, M. R. (2002): *The Ornament of the World: How Muslims, Jews and Christians Created a Culture of Tolerance in Medieval Spain*, Boston / New York: Back Bay Books.

Mirandola, P. (2012): *Oration on the Dignity of Man: a new translation and commentary*, ed. by Francesco Borghesi, Machael Papio & Massimo Riva. Cambridge: Cambridge University Press.

More, T. (2008): *Utopia*. In: *Three early Modern Utopias. Utopia. New Atlantis* and *The Isle of Pines*, ed. by Susan Bruce, Oxford World's Classics. Oxford: Oxford University Press. Translated with Introduction and Notes by Paul Turner. London: Penguin Books.

Poliakov, L. (1974): *The History of Anti-Semitism*, 4 volumes. London: Routledge & Kegan Paul.

Quisling, V. (1941): *Kampen mellom arier og jødemakt*. Frankfurt.

Saxlund, E. (1910): *Jøder og Gojim*, Christiania: J. Aass' Forlag.

Skorgen, T. (2010): "Toleransens grenser. Wergeland og jødeemansipasjonen i Europa." *Agora*, nr. 1-2.

Spinoza, B. (2000): *Ethics*, ed. and transl. by G. H. R. Parkinson. Oxford: Oxford University Press.

Spinoza, B. (2007): *Theological-political treatise*, transl. by Samuel Shirley: Introduction and Annotation by Seymour Feldman. Cambridge: Cambridge University Press.

Wergeland, H. (1844): *Jødinden. Elleve blomstrende Tornekivste*. Christiania: J. Aass' Forlag.

Wergeland H. (2000): *Wergeland på prosa. Henrik Wergelands tanker, brev og fortellinger I utvalg*. Oslo: Aschehoug.

Wergeland, H. (2008): *Henrik Wergelands Skrifter*, Leiv Amundsen & Didrik Arup Seip (ed.). Oslo: Cappelen Damm AS, 8 bd., bd. 2 og 8.

# Queering the Holocaust: Making the Impossible Possible

*Željka Švrljuga*

> The testimony is inherently a process of facing loss – of going through the pain of the act of witnessing, and of the ending of the act of witnessing – which entails yet another repetition of the experience of separation and loss (Laub in Felman and Laub 1992: 91).

> The "true" witnesses, the "complete witnesses," are those who did not bear witness and could not bear witness. They are those who "touched bottom" ... The survivors speak in their stead, by proxy, as pseudo-witnesses; they bear witness to a missing testimony (Agamben 1999: 34).

## Prelude

As an attack on humanity and on the Jewish segment of European populations in particular, the Holocaust is an unprecedented example of othering, whose burden is permanently imprinted on our collective memory. Literature, arts, and music tend this memory well after its last witnesses-survivors no longer are with us as a forewarning for the future. Concurrently, Holocaust studies with its ever-expanding focus on witnessing and testimonies has seen a gradual widening of scope: from the Jews, there has been a shift to other oppressed groups whose ethnic or cultural background, political or religious systems of belief, or sexual practices were thought to "pollute" the racial purity of Nazi Germany. The Holocaust experience of homosexuals, for example, had not only been repressed but remained silenced and condemned well after the war. As Michael Burleigh and Wolfgang Wippermann argue, "Homosexuals were not recognized as victims of the Nazi persecution in either post-war German state" (Burleigh and Wippermann 2003: 183), with reference to the suppressed history of outlawed same-sex relationship under the German Penal Code Paragraph 175 from 1871, which remained part of the Law for almost an entire century.

The military *Bruderschaft* of the Nazi regime inspired, indeed demanded, male bonding; homoeroticism, although forbidden and punishable, was relatively common among the military – its elite in particular. The unwritten rules like "Thou shalt love men, but not be homosexual" and "Thou shalt do what is forbidden, yet still be punished" not only voiced the Nazi fear of homosexuality but indicated that it was difficult to reveal and contain one's sexual orientation (Theweleit 1989: 339). As a taboo that outlived the system that punished its practitioners, the same-sex amorous conduct that was chastised under the criminal code has largely remained stifled. Homosexuality, which Michel Foucault deictically marks as "*that* love" in a different context (Foucault 1985: 193), implied a different or "deviant" sexuality in the Third Reich, whose focus on the family and family growth made clear that healthy sexuality portended procreative sexual practices and was not a private matter, but a responsibility to the state.[1] Despite its illegal status, a homosexual subculture secretly flourished, judging by some 40 gay clubs and meeting places in the inter-war Berlin (Burleigh and Wippermann 2003: 183). Moreover, Magnus Hirschfeld's Institute for Sexual Science (1919-1933) with its focus on sexual minorities, marital problems, and abortion provoked the Nazis, who saw in the sexologist "the big boss of the perverts" (Burleigh and Wippermann 2003: 187). The Nazi destruction of his work and library seems to have been governed by the belief that their public burning would eradicate their social and political effect. The S.S. Squad's verbal abuse aligned sexual politics with radicalism and Jewishness: Like Hirschfeld, "the Jewish swine Freud" was accused of defending criminal indecency, be it queer or straight sexuality, or psychoanalysis with its intrinsic connection to the unconscious and infantile sexuality (Burleigh and Wippermann 2003: 190, *Paragraph 175*, 2000). With the start of war and the increased raid rate, the persecution and encampment of all undesired segments of the population grew in scope. Very few documents of the concentration camp experience are available; even fewer are the accounts of homosexual Nazi work-camp survivors.

With the passing away of Gad Beck, "[the] last gay Jewish Holocaust survivor," in late June of 2012, to borrow from the title of his obituary (Weinthal

---

[1]    When, here, I take Foucault out of his context, it is to illustrate how deixis creates (and, in the case under discussion, underlines) spatial and ideological distance which, depending on articulation, may border on stigmatization. Since deictic words express otherness from the point of the one (who speaks or, as here, the ideology of a group), the *that* of "*that* love" seems to mark more than a physical distance.

2012), the era of living witnesses of a particular survivor group has come to an end. Yet, as the two epigraphs signal, there are different kinds of testimony. While, for example, Beck's testimony in the *Paragraph 175* documentary (2000) falls under the rubric of repeating "the pain of the act of witnessing," whose verbalization brings the past back into the present and makes him relive it, as Dori Laub suggests, there is also a so-called "impossible testimony" by "complete witnesses," which is how Giorgio Agamben designates *Muselmänner*, or the walking dead, who were anaesthetized by their experience of the extermination camp.[2] Since these impossible testimonies relate to those who cannot themselves give an account of their experience, survivors tread in their stead and tell the victims' stories by default. These are the "impossible" stories that the second part of my title refers to, stories which are similar to the stories that the literature of disaster brings up, creates, and performs. Or, more precisely, the stories are not impossible at the level of the statement, but at the level of the enunciation. In other words: one can speak about "hell," but to survive the hell of the Holocaust and still speak is impossible. The aporia of "impossible" witnessing lies in "the fact that it [the unobtainable testimony] is literally spoken from the ashes of a crematorium," to put it with Felman (qtd. in Felman and Laub 1992: 116 n.14). Literature is a similar case in point: Like testimony, it relies on discursive practices; yet its *modi operandi* allow testimony to become either the subject matter or a narrative means of literature (Felman in Felman and Laub 1992: 5).

Because they are not first-hand experience, many accounts of the Holocaust may fall under the rubric of "postmemory," to adopt Marianne Hirsch's trope for the politics of commemoration – "an intrasubjective transgenerational space of remembrance, linked specifically to cultural or collective trauma" (Hirsch 2001: 10). Postmemory is thus a painful memory we may wish to disown, a cultural memory of an event we wish never happened, which is ours as part of our cultural-political heritage, articulated "through an imaginative investment and creation" (Hirsch 1997: 22). Consequently, this specific type of memory relies on representation, mediation, translation, transformation, and transfiguration – all committed to the "transmission of cultural trauma" (Hirsch 2001:

---

2   Or, as Jean Améry defines this paradoxical figure, "The so-called *Muselmann*, as the camp language termed the prisoner who was giving up and was given up by his comrades, no longer had room in his consciousness for the contrasts good or bad, noble or base ... He was a staggering corpse, a bundle of physical functions in its last convulsions" (Améry in Agamben 1999: 41).

9). Just like the prefix "post-," the initial affix "trans-" – whose Latin etymology denotes "the farther side of, beyond, over" (*OED*) – suggests distance in space and time as well as movement, inferring a working through – both in fact and in effect. What postmemory of a disaster occasions and endless "trans-" functions complement is an aesthetically fashioned experience, a patchwork of memories and could-be memories, which, like quilting, makes use of old scraps to create a new whole.

## *For a Look or a Touch* as Textual Memory

The Seattle-based Music of Remembrance (MOR) with Mina Miller as artistic director at its helm has, for over a decade, committed itself to performing and commissioning work that speaks to issues of the Holocaust. Among its relatively recent productions is the chamber music drama *For a Look or a Touch* by the American composer Jake Heggie and librettist Gene Scheer, a musical memorial to homosexual Holocaust victims. From its world premiere in 2007 to its compact disc release by Naxos in 2008, music critics have struggled to classify it. Some consider it a "mini-opera" (Borchert 2007); for others, it is "a chamber opera, a theatre piece, or a quasi song cycle" (Moore 2008); for another critic, it is a "small-scale-theatre-piece," a mixture of "song cycle and melodrama" (Hugill 2008); and, for yet another, a "miniature operatic scene" (Briggs 2009). As a chamber opera for a lyric baritone and an actor, the work is haunted by an operatic legacy in its dramatic form, tragic love plot, and lyrical and dramatic arias. While these qualities may concur with the understanding that opera is a historical extension of the Greek tragedy, it is also an anachronism in the twenty-first century. Its generic survival Mladen Dolar sees as "the revival of a lost past" (Dolar 2002: 3), which implies a cultural nostalgia of sorts, as opposed to Heggie's revival of the past, which makes his mini-opera a work of mourning. The contemporary composer's untraditional syntax that blends the spoken word with an array of musical styles and idioms charges it with unprecedented energy, and ensures a nuanced depiction of the tragic love story.

The fact that the work resists being encapsulated in a single category contributes to its gender-political statement, for there is no doubt that the codes and coding of masculinity on the thematic level and as poetic expression and musical idiom queer the work: a gay teenage love affair that provides the narrative momentum takes us back to the early years of World War II, which haunt, and indeed become part of the narrated present, by way of the characters' individual memories and the group memory of "Crazy boys. Crazy queens," to quote from the libretto (Scheer 2008: 16). The musical idiom brackets together the themes of love, loss, and suffering in different musical styles: from nostalgic to melancholy tunes that trigger memories; to gay music in a double sense of the word, which recreates the pre-war *Zeitgeist* of Berlin dance halls and cabarets; and, finally, eruptions of dissonance, which musically illustrate and highlight the two torture scenes.

Based on a true story and crafted as a dialogue between two former lovers – Manfred and Gad, the young man who perished in the Holocaust yet returns in the shape of a ghost and his now eighty-year-old host, a camp survivor – this musical testament uses love as a means of working through the painful memory of the Holocaust. Heggie's *tour de force* is thus a specimen of a postmemory "genre" which stages testimony and witnessing of one of Europe's long silenced internal others sixty years after the event. Moreover, it stages the two types of testimony that the opening epigraphs refer to as theme and narrative technique, making the impossible possible at the level of artistic utterance. In keeping with the dramatic genre, dialogue and utterance inevitably blend the individual with the communal, the present of the utterance with the past of the experience. For, every drama is a "memory play" in its enactment of personal and cultural memories which by way of endless citations bring the past into the present as intertextuality and/or *ghosting* (Carlson 2003: 2). Thus, the already mentioned documentary *Paragraph 175* by Rob Epstein and Jeffrey Friedman, with its archival footage and oral testimonies of homosexual survivors of the Nazi regime (the late Gad Bech's story among others), haunts this mini-opera. Yet the documentary also points to the existence of another, equally significant text that complements the filmic testimonies: Manfred Lewin's handmade booklet of sketches and scanty poetry, *Erinnerst Du Dich, als* ("Do You Remember, When") from 1941, which he gave to his lover, the late Gad Beck, prior to his deportation. Not only does Lewin's mini-journal offer fragments of their intimate relationship and everyday activities of Jewish youth; it also lends its title to Heggie's Prelude. By interlacing the testimonies from the documentary with the fragments of the journal, Heggie and Scheer's music drama brings the two lovers back together, transforming the gift of love into love as a gift – other-oriented and with healing powers. The dead lover's invitation to remembrance – "Do You Remember, When" – consequently provides a plethora of interpretational possibilities which *For a Look or a Touch* already suggests with its title. For not only does it refer to longing, the nights of partying, lovemaking, and the lovers' final meeting before Manfred and his family are sent off to Auschwitz; it also suggests that "for a ['wrong'] look or a touch," if caught, one risked imprisonment, torture, and death.

While the work's narrated present has been identified with regard to the politics of time, space, and gender as well as intertextual references, the textual politics of the music drama still leaves some questions begging. Like the opera, Heggie's hybrid text is doubly encoded: Not only is it a musical transfiguration of the libretto – a "theatrical script designed to be set to music"; it is also a translation from page to stage, with performance at its core (Hutcheon and Hutcheon 1996: 5; 9). But, if cultural, historical, and social contexts help shape the operatic utterance, influences that impact it are also necessarily musical. As a product of a long tradition, the opera and its subgenres imply their own art of memory.

## Musical Memory: More than a Simple Transfiguration

If a particular historical moment and cultural setting trigger an historical tragedy, which in turn brings about personal catastrophes represented in the said music drama, then the musical legacy at the micro and macro levels needs to be explored as a constituent part of theme, time and setting, and its politics of representation. Because of its roots in factuality, *For a Look or a Touch* participates in a kind of documentary genre which exceeds the obvious testimonies that underpin the plot. The fact that the docu-opera genre, which the mini-opera resembles, is linked to factuality in no way diminishes its artistic achievement: In fact, the composer's first opera, *Dead Man Walking* (2000), which has brought him renown, is based on Helen Prejean's 1993 novelistic testimony with a telling subtitle – *An Eyewitness Account of the Death Penalty in The United* States.[3] Not only is it a commanding aesthetic-political musical

---

[3]    The contemporary US opera scene has, since the eighties, seen a burgeoning of the docu-opera whose history is considered to start with John Adams' *Nixon in China* (1987) and *The Death of Klinghoffer* (1985-87, first performed in 1991). The operas' mixed reviews may reflect the new "genre's" gimmick of going contemporary, political, and true to life. Thus the former's self-evident subject matter with an ironic twist becomes in the latter work an equally provoking rendition of the suffering of both Jews and Palestinians, even though its plot centers on the Palestinian hijacking of the passenger liner the *Achille Lauro* which led to the tragic death of wheel-chair bound, Jewish-American Leon Klinghoffer. *The Death*'s emotionally charged music and its unconventional ethnic politics eventually earned it recognition and prepared the ground for a series of operatic documentaries. Recent productions, like the young Nico Muhly's *Dark Sisters* (2010) and *Two Boys* (2011), testify to the genre's vigorous health in the twenty-first century.

denunciation of capital punishment, but its power resides in the performance of meaning – in its musical and discursive utterance. It is this kind of power that carries *For a Look or a Touch* to its artistic height.

Heggie is by far the only composer who has worked with the opera adaptations of literary and other texts that relate to the Holocaust. Nicholas Maw, for example, wrote his 2002 opera *Sophie's Choice* based on William Styron's Holocaust novel of the same title. Yet there is paucity of classical music texts that relate to issues of homosexuality and the war. A possible candidate is Benjamin Britten's *War Requiem* (1962) which draws on the poetry of World War I poet Wilfred Owen, whose homoerotic undertones have not remained unnoticed. For obvious historical reasons, however, Owens' poetry bears no relation to the Holocaust. While the composer's rumored sexual orientation is off the point in this discussion, the poet's tender feelings for friend or foe have been downplayed in favor of his anti-war sentiments. There is no doubt, however, that the personal is political and that politics lies at the heart of both issues.

Contemporary Norwegian composer, Ståle Kleiberg, inspired by Britten, crafts his *Requiem for the Victims of Nazi Persecution* (2004) around the Nazi concentration camp prisoners' triangular badges which mark their difference from the regime of the "normal": the yellow for Jews, the brown for Gypsies, and the pink for homosexuals. Following Britten's example, Kleiberg has put to music the poetry of the Glasgow poet laureate Edwin Morgan, fashioning his mass for the dead on an antithetical/"dialogical" principle, similar to the one we find in Britten. Ostensibly coded on a contrapuntal principle as a religious "call" and a popular "response," thus Latin and English verses, the requiem sets the universal language of the Liturgy against the vernacular – the language of minority groups. With the choral utterance vis-à-vis choric, discrete group statements, the requiem mass exhibits cultural valorization that is embedded in the genre, which creates a cleft between the solemn tone of prayers and the victims' group testimony, thus replacing the heaven/earth dichotomy with the heaven/hell nexus. To sample from Morgan's lyrics:

> We were the lowest of the low.
> Further down you could not go.
> Nature itself, they said, abhorred us.
> How should the Third Reich reward us?
> Flog them, scald them, batter them.
> Break their bones and scatter them.
>      …

Gay men returning had to shun
Stories of those terrible years.
Secrets and shames like unshed tears
Filled our hearts; we could not speak (Morgan 2004: n.pag.).

For lack of space, only a few fleeting remarks will be made here, which bear direct relevance to the argument that follows. On the one hand, the poet queers his iambic tetrameter as if underscoring with the irregularity of metric feet the "irregularity" of queer sexual identity with regard to heteronormativity. On the other hand, Britten's and Kleiberg's requiems can be said to queer the pitch of Latin in their individual attempts at adoption and adaptation of the traditional format, which expand the traditional religious agenda with a humanitarian plea. Is it not what Morgan and Kleiberg's textual politics suggests with its focus on Christian non-believers (Jews and Romani) and alternative sexual identities? Despite the affirmative answer, one cannot neglect the ideological, religious lining of the genre. For, might not a prayer to the Christian God almighty, even though it seeks protection of all, assume a doubt in the power of other deities, creeds, and rituals? Or, how about those who do not want to be part of the religious community of the person who prays for them, regardless of that person's good intentions? Might not one's acceptance to be included in the religious community of the other imply a betrayal of one's own community and faith?[4] The humanity argument may be a way out of such a suspicious reading, yet a potential embracing of *all* peoples, "races," religious beliefs, and sexual preferences under the protection of *one* is by no means innocent.

Kleiberg and Morgan's solution to the challenge is far from simple: The requiem's initial invocation on behalf of believers awaits no answer but hopes for a miracle. The "miracle," however, is not in the materialization of the plea, but in the workings of the poetic license: The victims, whose eternal rest the mass for the dead petitions, come back to life and speak of their suffering in the language of common people, as opposed to the language of the liturgy, which is not only foreign to minority groups, it is foreign to all but the Catholic

---

4    Following the tradition of *Missa pro defunctis* – "*Requiem aeternam dona eis, Domine, / et lux perpetua luceat eis*" – *Requiem* expresses hope for interminable rest for the deceased whom, as victims of Nazi persecutions, Kleiberg and Morgan's text brings back to life with their group testimonies. This skillful maneuver may not make amends for the loss of the victims' lives, but it invites the audience to imagine the torture that the victims had to go through.

Church. Consequently, there is no true communication between the prayer and the discourse of minority experience. The principle of othering is displayed yet not resolved; instead, the poems' statement avoids the pitfalls of the we/they dichotomy by transforming the "they" into an "it" – "the Third Reich," a synonym for inhumanity. The enemy's peremptory, rhythmically-executed commands echo physical punishment by beating, whose steady beat and repetition, the lines' rhythm and semantic priming, and the climbing crescendo of the musical phrase underscore. The narrative economy of an operatically enunciated word exceeds the economy of the spoken word which takes less time to perform. Musical enunciation, coloration, and repetition of the word underline its semantic value as much as they charge it with vigor and feelings. Thus, the concluding couplet of the already quoted stanza one – "Flog them, scald them, batter them. / Break their bones and scatter them" – brings the message home by way of the repetition of words, lines, and musical phrases, as well as by its quaint allussions to "*Confutatis maledictis*" of Mozart's *Requiem*.[5] As the quoted opening stanza of Kleiberg and Morgan's seventh section – "The Pink Triangle: Homosexuals" – confirms, the "we" of the victims are the system's pursued other whose elimination is codified in the sanitation program of the Nazi body politic.

The present critique may be considered unjust and unjustified, since Britten's and Kleiberg's requiems were commissioned and used in a religious context: Britten composed his work for the consecration of the restored Coventry Cathedral, whereas Kleiberg wrote his for Nidaros Domkor (the choir of the Nidaros Cathedral in Trondheim) in 2002, haunted by the memory of the wars in the Balkans and Afganistan, and the 9/11 attacks (Bruno 2004: n. pag.). The assigned historical-ideological parameters have in no way curbed Heggie's creative thrust. On the contrary, and in the true spirit of the task, the composer releases the form of potential music-historical constraints that genres like the requiem, for example, entail; at the same time, the release of the repressed history requires a format that would both be true to its guiding subtexts and its politics of emancipation.

---

5   The semantic proximity between the couplet and the opening lines of the first stanza of "*Confutatis maledictis*" ("The accursed are silenced") works as an intertextual reference which Kleiberg's musical phrases *qua* Mozartian allusions underline, by emphasizing different ways of inscribing cultural memories, which, in turn, depend on the specificity of artistic practices.

## Fatal Attraction

Since an estimate of 60-70 percent of homosexual camp inmates perished during the war, Gene Scheer deems sexual preference a sufficient enough reason for the Nazi banishment, and skirts references to the protagonists' Jewish background, which *Paragraph 175* brings up as part of its larger agenda. Yet beneath the text's declared theme, one discerns undercurrents of the Jewish pogrom: on the one hand, the list of characters in the liner notes makes explicit that Manfred Levin was killed in Auschwitz in 1942 (Scheer 2008: 14); on the other hand, textual references to the arrest of his family and their deportation point to his Jewishness.[6] The structure of the work can by no means be ignored: The seven sections of the music drama uncannily call to mind the seven branches of the menorah – the holy candelabrum – the symbol of Judaism and universal enlightenment. Heggie and Scheer's project has a clear educational agenda behind its aesthetic design: It brings to light what history has screened. "The Story of Joe" in its middle – a story of an eighteen-year-old youth whose only crime was his sexual preference for which he paid with his life – draws attention to the destiny of a number of carriers of the pink triangle – their torture and death included.[7] With the testimonies of "complete witnesses" lost in the ashes of the Holocaust, what is available are a few survivor stories which, for legal purposes, remained unvoiced until well after the war. Or as the Gad character puts it in an adequately named section – "Silence" – his need to speak of

---

[6]  Costume designs for two performances of *For a Look or a Touch*, whose fragments are available on YouTube, may illustrate the point more vividly: In the December 4, 2008 Santa Monica production and Morgan Smith's performance of the "Golden Years," the character of Manfred is clad in a camp uniform with a pink triangle affixed to his jacket; The "Der Singende Wald" aria with Colin Levin in the lead and the Boston Gay Men's Chorus recorded on March 25, 2012 also features Manfred in the uniform though with a different marking of otherness. His gender-inflected Star of David – a compound of equilateral pink and yellow triangles – highlights his ethnic belonging and sexual orientation; members of the choir, in turn, are all in black with a pink triangle on their breasts. The MOR choreography of the 15 March 2008 performance, which I saw at the Seattle Asian Art Museum with Morgan Smith as Manfred and the now-late Julian Patrick as Gad, features Manfred in flying shirttails, which not only suggests his ghostly existence, but appears to allude to a freer lifestyle and sexual conduct.

[7]  Like Morgan, Scheer honors the memory of other work camp prisoners, carriers of identification stigmata, starting with the most exposed and persecuted group – the Jews – yet also listing political prisoners, mentally retarded, and Jehovah's witnesses to acknowledge their suffering.

his camp experience was met with a "Leave it alone" advice, "It's over and done with" (15), signifying silence yet implying erasure and "disremembering." In order to prevent historical amnesia, Gad Bech decided to speak up and donate Manfred Lewin's journal to the US Holocaust Memorial Museum in Washington in 1999, where it is now part of an online exhibition.

Lewin's journal and Beck's testimony impact the music drama's plot and narrative format: the verse/narrative dichotomy of the two hypotexts becomes the drama's aria/spoken word composite. Not only does the versification of poem-songs echo parts of the journal; it also becomes what Shoshana Felman designates a "poetry as setting free," a poetic working through of a traumatic past (Felman in Felman and Laub 1992: 38). The rhyme "imperfection" of some of Scheer's lyrics may no doubt be attributed to his close following of Lewin's poetic style, whereas the free verse of others reflects the anguish and the chaotic reality of torture. It is as if language in the depicted scenes refuses to be harnessed in verse, and, in the most extreme cases, becomes meaningless, redundant and turns into screams at the level of human utterance, and brushes of atonality as its musical attribute or commentary. These scenes of torture which are most powerfully experienced and narrated by Manfred's revenant, warrant further attention with reference to politics of memory and of haunting.

With the work's centrepiece, "The Story of Joe," the text sheds light on the atrocities and mechanisms of the concentration camp torture: "good boy, Joe" is a sacrificial lamb in the system where "Horror and savagery are the law," and where the unthinkable is possible (Scheer 2008: 16). A graphic account of his bestial torture is rendered in the staccato rhythm of a minimalistic verbal phrase, whose graveness the string instruments' and the piano's accompanying chords punctuate. The lines are stripped of all redundancies, as is the victim of all his clothes:

> They strip him naked,
> Put a bucket on his head,
> Then sick their dogs on him.
> They bite his body,
> Tear at his thighs,
> Blood everywhere.
> His screams and cries
> Amplified by the bucket on his head.
> Ah! Ah!
>
> Goodbye, Joe.

If Scene Four is the thematic cornerstone of the work, line five of the nine-line quoted stanza obliquely relates to its underlying concern – sexuality.[8] At the core of this recitative lies the fact that the life of victims is immaterial in the camp environment, and that the way from "good boy, Joe" to "Goodbye, Joe," is painful and short, in fact, only a vowel "away." More importantly, the quoted lines problematize the issues of witnessing and testimony. As object of torture whose outcome is death, Joe is a material witness to the inhumanity of the persecutor; as witness to his friend's agony, Manfred is the embodiment of a *Muselmann*: "I am a silent, obedient shadow. / Dead to myself. Dead to the world. / A silent, obedient shadow." Accordingly, although he delivers his testimony, the text discloses its aporetic status as much as it points to different degrees of "deadness," which the testimony of Manfred's own death in "Der Singende Wald" aria illustrates. A striking absence of verbs in the quoted lines suggests the end of being, at the same time as it juxtaposes death with shadows – which return as androids in the final image of "The Story of Joe." Yet, an unexpected turn of the dramatic musical phrase – from the expression of pain to waltz – reveals that the tormentor himself is an automaton, insensitive to the pain of others. Despite the musical shift from discord to harmony, of which there is none in the camp life, Heggie dresses his tune in a melancholy guise, signing it with a signature of mourning.

"Der Singende Wald" aria that makes up Section Six is literally Manfred's answer to his friend's query: "What happened to you, Manfred?" (Scheer 2008: 17). The answer, even when repeated, makes as much sense as the inhuman torture that lies behind it. As a testimony of what he has gone through, Manfred's story leaves it open whether he is a witness to or a victim of a strappado torture, or both.[9] If both, his is an impossible testimony as subject and

---

[8]    My argument has so far fronted the role of the memory of the Holocaust, but the figurality of the present scene uncannily brings to mind the more-recent physical, psychological, and sexual assaults at Abu Ghraib, which the media have brought into our living rooms. Because of their recent date and numerous reprintings, these vivid images may speak more clearly to contemporary audiences, even though the horror of torture they communicate may be said to be of a different kind.

[9]    Strappado, or "bad-apple torture," is a means of punishment whereby the prisoner's hands are tied behind his body which is then hoisted and suddenly released so that his shoulder blades are dislocated and/or break. "Der Singende Wald" is thus a metaphor for group torture where the crying and screaming victims sound like a weeping forest. The entire scene closely follows the testimony of Heinz Dörmer from *Paragraph 175*, who explains that homosexuals were simply left hanging while the Jews were jerked, obviously to increase their pain.

object of narrative, which his ghostly existence nonetheless makes possible. Or, rather, it is language that makes it possible: the compact ekphrasis of the stanza details the torture procedure in which the "you" implies "one" at the level of the general, and "not-I" at the level of the particular. As the subject of experience and object of torture, "you" might suggest dissociation or even resignation, which is what passive constructions further highlight:

> There are holes in the ground,
> In each, a tall pole with a hook on top.
> Your hands tied behind your back
> Your wrists slung over the hook
> You are lifted up, posted high.
> Your shoulders snap and break
> And you swing and hang and scream.

When, following the repetition of the topical refrain which is coded as wailing, the "you" becomes a "they," there is an intimation that the victims are beyond language since physical pain resists it: "Physical pain has no voice," propounds Elaine Scarry, "but when it at last finds a voice, it begins to tell a story" (Scarry 1985: 3): The "I," "we," or, even, "you" can all be the subject of the utterance, whereas "they," who are beyond language, cannot, if utterance equals verbalization. Thus, what Sheer's libretto declares "Inexplicable. / Beyond comprehension," Heggie watermarks with another musical outpour of mourning.

*For a Look or a Touch*, however, refuses to associate homosexuality with ultimate suffering or to capitulate to the tragedy of the Shoah; instead, it balances it off with happy memories of the gay environment, which, by giving expression to the entire spectrum of the emotional palette, prevent the work from becoming a melodrama. Thus, references to pockets of joy and freedom, which the "Golden Years" aria highlights, offer an emotional relief even before the text zooms in on the torture scenes. What were for Gad endless possibilities, were for Manfred ultimate freedom and exuberance of the "Topsy turvy, joyful Berlin," where members of the gay community could "Meet and greet and eat and cheat and swing." Yet topsy-turvy is what the young men's lives become with their arrest by the Gestapo, which the semantic valency of a number of words underscores: Swinging and screaming from joy on the dance floor become swinging, hanging, and screaming on the torture pole. The sexual freedom which the golden years in Berlin celebrate with the musical styles of jazz and swing becomes physical torture with discreet implications of sexuality. The notion of freedom, too, is turned upside down when Manfred refuses to join Gad and escape the Gestapo, and returns to his apprehended family to get peace of mind: "If I leave my family now, I'll never be free again" (Scheer 2008: 17). The character of Manfred, however, is the prime example of topsy-turvying as the impossible witness of the Holocaust and a repository of memory, which he revives in his ghostly visitation.

The immediacy of the dramatic opening with Gad's question "Who is there?" and Manfred's response "Do you remember?" as an answer pulls the audience into the plot as if erasing the invisible line between the intra-mural and the extra-mural space of the drama (Scheer 2008: 14). With its subsequent reformulation ("Do you remember when night was for more than sleep?") and numerous repetitions and variations (19 in all, which was the age of the two young lovers when they got separated by the war), the initial question becomes an entreaty that grows into a demand – "Remember" – which is also the title of the work's final, seventh movement. Remember, then, is an imperative in both senses of the word with its double addressees – Gad and the audience. However, by way of repetition, it is also a textual revenant as a refrain that haunts the drama. Hailed by the ghost of history who demands attention and ethical commitment, the audience uncannily becomes a "witness" to history – if only as a witness to the story of the witness. Gad's grievance against the loss of stories that recount the sufferings of homosexual prisoners is a grievance against the lack of an ear that is willing to listen: "Nobody to talk to. Nobody to tell" become a silent appeal to the audience – to listen, remember, *and* tell (Scheer 2008: 16). Repression is no solution to painful memories which demand a working through by way of transference. Or, as Manfred expresses it in the last, most dramatic and lyric aria, the cure for grief is in solace and love:

> Will the last bonds of our community be torn apart?
> No, do not lament.
> Even though the fire torments your heart,
> There is one sure support:
> The voice of our love. Our love (Scheer 2008: 18).

Thus, love as an ontological imperative and memory as its hauntological manifestation suture the rift between the past and the present when, in the final section, Gad is finally able to say "love" and acknowledge the past with "Yes. Yes. I remember!" This assertion brings the plot full circle, because the opening question finally gets an answer; and its initial melancholy musical motif turns into a restatement in the drama's closing score. Yet, the final scene also harks back to the drama's opening in that the ghost's uncanny appearance is complemented with his even more uncanny exit – with Gad. If the lovers' humming away and the concurrent fading of lights and music, as stage directions indicate, imply a con-sensual contract which follows the final, dramatic aria – the *Liebestod* – they also revise the traditional *Liebestod* gender scenario from a heterosexual to homoerotic one.

One can, no doubt, commend the composer and his librettist for their adept handling of the subject matter, whereby the gender-political sheds light on the historical by skilfully avoiding the pitfalls of the melodramatic.[10] But the dynamics of the queering of the Holocaust also presupposes an inquiry into its existence and extent. We may still wonder how the Shoah was possible, and, like the character of Gad, have an obligation to remember the event and its banished others.

## Bibliography

Agamben, Giorgio (1999): *Remnants of Auschwitz: The Witness and the Archive.* Roazen, Daniel Heller (trans.). New York: Zone Books.

Borchert, Gavin (2007): "*For a Look or a Touch* Examines Seldom-Discussed Aspect of the Holocaust." *Seattle Weekly*, May 15, 2007. www.seattleweekly.com.

Briggs, Bob (2012): *MusicWeb International*, January 2009. www.naxos.com.

Bruno, Malcolm (2004): "Of Wars and Requiems." In: Kleiberg, Ståle: *Requiem for the Victims of Nazi Persecution.* Liner Notes. Grappa musikkforlag: Simax Classics.

Burleigh, Michael and Wolfgang Wippermann (2003): *The Racial State: Germany, 1933-1945.* Cambridge: Cambridge University Press.

Carlson, Marvin (2003): *The Haunted Stage: The Theatre as Memory Machine.* Ann Arbor: University of Michigan Press.

Dolar, Mladen (2002): "If Music Be the Food of Love." In: Žižek, Slavoj and Mladen Dolar (eds.): *Opera's Second Death.* New York: Routledge, 1-94.

Felman, Shoshana and Dori Laub (1992): *Testimony. Crisis of Witnessing in Literature, Psychoanalysis, and History.* New York: Routledge.

---

[10]  Having mentioned Hugill's characterization of the work as a mixture of "song cycle and melodrama," an explanation is here in place. It is not hard to agree with the music critic's view that Julian Patrick's interpretation of the Gad role is "too over-boiled," but the sentimentalism of the character's advanced age opens up for a melodramatic touch which serves as an apposite mnemonic device.

Foucault, Michel (1985): *The Use of Pleasure. The History of Sexuality*, vol. 2. Hurley, Robert (trans.). New York: Pantheon.

Heggie, Jake (2008): *For a Look or a Touch*. Libretto Scheer, Gene. Music of Remembrance. Naxos: American Classics.

Hirsch, Marianne (1997): *Family Frame: Photography, Narrative, and Postmemory*. Cambridge, Mass.: Harvard University Press.

Hirsch, Marianne (2001): "Surviving Images: Holocaust Photographs and the Work of Postmemory." *Yale Journal of Criticism*, 14 (1), 5-37.

Hugill, Robert (2012): *MusicWeb International*, July 2008. www.naxos.com.

Hutcheon, Linda and Michael Hutcheon (1996): *Opera: Desire, Disease, Death*. Lincoln: University of Nebraska Press.

Kleiberg, Ståle (2004): *Requiem for the Victims of Nazi Persecution*. Libretto Morgan, Edwin. Grappa musikkforlag: Simax Classics.

Lewin, Manfred (1941): *Erinnerst Du Dich, als* ("Do You Remember When"). United States Holocaust Memorial Museum, www.ushmm.org.

More, R. (2012): "*For a Look or a Touch* CD Review." www.naxos.com.

Morgan, Edwin (2001): "The Yellow Triangle: Gypsies." In: Kleiberg, Ståle: *Requiem for the Victims of Nazi Persecution*. Liner Notes. Grappa musikkforlag: Simax Classics.

*Oxford English Dictionary* (2012 [1989]). 2nd ed., online version, June 2012.

*Paragraph 175* (2000): Epstein, Rob and Jeffrey Friedman (dir.) and prod. research/assoc. prod. Klaus Müller, narr. by Rupert Everett, www.youtube.com.

Scarry, Elaine (1985): *The Body in Pain: The Making and Unmaking of the World*. New York: Oxford University Press.

Scheer, Gene (2008): *For a Look or a Touch*. Music Heggie, Jake. Music of Remembrance. Naxos: American Classics.

Theweleit, Klaus (1989): *Male Fantasies. Vol. 2. Male Bodies: Psychoanalyzing the White Terror*. Minneapolis: University of Minnesota Press.

Weinthal, Benjamin (2012): "Last Gay Jewish Holocaust Survivor Dies." *Jerusalem Post*, 25 June, www.jpost.com.

# Andorran Jews and Other Strangers: Narratives of Identity and Otherness in European Post-War Literature

*Sissel Lægreid*

> Jeder Mensch erfindet sich früher oder später eine Geschichte, die er oft, unter gewaltigen Opfern, für sein Leben hält (Max Frisch).

> Aber das Eigene muß so gut gelernt sein wie das Fremde (Friedrich Hölderlin).

In her description of the traumatic experience of estrangement Julia Kristeva argues that the stranger is "the hidden face of our identity, the space that ruins our resting place, the space in time where mutual understanding and instinctive fellow feeling become swallowed up". In order to prevent us from hating him in himself we must therefore first recognize the stranger within ourselves, become aware of our own difference and "acknowledge ourselves all to be strangers, rebels from ties and communities" (Kristeva 1991: 1).

Kristeva's point of departure is that the stranger seems to be suffering from a perpetual loss of identity, a condition which in turn makes him abject, all because of his inability to distinguish between a threatening outside and his own body, which as a consequence of this failure has become disgusting to him. Accordingly, in order to end this kind of suffering, the stranger must learn to recognise and love his own otherness, since only then, she argues, will he be able to accept the strangeness of others.

As indicated in the title of my paper, its focus will be on ways in which the dynamics of identity and otherness have been depicted in European literature written after 1945. Keeping the Kristevan description of the psychosomatic mechanisms of these dynamics in mind, let me start by quoting a fragment from a short prose sketch written by the Swiss novelist and dramatist Max Frisch (Frisch 1946-1949: 35):

In Andorra there lived a young man who was believed to be a Jew. It will be necessary to describe his presumed background, his daily contacts with the Andorrans, who saw the

Jewishness in him: the fixed image that meets him everywhere. Their distrust, for instance, of his depth of feeling – something that, as even an Andorran knows, no Jew can possibly have. A Jew has to rely on the sharpness of his intellect, which necessarily gets all the sharper because of it. Or his attitude toward money, an important matter even in Andorra [...]. He could not become like all the others, and so, having tried in vain not to make himself conspicuous, he began to wear his otherness with a certain air of defiance, of pride [...] (Frisch 1950: 35ff).[1]

Frisch called his prose sketch "Der Andorranische Jude" (The Andorran Jew) and in it tells the story of mistaken identity and its fatal consequences: a young man living in Andorra[2] believes himself to be a Jew, not because he is a Jew, but because the Andorrans see and treat him as one. When repeated attempts to be accepted as Andorran fail, he resigns and accepts his given, but false identity. From then on he looks upon himself as the Andorrans' other, starts behaving according to their image of 'the Jew' and finally gets killed for accepting himself to be what in fact he is not. After his death though, the Andorrans find out who his real parents were. Neither of them were Jews, and the young man had therefore been as much of an Andorran as the rest of them. But, as the story ironically ends, "the Andorrans every time they looked into the mirror, were astonished to see that they too had traits of the Jew ["des Judas"], each and every one of them."

The dynamics of this fatal play of and with identities is emphasized by the double implication of the German genitive form 'des Judas'. This literally means 'of the Jew' in the sense of something generic to him, like his voice, his face or his attitude and behaviour, such as his presumed lack of heart or soul (Gemüt), which, as Frisch ironically states, "all Andorrans knew" a Jew could never have. Moreover, it was general Andorran knowledge that a Jew could never be able to connect or show the warmth of mutual trust and confidentiality.[3]

---

1   When nothing else is noted, the following translations from German into English are my own (SL).

2   Frisch stresses that the name Andorra has got nothing to do with the small state of Andorra in the Pyrenees or for that matter with other small states; Andorra is the name of a model. Cf. Max Frisch: *Andorra. Text und Kommentar* 1999, 8.

3   Frisch, after having referred to the universal Andorran consensus about the fact that a Jew could never love, not in the Andorran way, since this was blocked by his typically Jewish cold rationality (die Kälte seines Verstandes), ironized as follows: "[...] es fehlte ihm das Gemüt, das Verbindende; es fehlte ihm, und das war unverkennbar, die Wärme des Vertrauens".

In addition, because it involves the word 'Judas', a stigmatized name in the Christian Bible, the phrase "traits of the Jew" (des Judas) is also associated with the name of Judas, the disciple who betrayed Jesus. In other words, when Frisch's Andorrans looked at themselves in the mirror, they saw traits of the Jew, as well as of Judas. On an unconscious level, they may thus have realized that both the betrayer and the estranged other had been living among them all along, both as the other part of and within themselves. Thus in the Kristevan sense, the Andorrans may be said to have recognized the stranger within themselves, but since they found what they saw disgusting, they repressed it, and were therefore unable to prevent the tragic death of an innocent man.

The irony of the semantics in this play was most likely intended by the author. Frisch wrote this prose sketch in 1946 in the wake of the Holocaust after a journey he had made through the devastated Germany, and about ten years later he turned it into a play called *Andorra*. Here the main character is given the name Andri, a significant name, since, because of its closeness to the German word 'der Andere' ('the other'), it indicates otherness. Like in the prose sketch, where the main character is nameless, his presumed otherness gets him excluded and finally killed.

*Andorra* is a play about a complexity of issues focussing on racial and national prejudice, stereotypes, identity and guilt on a personal as well as a collective level. In order to keep up appearances, a well-respected citizen lies about the identity of his own son, claims he is a Jew, names him Andri and by doing so gets him labelled as the Andorrans' other with traits they consider to be universally accepted as typically Jewish – such as cowardice, greed, sexual urges, and ambition.

However, in the course of the play the audience realises that these are all traits the Andorrans themselves have, but which they neither accept nor recognise in themselves. They therefore project what they do not like onto him, the Jew, whom they, as indicated above, at least on an unconscious level, both see and reject as their interior other. As a result of this projective strategy of identification, lodged in what is clearly a collective prejudice, the estranged Andri gets confused about his identity and finally adopts the image society has made of him.

Only after the play is over, do the Andorrans learn that he was the illegitimate son of the respected village teacher, and his mother was a Señora, one of the Blacks, the enemies south of the border, constantly threatening to invade Andorra. Too late the Andorrans realize that one of their own had told a petty lie to prevent the truth of his having a son out of wedlock from getting known. Although Andri at an earlier stage had met his mother and learnt the truth about his identity, this knowledge had not changed anything, for like in the prose sketch he refuses to give up his given identity as a Jew. In consequence, after the Blacks have occupied Andorra, he is finally taken away to be slaughtered on the pretext that the Andorrans have murdered the Señora. In other words in the end he gets killed by the Blacks for what he is, an Andorran, whom they (the Blacks) consider to be their other, interior or exterior, depending on whether or not they knew that he was one of them by birth, since his mother was a Black. The irony and tragic consequence of this foul play is everyone's death and suffering: the victim's father hangs himself and the sister, whom he initially, because of his mistaken identity, had planned to marry, goes insane.

After Andri's tragic death the Andorrans claim their innocence, apart from the priest, who admits his sin. The rest of the citizens argue that they couldn't possibly have known the truth about Andri's identity. And given the time in which the prose sketch, and later the play was written, post-war Europe in the wake of the Holocaust, the ironic intent of the author seems apparent: Frisch aims to investigate and show the destructive effects of the image we create of others as well as of ourselves through fear, self-interest, convenience. He efficiently uses the assumption that the central figure is a Jew, to reveal the selfish origins and tragic consequences of prejudice, its disastrous physical and spiritual effects on the victim. In his diary he has expressed the fundamental seriousness of this issue in the following way:

> Thou shalt not, it is said, make unto thee any graven image of God.
>
> The same commandment should apply when God is taken to mean the living part of every human being, the part that cannot be grasped. It is a sin that, however much it is committed against us, we almost continually commit ourselves – except when we love (Frisch 1950: 250).

Although *Andorra* may be read as a comment on the Holocaust and anti-Semitism, the play nevertheless addresses the fundamental problem of otherness on a more general level. This reading of the play is indicated by the ordinariness of its nameless figures, who apart from Andri and his sister Barblin, are not individual persons in their own right, but merely representatives of given social roles such as *the Mother, the Doctor, the Carpenter, the Teacher, the Priest, the Soldier,* and *Someone.* In short they are not there as individuals, but as representations of the average, depersonalized 'Everyman'.

Thus by stressing the ordinariness of the figures along with the initial events depicted in the play, Frisch succeeds in revealing how the petty weakness of everyday life with its lack of reflection upon the generally accepted rules and images of so-called normality, can lead to terrible consequences. In a comment on his play in the German weekly newspaper *Die Zeit* (3 November 1961) he talks about how its quintessence is the universal situation of guilt, because:

> … the guilty are never conscious of their guilt, are never punished, they have not com- mitted a crime. I do not want a beacon of hope at the end; I would rather end with this horror, with this cry of how scandalously people treat each other. Surely the guilty are seated in the stalls. They are the ones saying they did not want it to happen. They are the ones who became guilty, but who do not feel themselves to be accomplices to crime. They shall become startled, they shall, when they have seen the play, lie awake at night. The accomplices are everywhere.

## Invented Stories – Narrative Identities

To prevent a future Holocaust from happening, Frisch – in *Andorra* as well as in other parts of his work, argues that each individual carries the responsibility of accepting and affirming every person's unique being.

Kristeva's description of the traumatic experience of estrangement quoted above, and Frisch's affirmation that every person's unique being requires that we must recognise both the stranger within ourselves and our own fundamental difference from ourselves as well as from others. To each and every one of us the fundamental implication of this requirement is the recognition of who we are. First of all this requires knowing and distinguishing ourselves and our own biography as different from that of others. In order to *be* someone, we must be able to tell the story of our lives based on a mixture of what we remember or think we remember, and what we have been told about ourselves. In other words our identity and the narrative of who we are may be seen as the result of a dialectical process of fact and fiction. According to Frisch, the task at hand requires the ability to invent, tell and believe the story of one's life, since every "human being sooner or later invents a story, which he believes to be his life; or a whole chain of stories" (Frisch 1964: 74).

In this sense identity as the narrative of who we are may be said to be a creative construction of fact and fiction, or as Nietzsche put it in 1873 in his essay about truth and lies in the extra-moral sense, if conceived as *the* truth about someone, identity may be seen as a mobile army of metaphors, metonymies and anthropomorphisms, in short as a linguistic construction

(Nietzsche 1980: 880).[4] To Nietzsche the identity of a subject must therefore be conceived as fragmented or in truth as a multitude (Vielheit). Consequently, as the French symbolist Rimbaud put it in a letter to his friend and former teacher Georges Izambard, "I" must be another: "JE est un autre" (Rimbaud 1965: 267f) implying that the "I" in itself is both a construct and its constitutive other.

From a similar but clearly more ethically concerned angle Paul Ricoeur, who with reference to their ability to unmask, demystify, and expose the real from the apparent, called Nietzsche and critics like Marx and Freud "hermeneutics of suspicion", explores the hermeneutics of the self.[5]

Ricouer's contribution to the understanding of the self paved the road to a concept of identity, which implies both the essence of self-understanding and the understanding of the relation of the self to another. In *Time and Narrative* (Ricoeur: 1988), he explores the connection between the activity of telling a story and the temporal nature of human experience, and coins the term narrative identity. The term implies either the individual or collective entity addressed by questions such as who has done this or acted in that way, and to whom did these things happen?

In *Oneself as an Other* (Ricoeur 1992), Ricouer goes on to explore three categories of otherness: the otherness of the world, of another person (ego), and of the self to him or herself, both as a body and a conscience. He stresses the interrelation of these categories as intrinsic to the constitution of the self and by doing so highlights the ethical dimension of the self and its fundamental importance to the formation of the personal identity of every human being.

Essential to Ricoeur's notion of identity is the fundamental temporality of being, where the 'who' as a being in co-existence with others in a common world, transforms him- or herself in the course of a life history and only becomes who he or she is in the course of becoming him- or herself. In the Freudian sense this may be conceived as the becoming aware of oneself as a consciousness, which according to Freud comes into being instead of or places itself upon the trace of remembrance: "das Bewusstsein entstehe an Stelle der Erinnerungsspur" (Freud 1982: 235).

---

4    My reference is to the German version of the essay "Über Wahrheit und Lüge im ausser-moralischen Sinne". In Colli/Montinari (eds.): *Sämtliche Werke* 1980.

5    In his highly influential work on Freud, he states that "[t]hree masters, seemingly mutually exclusive, dominate the school of suspicion: Marx, Nietzsche, and Freud." (Ricoeur 1970: 32).

In his exploration of the concept of narrative identity Ricoeur stresses the essential importance of the temporality of human action and suffering and argues that the act of storytelling is the only way both can be prevented from being forgotten. His point of departure is that if there is such a thing as a story, it must be because there are people who act and suffer.

This concept of identity as an entity constituting itself in time is based on a distinction between identity as sameness (*idem*) and identity as selfhood (*ipse*), where the self is the *who* of a history, which is an identity given in the course of the narrative act. Identity as the self thus only comes into being by way of temporalization, as an entity constituting itself within the framework of time as and in the act of narration.

According to Ricoeur an individual or a collective entity can therefore only be identified by way of composing a narrative, whether it is fictive or historical. Therefore he argues: "To answer the question 'Who?' [...] is to tell a story of a life. The story told tells about the action of the 'who'. And the identity of this 'who' must therefore itself be narrative identity" (Ricoeur 1988: 246).

## I – Another: Traumas of Memory and Biography

In line both with the Kristevan description of the dynamics of identity and otherness, Frisch's words about man's invented life stories, and Ricoeur's concept of the narrative identity, the Hungarian-Jewish writer and 2002 Nobel Prize Laureate Imre Kertész (1929-) published a novel in German entitled *Ich – ein anderer*, in which he stated that "'I' is a fiction, where we are at best co-authors" (Kertész 2002: 25).[6]

In his novel Kertész, who survived both Auschwitz and Buchenwald, deals with the interaction of memory and biography, and asks "Who am I, what am I, and what is my unique story?" (Kertész 2002: 25). However, instead of answering this 'unanswerable question', he recapitulates one of the many fragments he remembers of what he has been told about his life. In so doing, he follows in the footsteps of Rilke's Malte Laurids Brigge (Rilke 1910), a young, estranged writer living in Paris at the turn of the 20th century. Brigge attempts to reconstruct his life and existence on the basis of fragments of his memories of childhood experiences and European history in order to prevent

---

6   I translate from and refer to the German version of the book and its motto "'Ich' ist eine Fiktion, bei der wir bestenfalls Miturheber sind".

it and consequently himself from dissolving. In a similar way the narrator in Kertész' novel goes on a time-spatial journey back and forth between reflections on fragmentary memory flashes from his life, as well as from the life and work of important figures in the history of European philosophy and literature – minute observations of people and events on the streets of cities like Berlin, Leipzig, Tel Aviv, Vienna, and Budapest.

At the end of the novel after a passage where he looks back on his unhappily married life with a woman, whom he loved and who, like the author Imre Kertész and/or his narrator, had survived a concentration camp. At this point he recognises that their life and love from the very beginning had been based on a kind of prison solidarity (Gefängnis-Solidarität) and suddenly realises:

> … that this world no longer *exists*, that I only have memories of it. And these memories are my memories, no *second dimension*, no evidence can verify it: perhaps that I have lived at all is not true, perhaps nothing is true. […] I almost get dizzy in view of the fact, that the past in a split second turns into what it is named: past, a depot of abandoned things, experiences, sounds and images, which long ago have been detached from their living origin, from the life which they had once borne and for some time kept intact. My story has fallen off of me: I am overcome by an intense feeling of vertigo as if I have lost my direction and have skidded out of time between past and future. […] my foot takes an indecisive step forwards. A step to where? No matter, because whoever takes the step, is already no longer I, but someone else … (Kertész 2002: 126-127).

Bearing these words by Kertész in mind, let us look at two examples of how the moral and traumatic dilemma of estrangement and otherness has been dealt with in German by two post-war writers like W. G. Sebald and Georges-Arthur Goldschmidt. Like Frisch and Kertész they both in their own unique way address the traumatic dynamics of identity and otherness in their work.

In the work of the German writer W. G. Sebald (1944-2001) the experience of estrangement and its consequences are a major topic. Like Frisch, he is not himself a Jew, but still many of his books evolve around the Jewish tragedy. After experiencing the lack of willingness to deal with the history of the tragedy in the first decades after the war, especially among German writers, he emigrated and lived in voluntary exile in England, where he was appointed Professor of European literature at the University of East Anglia.

Sebald is known to most as the author of *Austerlitz*, a novel he wrote in 2001, the same year he died in a car accident. The main character of the novel has been raised by a Calvinist family in a Welsh foster home during the 1940s under the name of Dafydd Elias, which as it turns out, is not his real name.

He knows little of his true origins, and from the start feels alienated from his foster family and surroundings.

But though he has dim memories of an earlier life, a period which ended before his fifth birthday, he spends his formative years stifling any curiosity as to what these recollections might portend. He is a middle-aged man by the time he starts to unravel the mystery of his own existence, and trace the path that leads him back to his childhood in Czechoslovakia, and his real name and identity Jack Austerlitz.

The last time the two of them meet, Austerlitz suffers a nervous breakdown, leaving the narrator with photographs and pieces of written and remembered oral information of their conversations. From this point on he takes on the task of retracing the biography and detecting the true identity of the man, who, as it turns out, is Jewish.

The structure of the book and its thematic fabric is complicated with a pattern typical of Sebald's way of writing and can also be seen in his other texts, such as in *The Emigrants*, where the main characters are Jews, who either die or commit suicide. Like in *Austerlitz* the narrator tries to retrace the story of their lives and unknown, hidden, and mistaken identity.

By means of photographs, family albums and fragments of written or told material, the narrator in *Austerlitz* as well as in *The Emigrants*, tries to restore and preserve the memory of the identity of the persons he meets or their presumed identity. The purpose of this process is to prevent them from being forgotten as victims and personifications of the tragedy of European history.

From an ethical perspective Sebald may be said to be in line with Frisch, who claimed that each individual carries the responsibility of preventing a future Holocaust by accepting and affirming every person's unique being. And by telling the story of people who have suffered because they were not accepted for who they were, Sebald's work also addresses Ricoeur's concept of the narrative identity. Because, as Ricoeur pointed out, if there is such a thing as a story, it must be because there are people who act and suffer, an individual or a collective entity, that can only be identified by way of composing a narrative, whether it be fictive or historical: "To answer the question 'Who?'[…] is to tell a story of a life. The story told tells about the action of the 'who'. And the identity of this 'who' must therefore itself be narrative identity" (Ricoeur 1988: 246).

In a different perspective the traumatic experience of estrangement and the tragedy of the Holocaust are also retraced and dealt with in the work of Georges-Arthur Goldschmidt or Jürgen-Arthur Goldschmidt (1928-). A German writer of Jewish heritage, he has lived in France since 1938, when at the age of ten, his parents sent him and his elder brother by train from their hometown Hamburg out of pre-war Germany via Italy to France, hoping they might survive. They both did, but they never saw their parents again. The mother died in 1942, the father was sent to Theresienstadt. He survived, but died in 1947, before the father and his sons had a chance to meet again.

During the war the two brothers lived in safety at a boarding school in the French Alps and both narrowly escaped the Germans in 1944. After his traumatic experience of being sent away from home and separated from his parents, Georges-Arthur Goldschmidt decided never to return to Germany. He moved to Paris, where he got his education as a high school teacher, got married to a French woman, and after some years started a career as a translator of German books into French. Later he wrote books, where the lines separating autobiographic facts from fragments of fiction are deliberately blurred.

In view of the traumas his books deal with, the writing strategy may to some extent function as a kind of therapy to the author. Goldschmidt himself has confirmed this to be the case in several interviews about his work. As with many Jews who survived the Holocaust, his relation to German as his mother tongue, had been compromised, and the natural link was somehow broken. In real life, both as a survivor of the Holocaust as well as on the level of fiction, he resorted to French, and today he sees himself not as German or Jewish, but as an integrated member of the French community. He started off writing books to deal with his traumatic life experience, first in French and then he let others translate them into German.

Although at some point in the nineties he started writing books in German, Goldschmidt still writes books in French, but now translates them into German himself.[7] In view of the dynamics of biography and identity as a narrative process of writing, fluctuating between the borders of fact and fiction as described above, the books dealing with his life in Germany were first written in French, and then translated into German. In other words they were written in such a way that the distance was strategically kept, not only in time and space, but also in the sense of languages and their borders, which had to be crossed in order to have safe conduct and return to and from the past.

Goldschmidt himself explains this choice of strategy as necessary in order for him to be able to deal with the traumatic experiences of his life. Since to

---

[7]    This was also the case with his autobiography, which he first wrote in French under the title *La traversée des Fleuves* (1999) and then some years later translated into German himself, naming it *Über die Flüsse* (2001).

him writing is also a therapeutic act that deals with the fact that his Jewish identity had been unknown to him until the catastrophe of the Holocaust, he admits that the story he tells about his life, at least in part, may be invented. With reference to the French writer Doubrosky, who first coined the term in his book *Le fils* (1977), Goldschmidt himself describes this kind of writing strategy as a deliberate violation of the borders between fact and fiction as "autofictional". He first used the strategy in 1991 when he began working on a trilogy of narratives dealing with his childhood experience and life in exile in France shortly before and during the war.

The estrangement experienced by Goldschmidt is shared by the main character and narrator of his autofictional trilogy. The first book of the trilogy was *Die Absonderung* (1991), implying disassociation and seclusion as well as excretion. In accordance with the reality of the experience referred to, the title indicates a parting and breaking of connections in a more physiological sense.

Like the two other books in the trilogy, *Die Aussetzung* (1996), which means abandonment, suspension or interruption, and the last one, *Die Befreiung* (2007), the liberation, the first book addresses the problem of identity and otherness lodged both in the dynamics of inclusion and exclusion, and the experience and consequences of estrangement for the individuals exposed to it.

*Die Absonderung* is the survival story of a young German Jewish boy in a boarding school in the French Alps during WWII. It is written a from the distance of the third person narrative, where forty years later, the survivor, swiftly moves back and forth between past and present, revisiting and remembering scenes from his traumatic childhood, all of them filtered through the eyes and language of a child.

From the outset the boy has difficulties coming to terms with his own identity. Like Goldschmidt, whose family generations before the Holocaust had converted to Protestantism, and therefore like many other German Jews considered themselves to be Germans, he is unaware of his Jewish ancestry. On the contrary, as he looks back forty years later, even in the train on the way to France via Munich and Florence, when travelling across the German railway bridges: "he had been proud to be German, proud of the fact that Germans had built such bridges to be driven across metallically, roaring" (Goldschmidt 1991: 16).

As he remembers, they had never talked about being Jewish at home, not until a few days before he was sent away. He remembers having heard them whisper the word 'Jew', only to stop talking as soon as he entered the room. But he did not at the time understand why, since it was just a word he knew from the Bible. And even in the train on the way to his refuge he thought the word 'J' (for Jew) on the passports of his fellow passengers, meant 'Jugendlich' (youth).

At first he had found this puzzling, since they were all adults. But later in the boarding school, he recalls, he had gradually started wondering if the letter could have something to do with being Jewish. Looking back he remembers, that at the time when he was still unaware of his own identity, he had not known any Jews, but he knew the word Jew had to do with murder "something uncanny (Unheimliches)[8] came into the bargain, a guilt, he was afraid of it, as if one might know, it was his own" (Goldschmidt 1991: 15).

According to the German racial laws, as a Jew he was guilty by birth (geburtsschuldig). He remembers that he at the time had believed the guilt must be caused by the discovery of his own sexuality, the "Er-Selbst-Sein" (Being himself), a sensation which, as he remembers, always had taken him by surprise and made him play with himself. And still a child and unaware of his true identity, and unable to understand the truth about why he must be sent away from home, he remembers he had made the misguided connection to the word Jew and had concluded:

> The year was 1938, he had not been allowed to stay at home: he was guilty, one already knew things about his person, he himself did not yet know: a paralysis from the inside out, every movement like plaster-cast; from now on again and again he had surprised himself at Being himself. He was guilty, proven guilty. He must be shipped away (Goldschmidt 1991: 14).

In the Kristevan sense of otherness referred to above, in a situation away from home and parents, the child of this story experiences a feeling of guilt, severe self-estrangement, and loss of identity. As a result of the exclusion and disassociation indicated in the title of the book, the condition of his homesickness lies at the core of this experience. The German word 'Heimweh', which functions as a leitmotif throughout the story, contains and emphasizes the constant longing for home and the feeling of pain (Weh) experienced at the loss of a place of belonging (Heim). The feeling is expressed in sentences like "In ihm würgte Heimweh" (Goldschmidt 1991: 29) and "das Heimweh

---

8   Cf. Freud's essay "Das Unheimliche", where he with reference to Schelling defines its opposite "Das Heimliche" as something that should have remained hidden and secret (Heimlich), but has come to light and concludes that unheimlich is a kind of Heimlich. In other words it merges into its opposite (Freud 1982: 248-250).

überkam ihn immer wieder" (Goldschmidt 1991: 52), indicating the suffocating pain he had felt, when he was repeatedly overwhelmed by the feeling of homesickness.

As an adult living in Paris, the narrator in retrospect still feels the pain of his childhood, for instance when standing at the Colline du Télégraph two meters higher than the Montmartre, he imagines himself, as he did then, to be able to see the towers of Hamburg from the Glinde, a hill outside of Hamburg. He now sees it all:

> … from an immeasurable distance, still above the horizon and sharp but none the less immediately recognizable: the spire of the St. Nicholas tower, the dome of St. Michael's and above all the tower of St. Catherine's, twice covering itself (Goldschmidt 1991: 32).

This glimpse into the past of the hometown of his childhood from the position of his present hometown Paris makes him feel the same pain of homesickness "it gets stuck in one's chest, one has to breathe deeply and for a timeless moment one is still at home" in Hamburg with the beech-trees rustling in the garden where "one hears the voice of the mother, sees her dress." And at this moment the memory of the childhood home "places itself on top of homesickness" (Goldschmidt 1991: 32).

Looking back, as he does repeatedly, the narrator remembers the view he had from the boarding school in the French Alps during the war: in one direction he could see a Swiss mountain range which, as he recalls, he had imagined to be the direction, where his parents must be. However, at the time "the trick" he remembers, "had been not to let them in any more" just like he had repeatedly had to defend himself against the others, the French children at the boarding school. Because they spoke a foreign language, he had not been able to communicate with them. He felt they immediately saw through him, seeing his guilt, they had punished him by pulling the chair way from under him and turned his bed upside down.

In this passage, as in many others in the book, the focus is on pain, both in a psychological and a physical sense. It shows how the one leads to the other in the mind of a child: repeatedly he combines repression with sadomasochistic physical aggression and punishment. In order to survive the emotional pain of homesickness and the loss of his parents, of belonging and identity, he seems to seek and enjoy the physical pain of being beaten as a means of escape.

In his essay *Ein Kind wird geschlagen* (A Child is Beaten) Freud makes the connection between the feeling of guilt and erotic sensation and states that:

... being beaten is the coming together of the feeling of guilt and erotic sensation; it is not merely the punishment for engaging in the forbidden genital connection but also constitutes its regressive substitution, and this latter source then in turn leads to the libidinal excitement, which from now on is part of him and results in acts of masturbation. This, however, is what masochism is all about (Freud 1982: 240-241).

In an interview in the German daily newspaper *Frankfurter Rundschau* (3.2.2001) Goldschmidt, with reference to Freud's essay, explains the sexual implications of this phenomenon in the following way:

To children being beaten it may function as a frightening rescue operation of the own identity, a limitation of the self, which proves to me that I exist. Freud probably understood it the same way. When this kind of [sexual, S.L.] excitement occurs, to a young boy it is something which is impossible to understand. It cannot be grasped. And the failure of understanding it may make a child feel deeply insecure and disturbed. How come that being punished excites me? This is a distorted world. In the way that every concept of authority, every notion of superiority is disturbed. The child's personality constitutes itself within this confusion.

An example of how some of this functions can be seen in a passage from the text, which starts with the recollection of one of a series of occasions, where he had been overwhelmed by the feeling of being threatened and trapped by the other children, and consequently severely punished by the school matron for reacting aggressively as a means of escape. This time, as he recalls, he had deliberately destroyed the precious leather sketchbook of a smaller and weaker boy, who after bursting into tears had accused him of being evil without a cause: "How evil you are, I never expected something like this from you, and I have never vexed you" (Goldschmidt 1991: 87).

Looking back on this scene, he remembers having realised this and in conclusion accepted his identity as guilty: "He was an evil person. The others had the right to vex him endlessly; they had detected the evil in him. They had always known, he was the evil one" (Goldschmidt 2001: 87). And the reason, as he saw it, had been that he at that moment had crossed the line and moved beyond forgiveness. From then on he could never be forgiven and "was not even entitled to the lovely crying," which up till then had been a kind of escape.

This time he remembers the punishment had been that he had had to kneel for half an hour on the edge of the ruler which normally was used to hit him across the fingers. The pain in his kneecaps had been so strong that he had felt himself to be not himself, but the mere edge of pain, reified as his own torture instrument, which as it thrust through him cut through his body.

When this punishment was over he could not stand up, but fell over with the others standing around him watching "as if he had shown them an option of themselves, the way he lay there coiled up screaming on the floor" (Goldschmidt 1991: 87).

After this memory of himself as a thing detached and estranged both from himself and the others, the narrator goes on to the next scene of punishment, which is the masochistic sequel of the one described. He remembers that after punishments he usually was sent to bed without supper, where he would lie in bed listening to empty plates rattling. But since he had been sent to bed as part of the punishment, he did not have to carry the plates in high stacks down into the kitchen, which was usually the case. Looking back, he recalls how he normally had had to walk with his arms stretched out in front of him while the others put one plate on top of the other on his hands, and how he had had a feeling of joy, because he was able to carry such a heavy load of plates. He remembers:

> … that every day he was able to carry more of them, a weight hardening inside of him, that more and more forced his arms downwards. […] He loved to carry heavy weights, his body quivered: Carrying, being pushed downwards, heavy stuff, that would close his chest; arms and stomach covered in clay (Goldschmidt 1991: 87).

The strength of this feeling makes him visualize himself being sexually abused and like in an erotic dream he imagines how he would not be able to move because:

> … like a stone he would be locked into himself; walled up, pushed down, round, throttled he would just lie there at the disposal of the others. They would take him, grab him, push him into themselves. He would be just a tiny bullet of consciousness between warm, naked thighs. He would be locked up, just a painted seat, flat printed onto the seat bolster; he would then feel through his own, roundly shaped frame surrounding himself under the flesh sitting on top of him. Under the weight of the flesh on top of him he would be just a seat, at any one's disposal (Goldschmidt 1991: 90).

Both this passage and other passages in the book show the traumatic dream vision of a person seeking a way out of his misery by way of a masochistic fantasy, where he lets himself be treated as a thing, excluded from himself as well as from the others in order to avoid the pain of loss and estrangement.

In other words the condition of loss and estrangement seems to have made him abject, which in the Kristevan sense can be seen as the result of his inability to distinguish between a threatening exterior and his own body, which has become disgusting to him. In short the main character and narrator of his own story seems to be suffering from a perpetual loss of identity and self-estrangement. Unable to recognise and love his own otherness, which in turn would have enabled him to accept the strangeness of others, he gradually becomes aggressive and in a self-destructive way turns his aggression towards others as well as towards himself.

Tragically, he starts behaving like an outsider living out his otherness in a continuous conflict with the other children, who, ironically enough, are unaware of his Jewish identity, but look upon him as a German. And in that respect, like the Andorrans in *The Andorran Jew*, they treat him both as a stranger not belonging and as belonging to an invading enemy, who is to be rejected and finally defeated. In both stories, as indicated above, the physical and spiritual effects on the victim turned out to be disastrous: Andri, the Andorran, who was treated as a Jew, got killed because he accepted his presumed, but mistaken otherness. The narrator in Goldschmidt's autofictional story survived and by way of autofictional writing strategies, still has to deal with the traumatic experience of estrangement by telling the story of his life, which in the Ricoeurian sense can only be told because there has been human activity and suffering.

## Bibliography

Colli, Giorgio and Mazzino Montinari (eds.): *Friedrich Nietzsche. Sämtliche Werke. Kritische Studienausgabe, Nachgelassene Schriften vol. I.* Dt. Taschenbuchverlag: München 1980.

Freud, Sigmund (1982): *Sigmund Freud. Studienausgabe, vol.I-X.* Mitscherlich, A. et al. (eds.). Frankfurt a. M.: Fischer Verlag.

Frisch, Max (1950): *Tagebuch 1946-1949.* Frankfurt a. M.: Suhrkamp Verlag.

Frisch, Max (1964): *Mein Name sei Gantenbein.* Frankfurt a. M.: Suhrkamp Verlag.

Frisch, Max (1999): *Andorra. Text und Kommentar.* Frankfurt a. M.: Suhrkamp BasisBibliothek.

Goldschmidt, Georges-Arthur (1991): *Die Absonderung. Erzählung. Mit einem Nachwort von Peter Handke.* Zürich: Amman Verlag.

Kertész, Imre (1997; 2002): *Ich – ein anderer.* Reinbek bei Hamburg: Rowohlt Taschenbuchverlag.

Goldschmidt, Georges-Arthur (1999): *La traversée des Fleuves.* Paris: Edition du Seuil.

Goldschmidt, Georges-Arthur (2001): *Über die Flüsse*. Zürich: Amman Verlag.

Kristeva, Julia (1991): *Strangers to Ourselves*, trans. Roudiez, L. New York / London: Harvester & Wheatsheaf.

Ricoeur, Paul (1970): *Freud and Philosophy: An Essay on Interpretation*. New Haven: Yale University Press.

Ricoeur, Paul (1988): *Time and Narrative*. 3 vols., trans. Blamey, K. and D. Pellauer. Chicago: University of Chicago Press.

Ricoeur, Paul (1990): *Oneself as an Other*, trans. Blamey, K. Chicago: University of Chicago Press.

Rilke, Rainer Maria (1910): *Die Aufzeichnungen des Malte Laurids Brigge*. Frankfurt a. M.: Insel Verlag.

Rimbaud, Arthur (1965): *Oeuvre completes*. Paris: Bibliothèque NFR de Pléiade.

Valdes, Mario, ed. (1991): *A Ricoeur Reader*. Toronto: University of Toronto Press.

# Jewishness as an Expression of the European Other in the Novels of Marguerite Duras

*Helge Vidar Holm*

Not being a Jew herself, the prolific and innovative French novelist, playwright, and filmmaker Marguerite Duras (1914-1996) was nonetheless deeply engaged in Jewish destiny. We find a large number of Jewish characters in her novels, and the way some of them are represented, emphasizes their position as 'the European other'. However, an identification process takes place in the novels, where the other becomes oneself, where identities are blurred, especially when it comes to relations between Jewish and non-Jewish characters. In this chapter, I shall investigate the fictional blurring of borders between European Jewish and non-Jewish identity, and I shall be looking for arguments both in some biographical facts from Duras' own life and from her style of writing.

In my attempt to analyse the self-identifying descriptions of the other, I am indebted to the French philosopher Paul Ricoeur, first of all to his essay *Oneself as Another* from 1990, but also to *Time and Narrative*, published in three volumes from 1983 to 1985.[1] I am especially concerned with his theory of the "Triple Mimesis", presented in the essay's first volume. Among the Durasian novels, I shall especially be looking at the following two: *Abahn Sabana David* (1970) and *Yann Andréa Steiner* (1992).[2]

Most of Duras' novels are unconventional, even the majority of those she explicitly calls novels herself. Regarding the two works that I have chosen, she has not insisted on any mention of genre. I take the liberty of calling them novels, since I read them as novels. This classification may well be contentious, but the genre question is not my main concern here, even if it is implied in some parts of my analysis.

As one may see from the two titles mentioned, a study of the proper names, the onomastics of the works, might be rewarding for somebody looking for the Jewishness in Duras' novels. I shall return to this point, since I first need to point out a language problem. Apparently, there is no word in English to cover the specific idea of the French word *judaïté*, which implies that you take

---

[1] My references are to the French originals: Ricoeur 1990 and Ricoeur 1983-1985.
[2] The English translations of French quotations are my own.

part in the Jewish reality, the Jewish condition, without necessarily being a Jew by your family or religion. In English, Jewishness covers both the fact of being Jewish by family or religion; which in French is rendered by *judéicité* (family) or *judéacité* (religion), as well as the idea of partaking in the Jewish condition, by solidarity or ideological engagement. Even though Marguerite Duras was neither a Jew by her family nor by religious conviction, the Jewishness of many of her novels is a fact – Jewishness understood in the meaning conveyed by the French word *judaïté*, an identification with the Jewish people by someone's own personal commitment and engagement. *Judaïté* may be translated by Jewish reality or Jewish condition in this sense, and apparently *Jewishness* also covers this meaning, but less distinctly than *judaïté* in French. There also exists another English term, *Judaisation*, but this is practically an anti-Semitic term implying cultural assimilation of non-Jewish populations, and it would consequently be misleading in the present context.

As for the onomastic aspect of the two titles of novels mentioned above, both of them seem Jewish, and both of them are. Or neither of them is. In fact, the Jewish names and the Jewish characters in Duras' novels are mostly in between, they are not clearly – or merely – Jewish, although they are part of the Jewishness of these novels. Let us take the title *Yann Andréa Steiner* as an example. Yann Andréa was Marguerite Duras' companion and lover during her last years; in fact they met in 1979, when he was 27 years old and she was 65. She wrote several books, mostly between fact and fiction genres, both *to* him and *with* him, or with somebody named like him as the main character. This is also the case in this novel, but its title implies somebody – or something – else. Steiner is a typical Jewish surname, and Duras has used it – or parts of it – on many literary occasions, in various forms. One is Stein, for example in *Le Ravissement de Lol V. Stein* (1964), where the Jewishness of the character is barely mentioned. Another would be *Détruire, dit-elle* (1969), where one of the main characters, Monsieur Stein, offers information about himself and the other main characters: "Nous sommes des Juifs allemands".[3] In 1969, when this novel was published, this utterance created a very special kind of intertextuality, which is worth looking into. The famous slogan, "Nous sommes tous des Juifs allemands", uttered by the Parisian student leader Daniel Cohn-Bendit during the riots of May -68, might in fact contain one of Duras' central ideas, expressed through several of her novels, namely that metaphorically speaking, we are all German Jews, that mankind as such is made up of

---

3    We are German Jews.

some strange equivalent of German Jews. Or, perhaps, that we are all both victims and executioners, as Marguerite Duras herself puts it directly:

> Nous sommes de la race de ceux qui sont brûlés dans les crématoires et des gazés de Maïdanek, nous sommes aussi de la race des nazis. Fonction égalitaire des crématoires de Buchenwald, de la faim, des fosses communes de Bergen-Belsen, dans ces fosses nous avons notre part, ces squelettes si extraordinairement identiques, ce sont ceux d'une famille européenne (Duras 1985: 60-61).[4]

In *Abahn Sabana David*, there is a deliberate confusion when it comes to the Jewishness of the characters. Two of the four main characters are clearly presented as Jews, whereas the two others have orders to execute one of the Jews, or at least to keep the Jew under control until his execution, which is to take place the next morning. The text is written as a long scene, with much dialogue and little summary. The scene starts in the Jew's house late on a winter evening and ends the following morning, when the protagonists leave the house. During the night, the non-Jews have become Jews, or at least they claim solidarity with the Jews and apparently leave the house with them, probably to protect them. Nothing of this is clearly shown or told; the whole text resembles an epic poem, where silence sometimes seems more important than words as in the following quotation:

> Silence. Abahn ne continue pas à parler. David attend.
> Le silence dure. Abahn a fermé les yeux à son tour. A son tour il paraît exténué. David s'aperçoit qu'il est seul. Il est décomposé.
> Puis Abahn reparle. Il dit:
> Je ne sais rien de sa vie.
> Silence. Rien ne bouge dans le visage lisse et blanc de David (p.127).[5]

---

[4]    We are of the same race as those who were burnt in the crematoriums and those who became gas victims at Maïdanek, we are also of the same race as the Nazis. Egalitarian functions of the Buchenwald crematories, the hunger, the mass graves of Bergen-Belsen, in these graves we have our part, these skeletons so very identical, they are those of a European family.

[5]    Silence. Abahn does not go on talking. David waits. The silence is lasting. Abahn has closed his eyes, in his turn. In his turn he looks exhausted. David realizes that he is not alone. He gets frustrated. Then Abahn starts talking again. He says: "I don't know anything about life." Silence. Nothing moves in David's smooth and white face.

In fact, one might say that Duras' style of writing is one of silences. Not of the word 'silence', as it is repeated three times in this quotation, but of what we might call 'narrative silences'. As may be seen from the quotation, her sentences are extremely short. She barely gives any factual information, and when she does, it may be to describe negations of conversation ("Abahn ne continue pas à parler … décomposé") and of movement ("Rien ne bouge dans le visage lisse et blanc de David"). This is a very special use of poetic language, practically without tropes like metaphor or metonymy, but with a genuine purity, apparently with an extraordinary simplicity. If we don't value this kind of poetic language in our interpretation, we won't be able to catch the meaning of silences in Duras, as I see it.

I have translated the following quotation in a footnote. However, the language is so original in all its simplicity, that any translation will also necessarily be an interpretation, like in good poetry. At the same time, the language as such seems quotidian, very simple:

> On l'appelle aussi Abahn le juif, Abahn le chien.
> Et aussi bien le juif? le chien?
> Oui.
> On appelle juifs les autres, ici?
> Oui.
> Et chiens?
> Les juifs – elle attend – et là d'où tu viens?
> Aussi (p. 20).[6]

Even if language is here reduced to a minimum, it nevertheless implies the entire history of European Jews, the interior other who is looked upon as less than a human being. To come to grips with this passage in its context, one has to know that there are two Jewish characters named Abahn in the novel, one called the Jew, the other called Abahn. At a first perusal of the book, you may think that there is only one Abahn, who is also the Jew in the text, but a closer reading shows that this is not so. In Duras' novels, the borders between characters are often blurred, as we also may see in *Yann Andréa Steiner*, where one of the main characters gets a Jewish surname, Steiner, and where the story

---

6   "He's also called Abahn the Jew, Abahn the dog", "Also the Jew? The dog?", "Yes", "The others are called Jews here?", "Yes", "And dogs?", "The Jews", she is waiting, "and there where you come from?", "Also".

develops from a love story between a young man and an elderly lady to that of the tragic destiny of some Jewish children. I shall quote a passage from *Yann Andréa Steiner*:

> (…) l'histoire entre le très jeune Yann Andréa Steiner et cette femme qui faisait des livres et qui, elle, était vieille et seul comme lui dans cet été grand à lui seul comme une Europe (p. 18).[7]

This is not daily language, even if the words look rather simple. What could be the implication of the last part of the quotation: "… in this summer by itself as big as a Europe"?

To comprehend this, we must go on reading the novel. We must read about the obsession that the young man has regarding one of the fictional characters of Duras, a young Jewish woman named Théodora Kats, who is mentioned in some of Duras' books, but who never really gets her own story. This fictional woman has a fate "as big as a Europe"; she is in many ways the incarnation of the European other(s) in Duras' works, *l'innommable*, the unnamed Jewish fate of which we all have our part:

> Vous n'écrirez jamais l'histoire de Théodora?
> J'ai dit que je n'étais jamais sûre de rien quant à ce que j'allais ou non écrire.
> Vous n'avez pas répondu.
> J'ai dit:
> Vous aimez Théodora.
> Vous n'avez pas souri, vous avez dit dans un souffle:
> Théodora c'est ce que j'ignore de vous, j'étais très jeune. Tout le reste je le sais. J'attends depuis trois ans que vous écriviez son histoire.
> (…) J'ai dit que sans doute je ne finirai jamais Théodora, le livre, que c'est presque sûr. Que c'était la seule fois de ma vie que ça m'était arrivé. Que tout ce que j'avais pu faire c'était de

---

7   The story of the very young Yann Andréa Steiner and this woman who made books and who, as for her, was old and alone like he was in this summer by itself as big as a Europe.

sauver cet extrait-là du manuscrit abandonné. Que c'était un livre que je ne pouvais pas écrire sans aussitôt m'égarer vers d'autres livres que jamais je n'avais décidé d'écrire (pp. 28-30).[8]

Now let's look at the closing of the text *Yann Andréa Steiner*:

> L'écriture s'était fermée avec son nom. Son nom à lui c'était toute l'écriture de Théodora Kats. Tout était dit avec. Ce nom.
>
> Et le blanc des robes et celui de sa peau.
>
> C'était peut-être quelque chose d'encore inconnu, Théodora Kats, un nouveau silence de l'écriture, celui des femmes et des Juifs (1992: 141).[9]

This is poetic, literary writing, a little different from that of *Abahn Sabana David*, but still minimalistic. Perhaps we have a metaphor in the last sentence (silence of writing), and metonymy in the middle one (the white of the dresses and of her skin). But I don't think so. The white, is the colour white, nothing else. And the new silence of writing is in my view just that, no metaphor. All the same, the language is poetic, very much so. And it tells us something which might be individual to each reader, but which most certainly is connected with the last word of the quotation, *Juifs*. And it may be connected to an earlier quotation from the book, where the issue was a "summer by itself as big as a Europe". During that summer, the narrator of the book tells several stories about children, Jewish and others, about deportation and camps. One of them ends like this:

---

8   "You will never write the story of Théodora?" I said that I was never sure about what I was going to write. You didn't answer. I said: "You loved Théodora" You didn't smile, you said in one breath: "Théodora is what I don't know about you, I was very young. All the rest I know. I have been waiting three years for you to write her story." […] I said that I probably never would finish Théodora, the book, that this was very likely. That it was the only time in my life that this had happened to me. That all I had been able to do was to save this passage of the abandoned manuscript. That it was a book I could not write without immediately go astray towards others books which I never had decided to write.

9   The writing had closed with her name. Her name, just her name, was the whole writing of Théodora Kats. All was thus said. That name. And the white of the dresses and of her skin. It was perhaps something still unknown, Theodora Kats, a new silence of writing, that of women and of Jews.

[…] elle a crié tout bas un mot que l'enfant a reconnu et qu'il a crié à son tour. Un mot qui ne s'écrit pas, qui se parle seulement entre les Juifs, depuis dix mille ans, depuis cent mille ans, on ne sait pas.

Sur Gdansk j'ai posé ma bouche et j'ai embrassé cet enfant juif et les enfants morts du ghetto de Vilna. Je les ai embrassés aussi dans mon esprit et dans mon corps (1992: 132).[10]

Marguerite Duras was born in Indochina at the time of the French colonies there, and she came to France and Paris as a young student. After WWII she joined the French communist party, from which she was expelled in 1950, together with her ex-husband, Robert Antelme, and her companion Dionys Mascolo, who was also a very close friend of Robert Antelme. Both of these men have written important books about the situation of the Jews in Europe, but none of them were Jews. As a resister, Robert Antelme was sent to the concentration camps, and at the end of the war he returned more dead than alive. In her Duras biography, Laure Adler tells how Duras and Mascolo helped Robert Antelme back to life through medical care, and how they started listening to his stories from the camps and, after a while, were completely transformed as human beings. They learned what man could do to man in the 20th century, on racial grounds. And through their engagement and their *judaïté*, their involvement in the Jewish reality and the Jewish condition, they became Jewish in their own way, even more than that: The son of Marguerite Duras and Dionys Mascolo tells that as a child, he thought for many years that he and his family really were Jewish![11]

The son's mistake is rather an amusing anecdote in a context which is all but amusing. The Jewishness of Marguerite Duras' novels certainly finds parts of its foundation here, in the relation to her ex-husband and her anti-nazi engagement with Dionys Mascolo. Another part of this background is most certainly to be found in her upbringing in the colonies, where she learnt a lot about social misery and injustice. Her many novels based on this experience show her concern for the other, for the poor and the helpless. However, what first of all marks her more than forty books of fiction, is an original, varied and very literary style of writing. If we now look to Paul Ricoeur's idea of the triple

---

10    […] she cried out quite silently a word which the child recognized and which, in his turn, he cried out. A word which cannot be written, which is spoken only among the Jews, for ten thousand years, for a hundred thousand years, nobody knows. On Gdansk I placed my mouth and I kissed this Jewish child and the dead children of the Vilna ghetto. I kissed them also in my spirit and in my body.

11    Adler 1998: 235.

mimesis, we could say that the prefiguration of the first mimesis, before the literary work takes form, is marked by these experiences, first in the colonies, then in France.

Another experience which definitely counts in this prefiguration, is that of the political situation in the Europe of 1968. Not only in May (cf. "Nous sommes tous des Juifs allemands", the Cohn-Bendit slogan quoted earlier), but even more so, in August. When Duras was writing her first version of *Abahn Sabana David*, she had just been profoundly shocked by the news concerning the Soviet invasion of Czechoslovakia, in August 1968. The character Gringo, an incarnation of evil in this novel, is in fact a communist leader as well as a Nazi, even if he officially is neither. One of the first titles given by Duras to this novel, is *Les Chiens de Prague* (The Dogs of Prague), and she hesitated for a long time between this title and the one she finally chose. She also tried out the title *La Forêt de Prague* (The Prague Forest). Clearly, the Soviet invasion of the Czeck capital plays a very important part in what Ricoeur would call the novel's prefiguration or its *mimesis 1*, and this historical event continues to influence strongly the *configuration* (or *mimesis 2*), especially in the first version of the book. If we look at the many different versions of the "tapuscripts" of the novel preserved at the IMEC[12], we discover that the titles *Les Chiens/La Forêt de Prague* are being kept in the majority of the versions. However, none of the two titles was kept in the published version, neither is there any direct mention of the Czeck situation in August 1968 to be found there. There is no doubt, however, that it underlies large parts of the text, especially the parts where Gringo plays an important role. But the dominating 'role', as it were, in the configuration, is played by the Durasian use of language, as we have seen in the examples given above. As for the third mimesis, or the *refiguration*, my interpretation in the present article of the two novels, suggests one form of reading, one that is stressing the Jewish element of the Durasian texts.

In terms of the basic idea in Ricoeur's essay from 1990, *Oneself as Another*, I don't think that the novels of Duras really are examples of autobiographical literature in the sense that Ricoeur sees the identity of the writer. His idea is that identity is constituted of both sameness (*mêmeté*) and selfhood (*ipseïté*), and that we may change our selfhood during time, without losing our basic personality, our *mêmeté*.

---

12    *L'Institut Mémoires de l'Edition Contemporaine* at the Abbaye d'Ardenne in Normandie in France, where an important collection of Duras' notes, tapuscripts and manuscripts is preserved.

According to Ricoeur, our *ipséité* implies a relation to others in such a way that it is practically impossible to separate selfhood and otherness. He challenges the Cartesien *cogito*, because it posits a single, independent subject, the grammatical first person subject, an 'I' or an 'Ego' (Cogito, ergo sum = Ego cogito, ergo sum), without reference to the other. One might add that in fact, Michaïl Bakhtin represents a similar opposition to the philosophy of the cogito, as do Martin Buber and Emmanuel Levinas.

Ricoeur states that in his essay, the word 'as' in *Oneself as Another* implies a closer connection than a mere comparison; it means that oneself becomes a part of another (in French: "un lien plus étroit que toute comparaison: soi-même en tant qu'*autre*".) When I first started working on this paper, my impresssion was that Ricoeur's statement here, describes what happens in the novels of Duras, an identification with the Jews, as if the author were a Jew herself.

But now, I am no longer so sure. As a person, Duras might identify with the Jews in a way that gives Ricoeur an excellent example of his idea in *Oneself as Another*. But I don't really think that this is the case in the novels, or let us rather say, in the *fiction*, of Duras. Ricoeur talks about a dialectic of the self and the other, which contradicts the Cartesian cogito. I agree with the idea that there is such a dialectic in the fiction of Duras, but it is an *immanent* dialectic, a dialectic between characters in novels. The author is implied in this, but only as an *implied author*, in the sense Wayne C. Booth gives to this term[13], not as a biographical person. Or perhaps not even as an implied *author*, because the dialectic is really between the characters, and my understanding of the Boothian term is that the implied author controls this dialectic from another level, from a level which implies as *surplus* of vision, as Michaïl Bakhtin would have said.[14]

In both novels that I have been discussing, the identity borders between the characters are vague and difficult to draw: who is a Jew and who is not? Is the same person both a Jew and a non-Jew?[15] In *Abahn Sabana David,* the character named Sabana, who is presented as a non-Jew, says towards the end of the book: "Whatever happens now, I'll stay with the Jews" (p. 148). David, who has a first name which refers to the common religious heritage of

---

13    See Booth 1961.
14    See "L'auteur et le héros" in Bakhtin 1979.
15    Cf. the composition of the name *Yann Andréa Steiner,* mentioned earlier in the present article.

the Christians and the Jews (the ancestor of Christ, the slayer of Goliath, the author of the Book of Psalmes in the Bible), changes from being the appointed executioner of Abahn the Jew to becoming his friend, apparently willing to share his fate.

In the novels of Marguerite Duras, there is identification with the other, especially with the Jews, and it evidently takes place on the level of selfhood (*ipséité*), not on the level of sameness (*mêmeté*). However, it is a fictional, literary identification, which enables the author to write something different from what we might encounter in the works of Jewish novelists, writing about Jewish fate in Europe, about the Shoah, about discrimination and persecution throughout the centuries. As implied author in her novels, Duras appears to be dominated by Jewish fate and thus by Jewishness, but not completely.

As mentioned above, to Paul Ricoeur the word 'as' in *Oneself as Another* implies a closer connection than a mere comparison.[16] I think this is what happens in some of Duras' novels, especially in *Abahn Sabana David* and *Yann Andréa Steiner*, where not only non-Jewish characters become Jewish on the level of selfhood (*ipséité*), but where European Jewish history constitutes the dominant background, the ultimate historical reference, for the triple mimesis process, both on the prefiguration level, where the novelist's own life experience is of signal importance, and on the refiguration level, where the reader's background plays its part. On the configuration level, we might say that Duras' novels give us examples of a certain form of Jewishness, where (and this *is* very Jewish) *language* is decisive, in the poetic, succinct form we have seen from the text examples analysed above, with the use of silences as one of its main stylistic features.

## Bibliography

Adler, L. (1998): *Marguerite Duras*. Paris: Gallimard.

Antelme, R. (1947): *L'Espèce humaine*. Paris: Gallimard.

Bakhtine, M. (1979): *Esthétique de la création verbale*. Paris: Gallimard.

Booth, W. C. (1961): *The Rhetoric of Fiction*. Chicago: The University of Chicago Press.

Duras, M. (1964): *Le Ravissement de Lol V. Stein*. Paris: Gallimard.

Duras, M. (1970): *Abahn Sabana David*. Paris: Gallimard.

Duras, M. (1985): *La Douleur*. Paris: P.O.L. et Gallimard, Coll. Folio.

---

16  Ricoeur 1990, back of cover.

Duras, M. (1992): *Yann Andréa Steiner.* Paris: P.O.L.

Ricoeur, P. (1983): *Temps et récit,* I. Paris: Coll. Points, Seuil.

Ricoeur, P. (1984): *Temps et récit,* II. Paris: Coll. Points, Seuil.

Ricoeur, P.(1985): *Temps et récit,* III. Paris: Coll. Points, Seuil.

Ricoeur, P. (1990): *Soi-même comme un autre.* Paris: Seuil.

Ricoeur, P. (1992): *Lectures 2. La contrée des philosophes.* Paris: Seuil.

# Part 3:
# Variations on the
# Interior Other(s)

# The Boomerang of Imperial Conquest: On Russia's Internal Orientals and the Colonization of One's Own

*Lillian Jorunn Helle*

In this chapter I will examine Russia's inner Oriental, or the internal colonization of the Russian Empire, topics that include intriguing examples of imaginaries, of othering, and the construction of cultural borders. In the process I shall also present an exciting field of research now achieving growing scholarly attention. Before I discuss these topics, however, I will look at some aspects of Russia's external colonization in order to establish a background for my discussions.

A characteristic trait in 19th century Russian literature is the abundance of motives related to boundary encounters and various representations of the other. A recurring theme is the meeting between Russia and Europe, a meeting stimulated by Peter the Great's founding of Saint Petersburg in 1703. The Tsar's founding of the city was seen, in the official rhetoric of the Petrine Empire, as an act of rationalist illumination, and the rule of the Romanovs from this time on became an emblem of westernized progress and Enlightenment. Such ideas are eloquently expressed in a famous saying by the Russian literary critic Vissarion Belinsky, who in biblical allusions exalts the founder of the reformed nation: "With his powerful 'Let there be!' Peter dispelled the chaos, separated the light from the darkness and called the country to its great, global destiny" (Belinsky V: 117).

When the autocrat set up his new "Northern capital" on the estuary of the Neva, at the outermost frontier of his realm, he opened a window towards Europe at the same time as he distanced himself (both in a symbolic and a geographical sense) from the medieval Muscovite regime. The building of the new metropolis therefore came to represent a total break with the old order, initiating in the post-Petrine cultural consciousness a chasm between the traditional Moscow mentality and a new Western way of thinking. As such, Saint Petersburg led to a division of the Russian nation, and the numerous founding myths, which from the very beginning sprang up around Peter's "creation", were divided into two versions; one panegyric with the Tsar as a God-like being, and one profane, in which the ruler and his city are demon-

ized as anti-Christian mirages.[1] These conflicting views on the europeanizing
deeds of the *Imperator* generated longstanding discourses about the country's
relations to the West – as in the famous disputes between the Slavophiles and
the Westernizers. It also established Europe as Russia's most significant other,
even "the main constituent other", against which the Romanov reign tried
"to construct a new Russian identity" (Tolz 2001: 1).[2] The Empire's complex
interaction and its constant contrasting with the "constituent other" became a
kind of *Ideensteinbruch* for cultural and literary activity.[3] This interaction was a
particularly decisive factor in the development of Russian literature – especially
concerning the so-called Saint Petersburg texts – from the odist Lomonosov
in the 18th century to the symbolists of Russia's *fin de siècle*. Some of these
texts apotheosize through "sublime" rhetoric the pro-imperial and pro-Petrine
ideology (Ram 2003). But more often than not they explore anti-Petrine sentiments, with their implied rejection of the European *alter*, a prevalent topic in
the fiction of the classical Russian masters and a theme to which I will later
return.

Another cross-cultural encounter, also of great importance to the evolution of Russian literature, resulting in new constructions of alterity, was
the multilevel contacts between the Empire and the Caucasus, contacts that
became the main motif in the Caucasus texts.[4] The historical backdrop of
these texts is the Russian colonial conquest of the region that began at the
end of the 1700-hundreds, reached a preliminary high point by the inclusion
of Georgia into the Empire in 1802, and abated after Shamil, the last leader
of the Chechens, was captured by the Russians in 1859.[5]

Against this historical setting, Russian writers of the first half of the 19th
century took part in a massive text and culture production, which from the

---

[1]   The epithet "Peter's creation" was coded by Aleksander Pushkin in his poem "The Bronze
      Horseman" (1834), to indicate the aspect of will and power behind the genesis of the new
      capital (see Helle 1995). On the founding myths of the Petrine state and on the semiotics
      of the new city, see especially the seminal works of Lotman (1984) and Toporov (1984).

[2]   On the idea of Europe as an other against which the idea of Russia is defined, cf. Neumann
      (1996: 1).

[3]   As Vera Tolz points out, this contrasting had problematic effects. Constant attempts to
      contrast and compare Russia and the West provided a powerful creative stimulus for Russian
      cultural figures, but proved dysfunctional as a tool of political analysis of Russia's develop-
      ment (Tolz 2001: 1).

[4]   On the development of the Caucasus texts and their myth making effect, see particularly
      Layton (1994) and Ram (2003).

[5]   On the history of the Caucasus during the Russian Empire, see Baddeley (1969).

very start was marked by a dichotomy between "us and them". In this process of dichotomous mythmaking the most striking aspect is the orientalization of the Caucasus. Stereotypes well known from Edward Saïd's seminal book *Orientalism* (1978) are projected onto the Caucasian highlands, and both places and peoples are reinvented within the frames of orientalizing schemata. These fictional reinventions culturally transformed the mountainous borderland into the other, the foreign, the primitive Asian and the antithesis of the westernized and progressive Romanov empire.[6]

Through such imaginaries the nation's ruling (and educated) élite – or the Petrovians, as they were sometimes ironically referred to – sought to distance themselves from the colonized Muslims.[7] The europeanized Russians insisted for instance on being regarded as a people of linear movement, in contrast to the colonized tribes and their cyclic, anti-modern perception of time. As the legal historian Konstantin Kavelin expressed it in 1847: "[W]e are a European people, capable of perfection, of development; we do not like to repeat ourselves or stand on the same spot for an endless number of centuries" (1989: 13). The clash between a Western dynamic way of looking at life and the Eastern "backwardness" is a topic often elaborated in the Caucasus texts. A good example is the following extract, which contains the reflections of an imperial officer returning home after a stay in the mountainous country of Dagestan:

> I am very glad that I will be leaving Asia [...] where the mind still remains in swaddling clothes. The static character of life in Asia is astounding [....] The Caucasian mountain chieftains are now just the same as they have been for two thousand years [...]. I am leaving the land of fruit to be born back to the land of work – that great inventor of everything useful, that animator of everything lofty, that alarm clock of the human soul which has fallen into a voluptuous sleep here in the bosom of that charmer, nature (Bestuzhev-Marlinsky 1995: 77).

The above passage articulates a seemingly standard imperial perspective on Eastern cultural retardation. But for the reader (certainly for a modern one) the opposition between the charmed land of fruit and the useful land of alarm clocks is somewhat undermined, creating a destabilising longing in the text for the first alternative, however 'backward'. This element of ambiguity can,

---

6   On Caucasus as the oriental other, see Helle (2009, 2012).

7   The reforms, it was claimed, changed Russia so radically that it ought to be renamed Petrovia, while the europeanized subjects were to be called Petrovians (cf. Riasanovsky 1985: 109).

in its turn, be seen in connection with the unstable status of the Russian eurocentric project in which so many uncertainties concerning national identity were embedded.

These uncertainties are to no small degree grounded in the problematic fact that the Empire, which in its colonizing quest emphasized its status as a civilized European power, was itself frequently viewed as Asiatic by the West. From the Enlightenment onwards the Western countries construed Eastern Europe as a semi-orientalized zone, a place simultaneously included into and excluded from Western Europe. As such, the Hegelian statement about the Slavic peoples from (Lectures on) *The Philosophy of History* (1837) is highly characteristic:

> A part of the slaves has been conquered by Occidental Reason. However these peoples remained excluded from our consideration, because hitherto it has not appeared as an independent element in the series of phases that Reason assumed in the world (Hegel 1956: 350).

It has been argued that the colonizing impulse of the Romanov rule was a result of the nation itself being culturally and politically colonized by the West. From the early beginning of Peter's regime the Russian élite became (and often forcibly) mentally colonized without having ever been a colonial subject. As Kalpana Sahni (1997: 15) has asserted, this "was the uniqueness of Russian history and created the inherent contradictions of Russian orientalism". In other words, the orientalist attitude directed at the Russian occidentalists was accepted by them and repeated as a pattern for downgrading the conquered people in a kind of compensatory urge. By the same token, the very encoding in the eurocentric post-Petrine mind of the Caucasus as a segment of the prototypal Orient "signalizes the deep interiorization in the Russian imperial consciousness of the borrowed European discourses, including the orientalist clichés" (Tlostanova 2008: 2). Likewise, these processes show how Russia, paradoxically, in order to emerge as a Western state, must move East. This intricate contrariness is caught in Fedor Dostoevsky's famous saying from 1881: "In Europe we were hangers-on and slaves, while in Asia we shall be the masters. In Europe we were Tatars, while in Asia we too are Europeans" (XIV: 508).

The West though often mocked this manner of mastering, from what they saw as a nation of secondary eurocentrism, regarding it as a secondary, mimicked orientalization. In this respect, the Russian imperial discourses "demonstrate the double-faced nature of this Empire which feels itself a colony in the presence of the West, at the same time acting as a [...] caricature 'civilizer' in its own non-European colonies" (Tlostanova 2008: 1). Typically, the

British politician and viceroy of India, George Curzon, tried to draw a line between the Western style of colonialism and the Russian mimicking one, by (condescendingly) describing the advances of Russia in Asia in the second half of the 19th century, as "a conquest of Orientals by Orientals" (1889: 392).

The many complexities connected to the post-Petrine imperial quest distort the traditional patterns of colonialism and make the country both an object – that is an other – and a subject in the colonizing processes. Moreover, the relationship between the Caucasian Orient and the imperial centre turns out to be less binarised and more multifaceted than it may initially seem. There is much to suggest that the Empire's secondary colonization – which intended to establish the Caucasus as a place inferior and for ever fixed and fallen out of history – did not always produce the expected clean-cut Saïdian schism between the Caucasian natives and their civilizing masters. Not least the literary representations of the Caucasian in the first decades of the 19th century offer a wide range of varieties in terms of constructions of the colonized other.

The equivocal attitude to the colonized Caucasian is expressed with particular poignancy in the works of Aleksander Pushkin, Mikhail Lermontov, and Aleksander Bestuzhev-Marlinsky, in whose writings we easily find descriptions of the highlanders that destabilize sharp cultural and national polarizations.[8] In their contribution to the Caucasian mythology, the Oriental is far from conceived as an absolute and abominable alien. The orientalized Caucasian or Asian – Caucasia and Asia is one and the same location in this imagined geography – is rather presented as an enigmatic Rousseauésque *noble savage,* a pure, brave and fearless defender of liberty and freedom and a potent, but suppressed alter ego. This is a secret ego that has been suppressed by the forced europeanization of the post-Petrine regime, and it is hiding behind a mask of European civilization. The Caucasus therefore becomes a return to a mythic Russian space, untouched by Western progress and the coercive norms of the civilizing European state.

Such ambivalent (literary) evaluations of the oriental other demonstrate amongst other things the paradoxes in the nation's colonizing endeavour and activate a characteristic dilemma of Russian orientalism. Even though Rus-

---

[8]  Examples of the opposite, texts that celebrate – in the name of a triumphant sublime imperialism – a clear cut divide between the colonizer and the colonized are also easy to find, like the panegyric odes from the 18th century. However, even this programmatic literature could be interpreted as less polarized and more ambiguous with regard to the oriental other than has usually been assumed, see Helle (2009, 2012).

sia was politically an imperialist nation, it was culturally speaking subject to a deep ambiguity.[9] Consequently, in addition to the usual Western stance of superiority towards the East, there was an extraordinary fascination and cryptic identification with it, illustrating the traditional idea of the Empire as a two-sided Janus, who looks "simultaneously toward Europe and Asia" (Bestuzhev-Marlinsky 1958: 599).[10] Such a Janus-faced outlook would not surprisingly open up to a diversity of cross cultural bonds between colonizer and colonized.[11]

Clearly, these ambiguous bonds tend to modify or disturb traditional orientalist discourses and make the relationship between rulers and colonized subjects less influenced by the "Manichean delirium" – to use Frantz Fanon's famous trope of colonial compartmentalization – than might be expected.[12] When the polarised oppositions are thus undermined, the focus shifts to cultural mingling. This is a shift which also represents a certain contrast to Fanon's negatively charged understanding of "the occult instability" of the zone "where the [colonized] people dwell" (1963: 227) towards a more positive evaluation

---

[9]    This ambiguity is evident even in the Empire's most chauvinistic periods, marked by constant attempts from the Tsarist side at creating a distinct divide between "us and them", where we find examples, however inconsistent, showing that the indigenous peoples of the Caucasus never became quite foreign. The highlander, for all his backwardness, never sank to the level of the Guinea Negro, but belonged, in spite of his childlike immaturity to "our" superior race, as the ultra conservative journalist Rotislav Fadeev phrased it, in a racist language typical for its time (cf. Layton 1994: 255).

[10]   The idea of the oscillating, two-faced personality of the Russian was a persistent one, and Rudyard Kipling gives his version in 1889: "As an Oriental [the Russian] is charming. It is only when he insists upon being treated as the most Easterly of Western peoples instead of the most Westerly of Eastern, that he becomes a racial anomaly extremely difficult to handle" (Kipling 1952: 28).

[11]   On Russia's position between East and West and the unique place of Asia in the Russian mind, see Bassin (1991) and Schimmelpenninck van der Oye (2010). Even if examples of ambivalent attractions between colonizer and colonized can be observed also in a Western European context, like the British Empire and its imaginations about exotic India (Inden 1990) or in French orientalism and its fascinations for colonized Africa (Hosford & Wojtkowski 2010), it still seems that the Russian ruling classes had feelings towards their Orient of an even more complicated and contradictory nature, see Helle (2012).

[12]   The "Manichean delirium" refers to a sharp dichotomy (along Saïdian lines) between the colonizer and the colonized. Since the 1950s the Fanonian term has been widely used to designate the compartmentalization of colonialism, but implies in a stricter sense that colonialist ideology produces a doubling of the mind of the colonized and a damaging cultural personality construction (cf. f. ex. Fanon 1967: 44-45, 183).

of the processes of colonial interaction.[13] For Fanon the occult instability fosters an inner psychological binarism in the colonized population with a fatal split of the personality and a destructive doubling of the consciousness. Homi Bhabha however has claimed that these mental effects of colonialism by its mere destabilising force contain a liberating potential. The splitting in the consciousness of the colonized between his own voice and the authoritative voice of the master, whereby the colonized turns into a mimicking double, can as Bhabha asserts, by its utter ambivalence be paradoxically creative, since such hybridizing mental constellations threaten to shake the hegemonic ideology of imperial power (1994: 85-92). Along such lines, recent (historical) research has focused on similar hybridizing phenomena and has shown, for instance, that cultural traffic between the Russian imperial centre and the colonized periphery was of a much more mixed nature than previously presumed in post-colonial studies. By the same token, colonization in the Caucasian mountains has been presented as a fluid mosaic of cultures rather than a clean-cut imperialist divide (Barrett 1999).

Hybridizing activities can be observed also in the Caucasus texts with their blurring of fixed national and cultural traits, and we might even talk about a certain internalization of the alien and wild man as a presence or a Bhabhaian "shadow" in the mental space of the fictionalized colonizing heroes.[14] As already pointed out, in classical Russian literature the Caucasus is often construed as a spiritual homeland where the (upper class) Russian officer or traveling gentleman regains his original ego and renews lost aspects of himself, thereby undermining the (constructed) dichotomy between Western superiority and Oriental stagnation, if rather subversively. Through the imaginative cultural contact and intermingling that go on in the invented border zones of the Caucasian highland, these fictitious Russian invaders and border crossers – plus their readers – might (however obliquely) gain new insights not only into the mechanisms of the culture of the other, but of their own as well. By implication, they could even confirm a central concept of the border-thinker Mikhail Bakhtin, that creative, new understanding is born only when we are located outside our own cultural sphere in the areas between ourselves and another, foreign culture:

---

[13] In Fanon, the concept of "occult instability" refers to the situation of uncertainty and personality splitting characterizing the life world of the colonized.

[14] On copying shadows as a result of the colonial doubling, see Bhabha (1994: 62).

> In the realm of culture, outsideness is a most powerful factor in understanding. A meaning only reveals its depth once it has encountered and come into contact with another, foreign meaning: they engage in a kind of dialogue which surmounts the closedness and onesidedness of these particular meanings, these cultures (1987: 7).

For Bakhtin then, every cultural act lives essentially on the boundaries, and it derives "its seriousness and significance from this fact. Separated [...] from these boundaries, it loses the ground of being and becomes vacuous, arrogant, it degenerates and dies" (1990: 274). But what happens when the borders are violently transgressed and those on the other side are forcibly invaded? Could some of the creative potential of the Bakhtinian border meeting (or the Bhabhaian hybridization) be carried over into invasive and bloody border confrontations so often depicted in the Caucasus texts? There is, I think, no simple answer to this. But it could be added that Jury Lotman has claimed that even in war there has to be a common language. As such, even if rather implicitly, also brutal imperialist intrusions are invested with certain possibilities for dialogue, which gradually opens up for, in Lotman's words "the creation of a new semiosphere of more elevated order in which both parties can be included as equals" (1990: 142).

In the Caucasus texts this goal of equality is still though an utopian dream. True enough, these texts demonstrate a considerable amount of reciprocal and hybridizing activity, a kind of dialogicity, also in the zones of military colonial actions. It could be said as well that this interaction – to some degree – subverts the Saïdian unidirectional transmission of Foucauldian power/knowledge. But it must be admitted that the hegemonic voice of Europe, albeit somewhat muted, is still the dominant one. Even supposing some (Bhabhaian) splitting, also in the consciousness of the colonizer, with the result that the foreign voice of the native produces a certain destabilizing ambivalence in the master's mind, the relationship is still asymmetrical. The Caucasian as Russia's oriental other possesses no real independent function but tends to play a part only as a mythological actor in the post-Petrine quest for a national identity, either in the role as foe or as friend, as an other, or as a twin brother.

With the end of tribal war, following the capture of Shamil in 1859, the literary constructions of the highlander as an enigmatic and controversial figure in the country's empire building increasingly lost its formidable attraction both for readers and writers. However, as the imaginaries of the colonized Caucasian as an *external* alter faded, other existing myths of orientalizing alterity, connected to the *internal* other, were growing stronger. In these imaginaries, developed by the post-Petrine ruling and educated élites, the Russian common

folk (enserfed until 1861) were transformed into an object of inner orientalization, an othering that took the form of an internal colonization that sometimes
has been described as a "white on white" imperialism (Thompson 2000).

The Prussian traveller August von Haxthausen was the first to use – in
1856 – the term internal colonization with regard to Russia in his well-known
utterance: "All the energy of the Government must be directed to the internal
colonization of the Russian Empire" (1856: 76).[15] Internal colonization is often
discussed in connection with the concept of "self-colonization", a concept
actualized by the historian Vasilii Kliuchevsky in the late 1800-hundreds, in
his enigmatic and famous aphorism: "Russia is the history of a country which
colonizes itself" (I: 31).[16] Kliuchevsky's focus was mainly on the pre-Petrine
period; more recently the theorist and thinker Boris Groys (1993) has written about the Petrine era as a unique deed of self-colonization of the Russian
people, manifested as a secondary, internal colonization by the westernized
state of its own territory and population. It is a movement that up to a certain
point coincided with the country's external conquest, in a highly complicated
relationship, and Russian rule in the Caucasus and Russian rule of its own
people were two colonial adventures, in permanent exchange. As has been
maintained, the Russian Empire was built by and through this exchange,
constituted by the same actions it performed (Etkind 2007: 626).[17]

The internal colonization of Russia, where methods of colonial rule from the
non-Russian provinces were employed to govern the nation's own core domains,
can be seen partly in light of the imperial boomerang, a term introduced by
Hanna Arendt (1970) in 1951. This term, later taken up by Michel Foucault
in an identical meaning, denotes the processes in which imperial powers bring

---

[15]  That internal colonization was conceived as analogous to external colonization is evident
from Haxthausen's following remark: "Russia would need like England, although in somewhat different sense, a Colonial minister" (1856: 76).

[16]  On this historiographic discussion, see Mjør (2012).

[17]  For recent research on Russia's internal colonization, see Etkind (2003, 2007, 2010, 2011).
Etkind's inspiring works on the topic – in particular his book *Internal Colonization: Russia's
Imperial Experience* – demonstrate how he exploits the concept of internal colonization
both as a metaphor and as a mechanism in a stimulating multidisciplinary reconstruction
of Tsarist Russia's colonialism and the Empire's colonial mentality.

their practices of coercion from their colonies back to the motherland.[18] Aimé Césaire in a similar language has called these processes the reverse shock of imperialism, to characterize the effects of colonial strategies returned home to the European countries.[19] In the Russian case, the return arch of the imperial boomerang contributed to establish on the imperial mainland an internal Orient and the Empire's Orientals became predominantly Russian nationals. Significantly enough, the foremost expert on Russia's external colonization, the historian Mikhail Pokrovsky, was in no doubt about the colonial character of the Empire's dealings with their own people. He claimed that the colonial system was applicable not only to the countries with "hot climate and coloured populations", but was possible no less in places like in the Siberian forests and in the Northern Russian marches (Pokrovsky 1922). The centre related to its inner colonies as it related to the external colonies – that is through hegemonic techniques of forced enlightenment and oppression.[20] There is even much to suggest that the level of brutality used by the Empire towards its Russian subjects in the heartland could be more severe than that applied towards the external colonized others. In this sense, the terrestrial Russian state demonstrated what Etkind (2011: 252) has termed a "reversed imperial gradient", a concept implying that the colonized people on the periphery lived better than those in the central provinces, while the colonized in home domains were

---

[18]  Cf. Foucault (2003: 103): "It should never be forgotten that while colonization […] transported models to other continents, it also had a considerable boomerang effect on the mechanisms of power in the West […]. A whole series of colonial models was brought back to the West, and the result was that the West could practise something resembling colonization, or an internal colonization, on itself".

[19]  The reverse shock of imperialism was a phenomenon Césaire (in a text originally published in 1955) saw manifested with particular force in the Holocaust, stating that Hitler "applied to Europe colonialist procedures which until then had been reserved exclusively for the Arabs of Algeria, the 'coolies' of India and the 'niggers' of Africa" (2000: 36).

[20]  The degree of repression and violence when colonial methods were transported home, varied. The aim of internal colonization was to civilize rural Russia, but the return of the representatives of the civilizing mission from the tamed areas of the Caucasus to their own land often had devastating effects. As the writer and provincial administrator Nikolai Saltykov-Shchedrin expressed it, these imperial representatives considered themselves "civilizers", but acted like "moving nightmares" (1970: 15).

treated with less respect and with more rudeness than were the non-Russians.[21] This development, with its inverse or even "perverse" colonialism (Rayfield 2012: 317) made the already complex exchange between Russia's inner and outer orientalism even more intricate and contradictory.

A decisive step in the implementation of internal colonization was the Petrine rule with its radical transformation of Russian society. The Petrine state, from one perspective also an internal other, foreign and frightening to the old Muscovite order, started its reign with a grand colonizing effort to civilize its own rural masses. One of the Tsar's founding acts was to invite foreigners to colonize the internal territories for the sake of giving the *muzhik* (serfs and other commoners) new models for copying westernized work and life. Another founding act was to coerce the country's élite to change their clothing, hair and beards, in order to distinguish themselves from the peasantry. Especially important was the decree or *ukaz* of enforced shaving (from 1698), a regulation which set a (small) part of Russians apart from the multitude of bearded peasants and signalized a belonging to the estate of europeanized nobility. The result of these often absurd eurocentric strivings was a culture where the official and beardless representative of the Empire took upon himself the shaved man's burden of transforming the unshaved man in the name of progress and rationality.[22]

The Petrine series of westernizing reforms laid the foundation for an extremely sophisticated net of differentiations between the rulers and the subjects, creating a growing hiatus between the ruling classes and the rural masses. In the course of the 19th century the image of the peasantry had developed into a fantastic ideological construction, and the idea of the Russian folk – *russky narod* – became probably the most vital mythic narrative

---

[21] Etkind sees the "the imperial gradient" as a complex sum of inequalities which was constitutive for traditional Western colonialism, resulting in the centres of empires enjoying "a better life than their colonies" (2011: 143). The Romanov Empire demonstrates a different or "reversed" version of this development and, as has been maintained, this internal oppression was a "remarkable feature of the socioethnic structure of Russia" (Kappeler 2001: 125).

[22] On the shaved man's burden and the importance of the beard in the cultural history of Russia, see Etkind (2010). Gradually some members of the ruling and educated classes started not to shave. Writers and thinkers or prophets (like Tolstoy and Dostoevsky) kept their beards as a sign indicating *inter alia* their opposition to the Petrine reforms and its eurocentrism. But in government and administrative circles the shaved man remained the rule.

in the cultural history of the country. In this mythmaking the *narod* was gradually reinvented (as were the Caucasian tribes) into images of the alien. This internal alien was discovered, it was claimed, in a manner that felt similar to the ways in which Columbus had discovered America (cf. Starr 1968: 479).[23] The exotic discovery of one's own domains with an increasing degree of directed missionary work, adventurous journeys, and ethnographic scholarship, constructed the characteristic phenomena of external colonialism inwards towards the alterity of the Russian village rather than outwards to non-Russian regions. Russian ethnography became an imperialistic investigation of one's own population perceived as the other, choosing as its object not distant wild men, but the "great Russian people", starting the study of the folk that was radicalized by the populists and socialists (cf. ex. Etkind 2010: 133).

In a process of estrangement (*ostranenie*), as the formalists might have put it, the people became strange and strangers, more of an "unknowable aborigine to the Russian ruling classes than the Muslim and pagan tribes" that the nation was conquering (Rayfield 2012: 317). The rural inhabitants of the Russian heartland were (felt to be) as different from the gentry and urban dwellers of Russian cities, as were those indigenous natives who worked in the plantations in the Caribbean, from the citizens of London or Paris (Etkind 2010: 129). A visit to the countryside seemed to the westernized Russian like an expedition into the dark heart of Africa, and the common men and women were endowed with features which made them highly uncivilized from the perspective of the civilized élite. In the gaze of the educated man they could even be seen as members of another race and they were generally called the "black people", *cherny narod*, to indicate their retarded and primitive position. Their backwardness in its turn legitimated the brutal rule to which they were often subjugated by their imperial masters.

Not all members of the educated classes complied with the harsh treatment of the folk. The intelligentsia in the first half of the 19th century, for example, was bothered by the cruel conditions of the (enserfed) population, comparing them to those of the slaves in the United States. Belinsky, an ardent critic of the imperial regime, insisted that the Russian system of "white negroes" was even more reprehensible, since the Russian masters did not have "the excuse

---

[23]   The first to compare the discovery of the *narod* with the discoveries of Columbus was the French historian Jules Michelet (1854: 35), in commenting on Haxthausen's travels in Russia.

so insidiously exploited by the American plantation owners who claim that the Negro is not a human being" (IX: 213).[24] Actually there were cases showing that the Russian "black people" was looked upon not as human figures, but as animals and bastards, excluded from the acculturated community of the Empire.[25] But such extreme forms of othering were rather rare, and it was usually accepted that the rural masses were humans and had a soul. At this time landowners even referred to them as "souls" for accounting purposes, as in Nikolai Gogol's novel *Dead souls* (*Mertvye dushi* 1842), about commercial transactions with deceased serf-peasants.[26]

Gogol's book thematizes amongst other things – and in a highly burlesque style – the ambivalences involved in buying and selling people that are in so many ways similar to you, making the walls construed between the lord and the *narod* rather unstable. Because not only did the peasants have a soul (and a white skin), they also shared the religion with the ruling classes, and it was widely recognized that the common population was especially devoted to the Orthodox faith. However, although it sometimes felt as a dilemma that Christians owned and disposed of other Christians, and not heathen creatures, the civilized society generally accepted this form of disturbing dissonances.

Also the shared Russian language must have added to a feeling of instability of the cultural borders. To a conspicuous degree the language of the lower masses was used by the higher classes without significant differences with regard to dialects or sociolects, likely making the constructiveness of the abyss between "us and them" both obvious and uncomfortable. After the Petrine reforms this embarrassing situation was increasingly compensated for by the élite's borrowing of French (and other foreign languages) as their main media

---

[24] While Belinsky refers to the peasants as "white negroes" the likewise radical minded Aleksander Herzen (1956: 302) called them – in a horrifying image – "nègres gelés" or "frozen negroes" (cf. also Etkind 2012: 105).

[25] Cf.: "Peasants are not far from domestic animals […], all of them are not human figures […]. They are all as if beyond the borders of our government's life, all as if illegitimate children of Russia, all are defeated by the sword of a conqueror not from the same tribe" (Lebedev 1888: 354).

[26] It was even claimed that this soul was the real soul of Russia and that the Russian folk were the only "God-fearing people on earth", a people with a messianic mission to bring true Christianity to the rest of humanity, as expressed by Dostoevsky (VII: 235) in the novel *The Possessed* (*Besy*) from 1872. Such elevated evaluations of the peasantry must have created paradoxical feelings in light of their low status in society.

of communication, something which together with the (noble men's) shaved faces was vital in distinguishing them from the black and backward folk.[27]

The fact that the colonies in which the internal other lived were disconcertingly near, and not in a remote land far across the wide ocean, also contributed to an atmosphere of uncertainties and paradoxes. Russian internal colonization was an arrangement, where the inner Orientals were everywhere, not only inhabiting communities secluded from the cities, but coexisting with their masters in urban surroundings of mansions and townhouses. The *narod* was exotic, but at the same time firmly and closely situated on native soil, ambiguously interacting with the europeanized Russians in a variety of different forms. Probably the intimate contacts with the hegemonic culture would produce a certain Fanonian doubling in the consciousness of the colonized peasants, in which mental imitations of the masters collided with traits belonging to their own (suppressed) traditions. In addition, such collisions accentuated the feeling of unstableness and flexibility connected to the system of internal colonization.

This flexibility is illustrated in an intriguing manner in the post-Petrine image of old Moscow which, as a result of the imperial civilizational drive to colonize its own, is split off from the europeanized centre. The ancient capital, the traditional core of the country, with its old fashioned, even archaic atmosphere was, by representatives of Saint Petersburg's governmental circles, subjected to well-known orientalizing categories, turned into an internal colony, distanced from the Empire's mainland and construed as a restless, hostile Caucasus. The advice from the westernized administrating élite was therefore, with regard to Moscow, to be vigilant and look out for the ambushes that lay in wait in its *auly*. As *auly* is the name for Caucasian mountain villages, the

---

[27]  An excellent illustration of this society where the higher classes predominantly spoke foreign languages, we find in the first version of Leo Tolstoy's novel *War and Peace* (*Voina i mir*) from 1869. A substantial part of the dialogue is in French with the fictive Russian aristocracy switching between the two languages. The element of French was felt so strongly by the readers that one critic claimed that "half of the characters speak in French and their entire correspondence is conducted in that language, so that almost a third of the book is written in French" (cf. Morson 1987: 47). Even if Tolstoy wanted to give a "realistic" picture of the Empire's language situation (false and borrowed, in the author's mind) at the very beginning of the 19th century, this situation had changed so much that in the second half of the 19th century French was no longer a common language for the reading public. In the following publications of the novel the French passages were therefore translated into Russian (and sometimes kept as footnotes in their original language).

orientalizing parallels between the internal other of Moscow and the external other of the Caucasus are made abundantly clear (cf. Pirozhkova 1997: 19). What is also evident, is that the question about what was internal and what was external in the post-Petrine period was an utterly complicated one. As the above mentioned historian Kluichevsky once expressed this bewildering dilemma, in the Russia of the Romanovs even "the centre is at the periphery" (2001: 58).

Actually, in Saint Petersburg, the Empire's peripheral and paradoxical centre, the colonizing processes of differentiation and dividing could be felt with remarkable intensity, and, as has been claimed, at "several levels, the development of the capital reproduced the script of internal colonization" (Etkind 2011: 101). This relates even to the architectonical outlook of the city, where behind the sublime europeanized facades we find the uncultivated domain of the dark and chaotic courtyards, both connected and not connected to the eurocentric life of the metropolis. In Russian literature (and thinking) the duality of Saint Petersburg is a predominant topic, combined with an almost unambiguous anti-Petrine ideology. As briefly touched upon already, the majority of writers from the 19th century onwards exploits in their works themes from the negative approach to the westernized state, transforming the Tsar's city into a symbol of the division in the mental space of the post-Petrine Russians.[28] This is a splitting which also destabilizes the fragile surface of the civilized imperial order and makes the new capital into what could be termed a zone of occult instability, a motive that prevails in the Saint Petersburg texts. Here the deception and violence that in the negative mythology are fused with Peter's (ungodly) "creation" seem to lurk beneath the harmonious palaces, infecting its dwellers with false dreams and absurd visions.[29]

---

[28] As has been pointed out, the classical writers' negative approach to Peter's Empire and their implicit critique of the situation of internal colonization, with its segregation and othering of the people, make their writings postcolonial not only *avant la lettre* but even before the Empire collapsed (see Etkind 2011: 255).

[29] Actually, in the most paradigmatic Petersburg text of all, Pushkin's famous poem "The Bronze Horseman" (1833), we find a double perspective on Peter's "creation". The pro-Petrine myth is gloriously elaborated in elevated images at the same time as the anti-Petrine myth is alluded to in dark descriptions of madness, death and destruction (cf. Helle 1995). But Pushkin is an exception and as a rule the great novelists of the 19th century expressed a one-sided negative view on Peter and his capital, contrasting the westernizing aspects of the Petrine state to the more authentic Russian dimension of old Moscow.

Although great classic authors like Nikolai Gogol and Fedor Dostoevsky have written beautiful and evocative descriptions of the Neva city, their basic idea is nonetheless the same: the new metropolis, brought forth against the God-given laws of nature as an instrument for an europeanizing colonization of the nation, is an infernal place which produces madness and moral dissolution in the inhabitants. It turns (especially poor and simple) Russians into loners, doubles, and ghosts, and leads to brain disorders, hallucinations and loss. This weird logic is particularly present in Gogol's five so-called "Petersburg Tales" in which the aspect of losing (and not least loosing illusions) is extremely prominent.[30] Despite the strong element of absurdities and satire in the tales, their main message is a tragic one, illustrating how the topos of the city is associated with *fantasmagoria*, nothingness, and diabolism. As the narrator warns us at the end of "Nevsky Prospect" (the most demonic of these texts), in Saint Petersburg everything "exudes deceit [...] and deceives at all hours of the day, but the worst time of all is at night [...] when the devil himself is abroad, kindling the street-lamps with one purpose only: to show everything in a false light" (Gogol 2008: 37).[31] Similar undertones of inauthenticity and fake are present also in Dostoevsky's novella *Notes from the Underground (Zapiski iz podpolia* 1864). This highly disillusioned story sees the misfortune of the ni-hilistic protagonist as related directly to Peter's capital, the "most reflective and scheming town on the entire planet" (IV: 455). The same twisted poetics can be observed no less in *Crime and Punishment (Prestuplenie i nakazanie 1866)*. It this novel, one of Dostoevsky's most famous, it is precisely Saint Petersburg's false and un-Russian atmosphere (in addition to westernized philosophy of history), that has invaded the mind of the ill-famed (anti)-hero Raskolnikov,

---

30  In the perhaps best known story, "The Overcoat" ("Shinel" 1842), the protagonist loses his new overcoat, in "The Portrait" ("Portret" 1835) he loses his artistic talent, in "The Nose" ("Nos" 1836) he loses his nose, in "A Diary of a Madman" ("Zapiski Sumasshedshego" 1835) he loses his mind and finally, in "Nevsky Prospect" ("Nevsky Prospekt") he loses his illusions and his life (through suicide).

31  "Nevsky Prospect" is an excellent example of the illusory, deceptive atmosphere of the city and its fatal consequences: A young lady with whom the protagonist meets in the capital's most glittering space, Nevsky Prospect, and believes to be a woman of the highest virtue, takes him into the dark courtyards of the back streets where it is made clear that she is a prostitute, a being from the underworld. This unmasking of the glaring demonism behind the beautiful scenes leads the protagonist to take his life (for an English translation of the tale, see Gogol 2008).

and made him into a bad copy of Hegel's "welthistorische Individen", permitting his morbid murders in the name of dialectical development.

The intricacy surrounding Saint Petersburg, a space culturally colonized by the West, yet also the motivating force for internal colonizing of the rest of Russia, demonstrates the dynamic processes of othering, of mimesis and multiple dualities which went on, not only between the europeanized classes and the common masses or between the centre and the periphery, but also within the centre and among the colonizing élite themselves. As already indicated, not all members of the educated and ruling society were comfortable with the treatment of the common people. In fact many of the shaved men (and not only those belonging to the radical intelligentsia) felt the burden of the civilizing mission as a heavy one, linked to feelings of differentiation and homelessness. As such, also the masters suffered from the abyss constructed within the Russian territory. The aristocratic poet Aleksander Griboedov thematized this situation in his essay "A Trip to the Country" ("Zagorodnaia poezdka") from 1826:

> How we are become alien to one another! The Finns are more likely to be accepted as brothers. While our people of one blood, of one language, are at odds with us, and for all time […]. A foreigner would think from the glaring difference in manners, that nobility and peasantry derive from two distinct tribes" (1953: 389).

Obviously, also the colonizing elite could experience problems of psychic instability and *Entfremdung*, seeing the Empire of the Romanovs as a place of fundamental doubling, imitativeness and false half-knowledge, all fatal results of the separation of the life of the higher estates from the life of the common population. "Where the society is doubled – a deadly formalism reigns the day", the Slavophile thinker Aleksei Khomiakov (1988: 139) claimed in 1847 with regard to the alienating effects of internal colonization. Likewise, the philosopher Peter Chaadaev (notwithstanding being a Westernizer who supported bringing the country into accord with developments in Europe) recognized the national traumas inflicted by Peter's new and mimicking regime: "Our memories do not go deeper than yesterday, we are foreign to ourselves […]. This is a natural consequence of a culture that is entirely borrowed and imitated (1914: 110, 113). Dostoevsky as well comments on the social and cultural gaps brought forth by the Petrine "instauration", asserting that the higher (civilizised) classes knew nothing of the real Russia, even "the moon was better explored" (XI: 12-13).[32]

Although the ruling and intellectual circles were sometimes pained by the many borders existing between their world and that of the Russian *narod*, the complex processes of hybridizing and othering involved in the border building also tended to destabilize these borders, undermining in a rather ambiguous manner patterns of fixed binarity. By implication, the common and colonized people could evoke in the governing classes emotions of both ambivalent affinity and shared identity – like we saw in the case of the Caucasian mountaineers. Members of the Russian ruling and educated élite often looked upon their inner Orient with both enthrallment and sympathy, feelings very similar to the way in which the Europeans (and the europeanized Russians) occasionally viewed their external Orient as a place of pilgrimage, an exotic, and especially attractive reality (cf. Saïd 1978: 168). Many of the over civilized occidentalists in the Empire's westernized metropolis were captivated by the folk's life and living, by their undeclared strengths, their frightening depths, mystical energy and untold wisdom The peasant became an enigmatic presence, and was in some cases even understood as a hidden ideal. In the cultural imagination he turned into the westernized Russians' own *noble savage*, representing like the Caucasian external other, a more genuine, pre-Petrine aspect of the psyche, thought to be more compassionate and sincere than the sophisticated, disenchanted europeanized ego.[33] Particularly intriguing was a supposed infinite love for suffering. According to Dostoevsky, who famously formulated this highly influential (and probably counterproductive) thesis, "the main and most fundamental quest of the Russian people is their craving for suffering, perpetual and unquenchable – everywhere and in everything" (XII: 42).

In the great classics of Russian literature the fascination for the suffering folk is a vital theme, and the encounter between the man of culture and

---

[32] On the Petrine "instauration", see Collis (2012). This study demonstrates the wide range of the Tsar's transformation of his country and how this was seen (in the official ideology of the 18th century) in light of the religious notion of instauration – a belief in the restoration of Adamic knowledge in the last age. Naturally, such high evaluations of Peter's reforms were far from the negative view held by the Orthodox Dostoevsky with his Slavophile convictions.

[33] An example of the myth of the uncorrupted peasant *savage*, we find in Ivan Turgenev's *A Sportsman's Sketches* (*Zapiski ochotnika*) from 1852, in which for the first time in Russian fiction the peasant (serf) is viewed as a human being no less talented or morally upstanding than his master.

the man of the people is a major topic. The fictional meeting between the colonizing master and the colonized *muzhik* is such a frequent motif that the classical Russian novel has been referred to as a "romance of internal colonization" (Etkind 2010). Bakhtin links this motif to the travel novel and relates it to the chronotype of the road. According to Bakhtin, in road fiction the hero always passes through "*familiar territory* and not through some exotic *alien world* [...]. It is the *sociohistorical heterogeneity* of one's own country that is revealed and depicted" (1994: 245). In such native surroundings, on journeys, trips and adventures, the man of culture discovers new dimensions of his own land and is confronted with the man of the people, to whom he is usually counterposed: A man of the people appears in the text as "the one who holds the correct attitude toward life and death, an attitude lost by the ruling classes" (Bahktin 1994: 235). A good illustration to Bakhtin here are the works of Leo Tolstoy in which the travelling nobleman's interactions with idealized representatives of the *narod* are often described. The chronotype of the road is, for example, elaborated in his great epic *War and Peace* (*Voina i mir 1869*), in which the prince Pierre Bezukhov – during his wanderings near the battlegrounds of the Napoleonic wars – meets the peasant Platon Karataev and establishes a contact that contains the dominant ideology of the book. Through the company and the conversations with Karataev, while they are both prisoners of the retreating French invaders, the aristocrat learns the wisdom (*mudrost*) of the Russian people and the internal other becomes a soul brother, or even a better version of the colonizer's self. Typically, the author creates Karataev as a Rousseauesque hero of nature, untouched by the damaging mental intrusion of westernized society. In contrast to the tormented prince who is divided and infected by eurocentric acculturation and progress, the peasant is depicted as a wholly harmonious individual, a self-contained human being resting confidently in himself.[34]

However, and this was also a major literary topic of the time, when representatives of the masses are drawn into the (occult) contact zones between their own world and that of the educated classes, their pure souls could easily be contaminated. The disruptive voice of civilization settles into their

---

[34]    On Tolstoy's pre-hermeneutic belief in the possibility of achieving knowledge pure and untainted by the perverting influences of (westernized) "civilization", see Helle (1997a).

consciousness, as an occupant, and the division begins.[35] In Tolstoy, the invading voice of the colonizer seems to result in a fatal Fanonian doubling (more than a creative Bhabhaian hybridizing), a development we can glimpse in his masterpiece *The Death of Ivan Ilich (Smert' Ivana Ilicha* 1886*)*. In this novella the peasant youth Gerasim is the only good person near the mortally ill upper class lawyer Ivan Ilich. Gerasim is newly arrived from the country and still retains a purity of mind and body. He is, as Tolstoy writes, the only one that "did not lie"; the only one that "pitied his sick master" (1964: 93). But even in the portrait of Gerasim we get hints from the author that the distorting consequences of copying the life of civilized society have begun: The "clean, fresh peasant lad had grown stout on town food" and he has "learnt from the townsfolk how to talk to gentlefolk" (1964: 96-97), thereby substituting his own simple and truthful peasant words with the affected phrases of the *beau monde*.[36] In this manner Tolstoy lets us understand (more than clearly) that the colonizing forces that one day will make this ideal internal other into a mimicry of the educated westernizers have already started their damaging work.

The effects of mimicry, whereby the innocent peasantry becomes as morally degraded as their eurocentric rulers, are presented by Tolstoy with particular intensity in his last novel *Resurrection (Voskresenie)* from 1899. This perverting process we can detect in the following extract, in which the protagonist, prince Nekhliuodov, observes – with a very biazed gaze – the people' corruption after being moved from the periphery and integrated into urban culture:

---

[35]  In a somewhat different setting, the result of the other invading the consciousness can be observed with devastating results in Dostoevsky's novella "The Double", in which the voice of the other – or the double – completely conquers the personality of the protagonist. While Bakthin in his analysis tends to see a creative (and dialogic) dimension in the text's double voiced inner discourses, Etkind regards this text as a blueprint of post totalitarian anti-utopia and a document of human collapse when the other is purged (Etkind 2011: 248).

[36]  Tolstoy was – somewhat astonishing for a writer of 90 volumes of collected works – programmatically against our (conventional) words, which he, from a pre-linguistic position with a clear divide between language and reality, regarded as an instrument for lies and deception, removing people from an inner and essential truth. He was particularly critical towards foreign languages with their double deceptiveness and preferred the peasant's simple talk, in which he saw a greater correspondence between the inner and the outer world, between content and expression. The best language for Tolstoy was the language of bodily signs, and in his writings the real communication between people goes on in non-verbal, contra-semiotic ways. On the role of contra-semiosis in Tolstoy, see Helle (1997b).

As he passed [...] the ready made clothiers', he was struck again [...] by the well-fed appearance of such immense number of clean, fat shopkeepers, the like of whom simply did not exist in the country, – the coachmen with their huge backsides and rows of buttons behind looked just as well-fed, so did the houseporters in their caps with gold braid, so did the chambermaids with their curled fringes and their aprons, and so especially did the dare-devil cab-drivers with the nape of their necks clean-shaven, lolling back in their seats and staring insolently at pedestrians. In all these people, Nekhlyudov could not help seeing peasants who had been driven to the town [...] and adapted themselves to city living (1996: 306-307).

The striking cleanness and well-fed state of the peasants' bodies are needless to say ironic signs of inner emptiness and moral lapsus, the inevitable result of internalizing the life of the colonizing élite. Furthermore, the above depiction illustrates the splitting that takes place in the consciousness of the colonized, changing them into (parodic) pseudo-versions of their colonizers. More horrifying cases of such division can be found in the same novel's narration of cannibalism among poor run away prisoners in the taiga of Siberia. As the text explicitly asserts, it is not natural for the simple Russian man to eat the flesh of one's brother (1996: 527). It is not "the heart of darkness" or some deep Dionysian drive of the unbridled folk that has created such monstrous acts. Quite on the contrary, in Tolstoy's interpretation, this monstrosity is a consequence of the *narod* taking over the dehumanizing practises of the europeanized state; they have in other words become doubles of the darkest sides of our "civilized" society: "Nekhluydov saw that cannibalism began, not in the Siberian marshes, but in the ministerial offices and government departments: it only found consummation in the marshes" (1996: 529).

In this last example Tolstoy's glorified hero of the people, the wise, mild and soft-speaking *muzhik*, has turned into a demonic and dangerous being. This is a being that has mimicked (albeit in a most perverted form) the violent, inhuman aspects of the colonizing Empire and, as the narrator points out, its unchristian thinking, anticipating Nietzsche's doctrine that "everything is permissible and nothing is forbidden" (1996: 527). The theme of the Russian common man as an individual no longer meek and obedient is a topos we recognize also in the portrait of Parfion Ragozhin, Dostoevsky's infernal anti-hero from *The Idiot (Idiot* 1868-1869), an apocalyptic figure foreshadowing the bloody and revolutionary end of the eurocentric Petrine regime. In this cataclysmic event the nation's own Orientals, the victims of the Empire's internal colonization, turned their energy against their oppressors in a mighty counter movement, full of destruction and hatred. Quite possibly, the coercion and cynicism with which Romanov Russia had treated its colonized commons can explain the brutality of the 1917-revolution, in which waves of violence boomeranged back to the centre, the city, and the state (see also Etkind 2011: 24). Rather ironically, though, the victory of the Russian masses made possible new constructions of hegemonic constellations between masters and internal others, between colonizers and colonized, but now in a Bolshevik setting.[37] There is regrettably much to indicate that the colonizing practises of the old imperial rule were partially reproduced in the Soviet Union. Methods of internal colonization were copied and borrowed to create a Soviet form of occult instability in the mental (and geographical) space of the citizens living in the ideal zone of Communist utopia.[38] But this is another intriguing post-colonial tale that cannot be told – only hinted at – within the borders of the present chapter.

## Bibliography

Arendt, H. (1970): *On Violence*. Orlando, Florida: Harcourt.

Bakhtin, M. (1987): *Speech Genres and Other Late Essays*. Austin, Texas: University of Texas Press.

Bakhtin, M. (1990): *Art and Answerability: Early Philosophical Essays*. Austin, Texas: University of Texas Press.

Bakhtin, M. (1994): *The Dialogic Imagination. Four Essays*. Austin, Texas: University of Texas Press.

Baddeley, J. (1969): *The Russian Conquest of the Caucasus*. New York: Russel & Russel.

Barrett, T. (1999): *At The Edge of Empire: The Terek Cossacks and the North Caucasus Frontier, 1700-1860*. Boulder, Colorado: Westview Press.

Bassin, M. (1991): "Russia between Europe and Asia: The Ideological Construction of Geographical Space." *Slavic Review*, 50, 1-17.

---

[37]  The cultural colonization of the *narod* continued, also in the Bolshevik state, and in 1927, during a visit to Moscow, Walter Benjamin follows up on this development by reproducing an orientalizing child image of the Russian peasants. In his article on the present situation in Russian film, he claims regarding the peasants meeting with the new media, that they can grasp only "a single series of images that must unfold chronologically", being incapable of understanding "two simultaneous narrative strands" (1999: 13-14).

[38]  The massive repressions of the GULAG system and the widespread Siberian network of prison communities are examples of the continuing internal colonization of the (Soviet)-Russian population, see Viola (2009: 34-56).

Belinsky, V. (1953-1959): *Polnoe sobranie sochinenii v 13 tomakh.* Moscow: ANSSR

Benjamin, R. (2003): *Orientalist Aesthetics: Art, Colonialism, and French North Africa, 1880-1939.* Berkeley and London: University of California Press.

Benjamin, W. (1999): *Selected Writings,* vol. 2. part 1. 1927-1930. Cambridge, Mass.: Belknap.

Bestuzhev-Marlinsky, A. (1995): *Kavkazskie povesti.* Saint Petersburg: Nauka.

Bestuzhev-Marlinsky, A. (1958): *Sochinenia v 2 tomakh,* vol. 2. Moscow: Chudozhestvennaia literatura.

Bhabha, H. K. (1994): *The Location of Culture.* London: Routledge.

Césaire, A. (2000): *Discourse on Colonialism.* New York: Monthly Review Press.

Chaadaev, P. (1914): *Sochineniia i pis'ma P. Ja. Chaadaeva,* vol. 2. Moscow: Tip. A. I. Mamontova.

Clifford, J. (1988): *The Predicament of Culture: Twentieth-Century Ethnography, Literature, and Art.* Cambridge, Mass.: Harvard University Press.

Collis, R. (2012): *The Petrine Instauration: Religion, Esotericism and Science at the Court of Peter the Great.* Leiden: Brill Academic Publishers.

Curzon, G. (1889): *Russia in Central Asia in 1889 and the Anglo-Russian Questions.* London: Frank Cass & Co.

Dostoyevsky, F. (1988-1996): *Sobranie sochinenii v 15 tomakh.* Leningrad / Saint Petersburg: Nauka.

Etkind, A. (2011): *Internal Colonization. Russia's Imperial Experience.* Cambridge: Polity Press.

Etkind, A. (2007): "Orientalism Reversed: Russian Literature in the Times of Empires." *Modern Intellectual History,* 4 (3), 617-628.

Etkind, A. (2010): "The Shaved Man's Burden. The Russian Novel as a Romance of Internal Colonization." In: *Critical Theory in Russia and the West,* ed. by Alastair Renfrew and Galin Tihanov. London / New York: Routledge, 125-152.

Etkind, A. (2003): "Whirling with the Other. Russian Populism and Religious Sects." *The Russian Review,* 62 (4), 565-588.

Fanon, F. (1967): *Black Skin, White Masks.* New York: Grove Press.

Fanon, F. (1963): *The Wretched of the Earth.* New York: Grove Press.

Foucault, M. (2003): *Society Must Be Defended.* New York: Vintage.

Gogol, N. (2008): *Plays and Petersburg Tales.* Oxford / New York: Oxford University Press.

Griboedov, A. (1953): *Sochineniia.* Moscow: GIKhL.

Groys, B. (1993): *Utopia i obmen,* Moskva: Znak.

Haxthausen, A. (1856): *The Russian Empire, Its People, Institutions, and Resources.* Vol II. London: Chapman & Hall.

Hegel, G.W.F. (1956): *The Philosophy of History.* New York: Dover.

Helle, L. (2012): "The Colonizer and the Colonized: On the Orientalized Caucasus as Alter and Alternative Ego in Russian Classical Literature." In: *The Borders of Europe: Hegemony, Aesthetics and Border Poetics*, ed. by Helge Vidar Holm, Sissel Lægreid and Torgeir Skorgen. Aarhus: Aarhus University Press, 151-165.

Helle, L. (2009): "The Multiple Meaning of Boundary Encounters: On the Caucasus as the Oriental Other in Russian Nineteenth Century Literature." In: *The Arts in Dialogue*, ed. by Johanna Lindbladh, Terho Paulsson, Karen Sarsenov et al. Lund: Lunds Universitet (=*Slavica Lundensia 24*), 65-79.

Helle, L. (1997a): "Tolstoy and the Other. Some Comments on the Role of Dialogue in Voskresenie." In: *Life and Text. Essays in Honour of Geir Kjetsaa on the Occasion of his 60th Birthday*, ed. by Erik Egeberg, Audun Mørch and Ole Selberg. Oslo: Universitetet i Oslo (=*Meddelelser* 79), 147-159.

Helle, L. (1997b): "The Dream of a Wordless Paradise: On the role of Conta-Semiosis in Tolstoj's *Voskresenie*." *Scando-Slavica*, 43, 18-31.

Helle, L. (1995): "The City as Myth and Symbol in Alexander Pushkin's Poem 'The Bronze Horseman." *Scando-Slavica*, 41, 22-41.

Hosford, D. and C. J. Wojtkowski (2010): *French Orientalism: Culture, Politics, and the Imagined Other*. Newcastle: Cambridge Scholars Publishing.

Inden, R. (1990): *Imagining India*. Oxford: Blackwell.

Kappeler, A. (2001): *The Russian Empire: A Multiethnic History*. Harlow: Longman.

Kavelin, K. (1989): *Nash umstvennyi stroi: Stat'i po filosofii russkoi istorii i kul'tury*. Moscow: Pravda.

Khomiakov, A. (1988): *O starom i novom. Stat'i i ocherki*. Moscow: Sovremennik.

Kipling, K. (1952): *A Choice of Kipling's Prose*. London: Macmilan.

Kliuchevsky, V. (1955-1959): *Sochineniia v 8 tomach*. Moscow: Gosudarstvennoe izdatel'stvo politicheskoi literaturoi.

Kliuchevsky, V. (2001): *Tetrad's aforizmami*. Moscow: EKSMO.

Layton, S. (1994): *Russian Literature and Empire. Conquest of Caucasus from Pushkin to Tolstoy*. New York: Cambridge University Press.

Lebedev, K. (1888): "Iz zapisok senatora K. N. Lebedeva: 1854-i god." *Russkii arkhiv*, vol. 7, 345-366.

Lotman, Ju. (1990): *The Universe of the Mind. A Semiotic Theory of Culture*. London / New York: I. B. Tauris & Co.

Lotman, J. (1984): "Simvolika Peterburga i problemy semiotiki goroda." *Uchenye zapiski TGU*, 664, 30-46.

Michelet, J. (1954): *Légendes démocratiques du Nord*. Paris: Garnier Frères, Libraires-Éditeurs.

Morson, G. (1987): *Hidden in Plain View: Narrative and Creative Potentials in 'War and Peace'*. Stanford, California: Stanford University Press.

Mjør, K. J. (2012): "Russian History and European Ideas." In: *The Borders of Europe: Hegemony, Aesthetics and Border Poetics,* ed. by Helge Vidar Holm, Sissel Lægreid and Torgeir Skorgen. Aarhus: Aarhus University Press, 71-92.

Neumann, I. B. (1996): *Russia and the Idea of Europe: A Study of Identity and International Relations.* London: Routledge.

Pokrovsky, M. (1995): "Zavoevanie Kavkaza," *Zvezda,* 3, 126-143.

Pokrovsky, M. (1922): "Svoeobrazie russkogo istoricheskogo protsessa i pervaia bukva marksizma". *Pravda,* July 5.

Pirozhkova, T. (1997): *Slavianofil'skaia zhurnalistika.* Moscow: MGU.

Ram, H. (2003): *The Imperial Sublime: A Russian Poetics of Empire.* Madison, Wisc: The University of Wisconsin Press.

Rayfield, D. (2012): "Book Review: Internal Colonization. Russia's Imperial Experience." *Journal of European Studies,* 42 (3), 317-318.

Riasanovsky, N. (1985): *The Image of Peter the Great in Russian History and Thought.* Oxford: Oxford University Press.

Sahni, K. (1997): *Crucifying the Orient. Russian Orientalism and the Colonization of Caucasus and Central Asia.* Bangkok and Oslo: White Orchid Press.

Saïd, E. (1978): *Orientalism.* New York: Vintage Books.

Saltykov-Shchedrin, M. (1970): *Sobranie sochinenii v 20 tomakh,* vol. 10. Moscow: Chudozhestvennaia literatura.

Schimmelpenninck van der Oye, D. (2010): *Russian Orientalism. Asia in the Russian Mind from Peter the Great to the Emigration.* New Haven & London: Yale University Press.

Starr, S. F (1968): "August von Haxthausen and Russia." *The Slavonic and East European Review,* vol. 46, no 107, 479-480.

Thompson, E. (2000): *Imperial Knowledge: Russian Literature and Colonialism.* Westport, Conn. and London: Greenwood Press.

Tlostanova, M. (2008): "The Janus-faced Empire Distorting Orientalist Discourses." *Worlds & Knowlewdge Otherwise,* vol. 2: 2, 1-11.

Tolz, V. (2001): *Russia: Inventing the Nation.* London: Arnold/Hodder Headline Group.

Tolstoy, L. (1996): *Resurrection.* London: Penguin Books.

Tolstoy, L. (1964): *Sobranie sochinenii,* vol. 12. Moscow: Chudozhestvennaia literatura.

Toporov, V. (1964): "Peterburg i peterburgskij tekst russkoj literatury." *Uchenye zapiski TGU,* 664, 4-30.

Viola, L. (2009): "Die Selbstkolonisierung der Sowjetunion und der Gulag der 1930er Jahre." *Transit. Europäische Revue,* 38, 34-56.

# Scenic Landscapes and Dialogic Spaces on the Outskirts of Europe: Arctic Drama and Polar Surrealism in the Arts – a Cross-disciplinary Approach

*Knut Ove Arntzen*

It seems to me to be of interest to notify, that Knut Hamsun has spent a great part of his childhood and early youth in Nordland. The fantastic, exotic in Hamsun may be seen in connection with his young years in Nordland. Like Kipling in his authorship has been marked by India, the same way it seems to me, that Hamsun's authorship has been coloured by Nordland: The nature of the north, the sky and the sea, the high mountains, the strong and thriving sun, the deep darkness. The nature has a very wild representation in Hamsun's writing, stronger than anybody else in our artistic world, something wild, untamed, original human which not the least breaks through in Pan and in The Play of Life (Christensen 1902: 38, my translation).

This chapter on scenic landscapes in the context of dialogic spaces in the arctic outskirts of Europe is a cross-disciplinary approach to the arts, which also touches on the concept of a polar surrealism. Dialogic space is a concept describing artistic creation and communication between partners in an exchange situation reflecting the spiritual, the vernacular, and the political (Arntzen 2012).

## Arctic drama and the spiritual: Zogbaum to Ibsen, Hamsun to indigenous dramaturgy

A spiritual awakening in the arts came about by the end of the 19th century, to a large extent expressed through a strong interest in the landscape painting of the romantic period. Ever since the French *La Recherche* expedition to Finnmark and Spitsbergen/Svalbard in the 1830s, a new scientific fascination for the Arctic regions has been steadily growing. The interest in the Arctic that emerged from the Copenhagen symbolist milieu around 1900 (Wivel 2004), which was rooted in classical and romantic landscape painting, initiated a new search for spiritual landscapes. This contributed to the organization of 'literary expeditions' with artists going to arctic Greenland. Polar researcher and writer, Ludvig Mylius-Erichsen (1872-1907) headed one of the expeditions during the years 1902-1904 (Rifbjerg 2004).

Arctic drama may on concrete as well as a metaphorical levels, be defined as the experience of excitement connected to polar expeditions, hunting tours or mountain climbing in spiritual or vernacular modes. Experiences of dialogic spaces related to nature are expressed in reflections of arctic landscape transformed into scenic or artistic landscape. This has a certain impact on artistic work from romanticism to modernism and the avant-garde. Some of the creative force within modernism is lodged in the discovery of nature as a mirror of the spiritual landscape.

The term *arctic drama* was studied and researched by the International Association for Scandinavian Studies-conference (IASS) in Gdansk 2008: *Nordic Drama. Renewals and Transgressions*. This proves that the challenge consists in searching for – and describing – other narrative traditions and dramaturgic techniques that often exist in the range between epical techniques of drama, shamanism, and Ulla Ryum's circular and spiral dramaturgy of a non-linear and mythological kind (Ryum 1986). David Schuler showed how the Sámi chanting form, the *joik*, was a source of inspiration for arctic drama, mentioning Finnish-Sàmi multi-artist Nils-Aslak Valkeapää's (1943-2001) play *Ridn'oaivi ja nieguid oaidni* (Den rimhårede og drømmeseeren, 'The Icyhaired and The Dream Seer'). It is about a young reindeer herder meeting an old seer or shaman, and is a play developed in a dialogue with Japanese Noh Theatre. Beàivvas Sami Theater produced it in 2007. This play it is an example of a Sàmi drama built up around the narrative structure of the joik (Schuler 2008: 104-105). Let us go back in time to get an overall perspective. Hans Lindkjølen (2008: 79-81) comes up with a contribution that locates an historical arctic drama within the Scandinavian main stream by speaking of the schoolteacher and author Emilie Zogbaum (1843-1897), originally from Horten at the Oslo Fjord. She was teaching in primary school in Hammerfest around the 1850s and was a friend of Henrik Ibsen, who produced her play *Atten År efter* ('Eighteen Years Later') at Kristiania Norske Teater in 1861. The play was written under the pseudonym Thorbjørn Bjelle in the romantic tradition, inspired by the German Theodor Mügge who travelled to Finnmark in the summer of 1840 and wrote a book entitled *Skizzen aus dem Norden* (*Sketches from the North*), based on his experiences. According to Lindkjølen, Mügge here describes the Sámi as a people still not influenced by civilization. Later on, Mügge concretizes this in the novel *Afraja* (1854) about a "Sámi chief" whose daughter falls in love with a Danish merchant, and focuses on how difficult or even impossible such an affair was. Zogbaum then catches this theme in her play about the young Sámi woman Zirsa who is falling in love with the Danish merchant Steen. This conflict may be a source of inspiration for the conflict in Henrik Ibsen's *Rosmersholm* (1886) about the young half-Sámi woman Rebekka West. Lindkjølen (2008: 81), shows a similar conflict in *Fruen fra havet* ('The Lady From the Sea', 1888).

In *Livets spill* ('Play of Life', 1896), Knut Hamsun (1859-1952) displays a landscape or topos in the Lofoten and Vesterålen archipelagos in the Nordland County in Northern Norway. The drama is about the philosopher Ivar Kareno, seeking a tower on a cliff, where he could write his dissertation, virtually takes place on a cliff situated in a little coastal town. The town with its market is surrounded by a coastal landscape that is most likely inspired by marketing towns in Lofoten and Vesterålen, such as Kabelvåg, Melbu, and Stokmarknes. Nature is the creative force and the perspective is that of the mystical and spiritual aspects of nature and the desire for insight into these realms. Hamsun's literature reflects nature in general, by using the coastal town and its surrounding nature as a scene both metaphorically and concretely. This topography is characterised by a kind of urban feeling through tourism and a growing industrialisation. At the same time this topography remains close to nature.

Cabaret dramaturgy and cabaret culture had a great impact on Hamsun as playwright, since he experienced it especially when he lived in Kristiania (Oslo) and Copenhagen in many cafés and clubs of the burlesque and spectacular kind. He was concerned with gaining deeper spiritual insight through contact with nature in landscapes marked by the spiritual, which came to expression in his tendency towards symbolism. Dramaturgically, his dramatic texts reflected a cabaret structure with numbers and fragmented sequences. This indeed also applies to *Livets spill*. The arctic landscape can be seen as converging with a wild and untamed nature of an imaginative kind, which contributes to the viewing of Hamsun's dramatic writing in the context of the landscape paradigm (cf. Fuchs and Chauduri 2005). This paradigm reflects a dramatic structure more circular than linear, and based on situations and portraits of situations. Cyclical composition may also be seen as corresponding to the four seasons. In his article on the Kareno-trilogy, which *Livets spill* was a part of, Even Arntzen refers to one of the few large studies of the play, namely Simon Grabowski's *Kareno in Nordland. A Study of 'Play of Life'*:

> ... In thread with Grabowski we may see *four* basic and powerful life forces that govern the situations occurring in *Play of Life; Logos, Eros, Mammon and Nature*... The three

first powers we may understand respectively as human longings and dreams: dreams of total understanding of life, the dream of all embracing love and the dream of great riches (Grabowski quoted by E. Arntzen 2002: 235).

In his article, Even Arntzen describes how the philosopher Ivar Kareno from Kristiania (Oslo) travels to Nordland to find his (in my words) dialogic space for reflections on the 'Nietzschean' strong man. He discusses "the expressionistic and intertextual space in *Livets spill*' (Play of Life) and classifies it as a very neo-romantic text in direction of being "psychologizing spiritual poetry, … with onsets to individualistic vitalism coupled with a mystified view of nature" (E. Arntzen 2002: 236-237).

In Knut Hamsun's dramatic works action mostly takes place in a dense Northern Norwegian landscape, or else it takes place in the bourgeois saloons and palm gardens of Kristiania (Oslo), as is the case in *Ved rikets port* (At the Gate of the Kingdom, 1895) and *Aftenrøde* (Sunset Glow, 1898), or for that matter the grotesque *Livet i Vold* ('In the Grip of Life', 1910).

… We see a play for closed doors, a play about vital forces and death. Slowly we understand that this is a dream play (Bang-Hansen 1987: 11).

It is not only a dream play, as Kjetil Bang-Hansen states in connection with his staging of this play at Nationaltheatret (The National Theatre) in Oslo in 1987. Furthermore it is a theatrical dream play about an aging cabaret singer and actress looking back at her life. As a dream play it also reflects the Arctic in a metaphorical way, in the sense that the Arctic represents nature and circular structures reflecting spiritual conditions.

Generally speaking, the term arctic drama may concretely describe humans in dialogic spaces in polar or arctic climate, which can be seen as related to scenic reflections and dialogue with nature. In a larger context we realise that arctic artistic receptions may be inserted into romanticism, symbolism as well as expressionism. The investigation of spiritual landscapes should be seen in relation to, or in confrontation with, the forces of nature. Arctic drama thus may historically be comprehended through a director's artistic receptions or through performativity, as well as in relation to different artistic expressions of polar experiences and events.

Even conventional plays with arctic themes are related to hunting trip situations, mining situations, and polar expeditions. Arctic drama may be a drama, which touches upon arctic relations and dialogic spaces, both concretely and metaphorically, through its description of polar nature. Moreover, it addresses social and political relations in the arctic areas as a basis for promoting the drama of people in coastal areas. This is also expressed in the theatre and visual art of indigenous populations, like the Sàmi in northern Scandinavia or the Inuit in Greenland, both closely related to landscapes and its mythological impact.

## The vernacular and political in local cabaret culture: revues and polar surrealism

Cabaret culture can find expression outside the metropolitan centres, for instance in local vernacular shows or revues applying local dialects. Historically such entertainment culture spread northwards to areas that had no theatre life in the professional sense, like small coastal towns, fishing villages, and market places. There was a high frequency of travelling artists and traders in northern Scandinavian and arctic areas (Rosenquist 2008). In the 1860s entertaining programmes were referred to as 'magic-comical' and spoken of as 'Kunstforevisning' (artistic performance) in Hammerfest and Tromsø (Berg 2008: 323). Drama societies had been established in Tromsø and Hammerfest in the early 19th century (Eilertsen 2004: 29-43).

When it comes to local revues, especially Honningsvåg at the barren island of Magerøya in western Finnmark is well known for its revue since the early 1900s, referred to as *Turnrevyen* (the Revue of the Gymnastic Hall) or Honningsvågrevyen (The Honningsvåg Revue). Such vernacular revues became well established in the fishing villages and smaller towns of the North. The revue shows can be seen as cabaret- cultural expression reflecting and expressing local identity in areas that had no access to professional theatre, except for visits by travelling companies like Riksteateret (The Norwegian Touring Company) since its foundation in 1949. The revue shows reflected local identity, and assimilated international stylistic features, such as was the case with the revue shows in Honningsvåg since the 1920s. From old photos one can see that the stage decorations had stylistic features from futurism (cf. Jensen and Kristiansen 1985). The humour in the shows and their texts expressed a wit formed by hardships of life in barren landscapes, transformed into non-sense close to surrealism. Pantomimes, poses and tableaus were important stylistic features. Knowledge of international trends was intermediated by extensive travelling done by parts of the population. Merchants, fishermen, and sailors visited cities on the European continent and the Russian White Sea region.

There is also an example of a Jewish dance instructor specialised in revue ballet, Salomon Shotland (referred to as Schotland in Jensen and Kristiansen

1985: 35), who took active part in the revue since 1929. He was among those Jews who were deported from Norway to Auschwitz in 1942 (Ottosen 1994: 358). So, it was a local coastal environment of an international orientation that inspired the revue shows. They were later on politically inspired, such as the show *The Face of the Town* in 1950, with mainly local communists in charge. The jokes were, however, not explicitly political, with titles like *Chaplin*, *Chiu-Chiu* and *Hawaii* (Jensen and Kristiansen 1985: 107; quoting of newspaper cutting).

The revue milieu became a major source of inspiration to artists like film director Knut Erik Jensen (1940-) and visual artist, painter Bjarne Holst (1944-1993). It was at home in Honningsvåg they started their artistic careers as young men in the 1960s. Liv Lundberg has written about a 'strange' artist environment that came about in Honningsvåg in the 1960s and early 1970s. Young people of the town, who had travelled the world for educational purposes, returned during the summer time and established the gallery and fish restaurant Aquarius (Lundberg: website). This artistic environment in Honningsvåg sought to define its identity in local positions, more than in a national one, and they wanted to research and express international avantgarde movements. This position was stated in a magazine by the strange title of *Liigtaarnen* (Corns). Jensen returned home from language studies in Leningrad and film studies in London, and Holst from studies at the State Design School in Oslo.

Bjarne Holst is defined as one of the first surrealist visual artists in Norwegian professional painting. He participated in the exhibition "Norwegian Surrealists" at Charlottenborg in Copenhagen in 1968 (websites: Museumsnettverk, Bjarne Holst- www.snl.no). In 1981 Bjarne Holst and Knut Erik Jensen directed a short film titled *Fiolplukkerne* (*The Violet Pickers*) together (NRK Tromsø), based on Bjarne Holst's painting of the same title.

> … Among Holst's main works from this period is the film *Fiolplukkerne* (*The Violet Pickers*). The theme is surrealist: people who are looking for violets at Finnmarksvidda – where violets never grow. This may be interpreted as a symbolic presentation of modern human beings and their hopeless quest for material values: power, money and prestige. In the end we all fall into the abyss! (website: museumsnettverk).

The film was shot by Knut Erik Jensen at Magerøya in wintertime, and the recordings alone must have been as challenging as a piece of performance art under very difficult conditions in a snowy landscape. The film presents installation-like tableaus in the landscape, set up in theatrical ways before the recordings were shot. This apparently surrealist film has to my mind a large impact on how polar surrealism can be defined. It is possible to find off-spring of this kind of polar surrealism and later experiments in site-specific and landscape based dance, such as the projects of the dance company Stellaris DansTeater based in Hammerfest, founded in 1980 by dancer and choreographer Solveig Leinan Hermo.

Knut Erik Jensen himself has since reached a large audience both in Norway and abroad. This applies especially to the later film *Heftig og begeistret* (*A Strong and Joyful Temperament*) from 2001, a portrait of the Mens' Choir Society at the fishing village of Berlevåg, and the choir's concert tour to Murmansk in Russia. Moreover, Jensen has portrayed the revue milieu in Honningsvåg in the film entitled *På hau i havet* (*Head Down in the Sea*, 2004). These films are of great importance to the understanding of how coastal areas with strong and violent nature can come to expression in dreamlike and surrealist images in a fragmented dramaturgy. Likewise we find a polar surrealism in the novel *Den siste skriftekaren* (*The Last Clerk*, 1964) by Egil Rasmussen from Alta (1903-1964). He wished to express that the dream always will have more impact than reality. However, it is difficult to evoke reconciliation between spiritual life and everyday life, just as Snefrid Larsen has pointed out (Larsen 1983: 80-81). Rasmussen can be compared to other forms of literary magic realism, and could be seen as antipodal to magic realism in Latin American literature.

## Situationism, arctic labyrinths and folk art

The artistic environment in Copenhagen was central to the Nordic artist milieu, not only around the previous turn of the century, but also in the 1940s, 1950s and 1960s when new impulses were translated to Scandinavia. The Danish participation in the COBRA art group (Copenhagen-Brussels-Amsterdam, 1948-1951) was significant. COBRA wanted to cultivate the spontaneous art of fantasy, apparently breaking away from surrealism and other '-isms', but still carrying on the avant-garde heritage. The Danish visual artist, writer and philosopher, Asger Jorn (1914-1973), was at first a member of the COBRA, and then a member of the Situationist International (1957-1972), whose Danish branch took an interest in folklore art and the pre-history of northern Scandinavia. The Situationist Movement found it important to be able to explore the arctic stone labyrinths from pre-historic times that could be found many places in arctic Scandinavia. Lech Tomaszewski, a Polish philosopher and researcher shared these ideas and became associated with the situationists. In an article in The International Situationist Times he launched the theory of labyrinths as topographic symbols in landscapes (Tomaszewski 1964).

Asger Jorn and the French philosopher and political actionist, Guy Debord, sought to lay the foundation of a freedom of expression uninhibited by economical and commercial interests. Jorn wanted to realize an expressivity in the situationistic actions for the purpose of liberating the individual through participatory action art. The intention was to create a kind of personal free zones, which could also be seen as related to the experience of vast landscapes, thereby turning spectators into participators of actions and events. This was also to be achieved via contextual and psycho-geographical strategies such as walkabouts to experience the topography of landscapes and architecture. Quite rebelliously, the human being should be activated and experience the geographically and culturally marginal, and thus the world would be perceived as authentic (Jorn 1990).

In such a perspective art contributed to the disintegration of power hierarchies, which also became a challenge to the traditional centres and contributed to disintegrating them. The breach with centrism and power hierarchies was essential to the criticism of established views on taste and existing '-isms'. Geographically peripheral areas in Europe became visible in a new and different manner, like in the case of Scandinavia, which had gained focus through the COBRA-group. In the 1940s and 1950s Europe, even Copenhagen, Amsterdam, and Brussels were still perceived as peripheral, and the north of Scandinavia was seen as extremely peripheral. In opposition to this, a view was opened up to an artistic gaze on the North, which was not merely of the traditional exotic kind. Moreover, the arctic with its supposed folklore and stone labyrinths came into focus. Actionist artist and member of the Danish branch of the Situationist Movement, Jens-Jørgen Thorsen (1932-2000), described this process in relation to the combination of freedom and the foundation of folk art:

> ... With its attempts at uniting the folklore of fairy tales with modern imagination Cobra carried Danish wood to the European colour-bonfire that in the 1950s tried to burn all authoritative formalism. This was done by a hitherto unseen cooperation across national boundaries out of the 'Tendency without -Ism' that worked according to the principle of freedom and on the common foundation of folk art (Thorsen 1965: 103).

This was yet another inspiration to take an interest in defining global regions, primarily through the search for the vernacular, a search that also created new interest in original populations in artistic environments. In this context the Northern areas with their culture and artistic expressions came into focus.

## Wreckage art from drift wood to sculptural landscapes in-between the local and the global

The way dialogic spaces are researched in and expressed in artistic works can be seen as something nomadic. One way of speaking about it is by using the term 'rækved-kunst', meaning wreckage art from drifting Siberian timber alongside the Arctic coasts. It can be used as construction materials or for carving or making installation art alike. Metaphorically speaking it can be seen as reflecting the drifting of cultural impulses.

Wreckage art from drifting timber is artistically used as a material by for instance Iver Jåks (1932-2007), a well known Sàmi visual artist working a lot with the carving of small figures and statues. So, in his case it is very concrete. In the case of Inghild Karlsen (1952-), visual artist from Tromsø, living in Oslo, the term wreckage art may be used metaphorically to describe a nomadic aesthetics as such. Her material felt can also be perceived as a 'nomadic material', created through the process of turning wool into felt using water and fat. This is a process that takes place through physical activity, particularly by hand. Felt has been in focus among Inghild Karlsen's materials in performance art and installation work. Karlsen is one of the participators in the project *Skulpturlandskap Nordland* (Artscape Nordland) carried out in the years 1992-1998 by the Cultural Administration of the County of Nordland. She participated with the sculptures *Etterbilder* (After images) in Nyksund and Myre in Vesterålen, sculptures which according to Susanne Rajka show how generations of coastal women are reflected in the women of present day coastal areas of Nordland. *Etterbilder* consists of two "lightstaffs", of which the one in Nyksund:

> ...is like a tombstone throwing shadows on the field in front of the abandoned settlements at Nyksund. It tells of a life form heavily loaded with traditions, a life form which is not returning and is just as 'dying' as the traditional technique of making wool into felt (Rajka 2008: 206-207).

According to Oddrun Sæter (cf. Sæter 1995), this process caused a lot of discussion in the local towns where the sculpture landscape was going to be established. Sæter pointed to the fact that conflicts related to the public space

*Inghild Karlsen's "Etterbilder" (After images) in Nyksund and Myre, a part of Skulptur-landskap Nordland (Artscape Nordland), 1992-1998. Copyright: Inghild Karlsen.*

often have taken place in urban environments, but in the case of Artscape Nordland the conditions of the surrounding nature were taken into consideration. Anthropologist Marianne Gullestad has stated that to Northern Norwegians nature is not primarily aesthetics but marked by existence, livelihood and symbol, which is quoted by Sæter in the following statement: "… nature exists as part of the basic values of the region both in the pragmatic and the mythological sense" (Sæter 1995: 163). This has an impact on the understanding of the relation between art and the identity.

I would also like to draw attention to a wider global horizon of the Arctic and the Sub-Arctic in the understanding of art and landscape dialogues. The Danish visual artist Kirsten Justesen (1943-) has been doing project work in Greenland, Finland and Canada entitled *Smeltetid* (Melting Time), a series of 11 projects that were included in a dialogue with glacier research to be viewed as a study of time and change of conditions, or of the expression of time through the melting of ice. The notion of time is part of the work on two levels, and as Anne Ring Petersen says, we see time both as linear and cyclical (Petersen 2009: 235).

In her series of projects, Kirsten Justesen has been working with ice on concrete and metaphorical levels in her installation work, also marked by performativity as in "episodes" with naked actors dressed in black gloves and moving in ice coated landscapes in Greenland. She also made these projects with ice cubes in indoor galleries (Justesen 2003). Justesen has a background in the avant-garde groups of the 1960s and 1970s Denmark.

Another example of global dialogic spaces in scenic landscapes, is The *3e Symposium en arts visuels de l'Abitibi-Témiscamingue,* an art project and a symposium which sought to connect nature conditioned relations in the form of the interaction between landscape, geology and culture in a Canadian and Scandinavian perspective. It was arranged in July 1997 in Canada, in the region of Abitibi-Temiscamingue, which is situated in North Western Quebec. The symposium took place in the small town of Amos at the border between the landscapes of tundra and taiga, situated not far from Hudson Bay. The aim of this symposium was to join together artists from Canada and Quebec as well as Scandinavian artists, in co-operation with Museet for Samtidskunst in Roskilde (Roskilde Museum of Contemporary Art) in Denmark (Catalogue 1998). The idea behind the symposium was that culture in cooperation with nature should find a common platform between Scandinavia and Canada, and it showed that the Canadian and Scandinavian artists had something in common. Geography and geology were important parts of the concept behind the symposium, and focused on the volcanic rocks from earlier geological periods which had been moved by the ice in the enormous landscape in this part of Canada, geologically referred to as l'Esker.

In this setting Inghild Karlsen and the Danish plaster cast artist Bo Bisgaard, presented an art installation in the Rotary Park at the Hurricana River. The installation consisted of a group of red-eyed albino watchdogs made of plaster, and was cast in a series as an on-going project. One of the red-eyed plaster dogs was placed on top of a hunter's tower built in wooden materials. The five other dogs were positioned lying on the field beneath the hunter's tower. The white plaster dogs were then cast in white concrete.

Art events in different cultures and in different dialogic spaces globally, may be compared to show similarities and differences. Thus we find the extensions of art and its deeper meaning in scenic landscapes like in the Arctic, while playing with and understanding it in a global dialogic space. This dialogic space is both cultural and social as well as spiritual, vernacular, and political.

On a concluding note I would say there are dialogic spaces in between antipodes of the southern and the northern orientation. One particular antipode is the one Hjalmar Christensen (1869-1925) expressed in his stunning comparison between Knut Hamsun's experiences of Nordland and Rudyard Kipling's of India. Maybe Christensen was not so conscious of global antipodes, and a concept of polar surrealism belongs to a more recent time than his, but

*Inghild Karlsen and Bo Bisgaard "Painted dogs" installation at the Rotary Park at the Hurricana River, 1997. Copyright: Inghild Karlsen.*

in spite of the orientalism in the quotation at the beginning of this chapter, there was an element of what we understand as polar surrealism.

## Bibliography

Arntzen, E. (2002): "Venstrehåndsarbeider? Noen betraktninger rundt Kareno-trilogien".
    In: Arntzen, E. (ed.): Knut Hamsun og 1890-tallet. 10 foredrag fra Hamsundagene på
    Hamarøy 2002, Hamarøy: Hamsun-Selskapet.

Arntzen, K. O. (2012): "A metaphorical View on Cultural Dialogues: Struve's Meridian Arc
    and Reflections on Memories in Eastern and Northern Borderlands." In: Holm, H. V., S.
    Lægereid, T. Skorgen (eds.): *The Borders of Europe. Hegemony, Asthetics and Border Poetics.*
    Aarhus: Aarhus University Press.

Bang-Hansen, K. (1987): "Hamsun, teatret og 'Livet i vold'," program for "Hamsun-høst".
    Oslo: Nationaltheatret.

Berg, T. (2008): "Teater og underholdning i Tromsø, Hammerfest og Vadsø." In: Rosenqvist,
    C. (ed.): *Artister i norr: bottnisk och nordnorsk teater och underhållning på 1800-talet.*
    Umeå: Kungliga Skytteanska samfundet/Umeå University.

Catalogue (1998): 3e Symposium en arts visuels de l'Abitibi-Témiscamingue, vingt mille
    lieu(es) sur l'Esker, Centre d'exposition d'Amos, 222, 1re Avenue Est.

Christensen, H. (1902): *Vort litterære liv.* Kristiania: Det norske aktieforlag.

Eilertsen, J. H. (2004): *Teater utenfor folkeskikken. Nordnorsk teaterhistorie fra istid til 1971.* Stamsund: Orkana forlag.

Fuchs, E. and U. Chauduri, eds. (2005): *Land/Scape/Theatre.* Ann Arbor: The University of Michigan Press.

Jaukkuri, M. (1999): *Skulpturlandskap Nordland.* Oslo: Geelmuyden. Kiese.

Jensen, K. E. and V. B. Kristiansen (1985): *E'du me' på den? Scener fra revylivet i Nordkapp.* Regissert av Jensen, Knut Erik og Viggo Bj. Kristiansen. Honningsvåg: Nordkapp historie og museumslag.

Justesen, K., ed. (2003): *Melting time # 11.* Catalogue. Åbenrå: Art Museum/Kunstmuseet.

Jorn, A. (1990): "Der grosse Schlaf und seine Kunden." In: *Situationistische Texte zur Kunst.* Hamburg: Nautilus Verlag.

Lindkjølen, H (2008): "Arktisk teater og drama. Fra Theodor Mügge til Henrik Ibsen. Nordlandsromantikk – et litterært tema." International Association of Scandinavia Studies, IASS abstractbook 1, pdf for 27. IASS-konference: Nordic Drama: Renewal and transgression, 4.-9.08.2008, University of Gdansk.

Schuler, D. (2008): "East meets west: Joik-driven dramaturgy and Noh theatre in the Beaivvás Sámi Teáhter's production of 'The Frost-Haired and the Dream-Seer'." International Association of Scandinavia Studies, IASS abstract book 1, pdf for 27. IASS-konference: Nordic Drama: Renewal and transgression, 4.-9.08.2008, University of Gdansk.

Sæter, O. (1995): "Samtidskunst i nordlandske landskaper – et umulig møte?" In: D. Sveen (ed.): *Møtesteder I: Om kunst og kunstforstålse.* Oslo: Pax forlag.

Ottosen, K. (1994): *I en slik natt. Deportasjon av jøder fra Norge.* Oslo: Aschehoug.

Larsen, S. (1983): 'Den siste skrivekaren' sett i lys av Egil Rasmussens kunst-filosofiske skrifter. Universitetet i Trondheim/University of Trondheim: Diploma dissertation.

Petersen, A. R. (2009): *Installationskunsten mellem billede og scene.* København: Museum Tusculanemums Forlag.

Rajka, S. (2008): Billedkunstneren Inghild Karlsens multimediaprosjekter 1979-1999. Universitetet i Bergen/University of Bergen: Avhandling for doctor philosophiae (dr. philos.)/PhD dissertation.

Rifbjerg, K. (2004): "Den store manøvre." In: H. Wivel (ed.): *Drømmetid.* København: Gads Forlag.

Rosenqvist, C., ed. (2008): *Artister i norr: bottnisk och nordnorsk teater och underhållning på 1800-talet.* Umeå: Kungliga Skytteanska samfundet/Umeå University.

Thorsen, J.-J. (1965): *Modernisme i dansk kunst, specielt efter 1940.* Thaning & Appel.

Tomaszewski, L. (1963): "Nonorientable Surfaces." *The Situationist Times, no 5.* Paris/København: Jaqueline de Jong/Rhodos.

Wivel, H. (2004): "Verden er dyb." In: H. Wivel (ed.): *Drømmetid.* København: Gads Forlag.

## Websites

Lundberg, Liv. www.hum.uit.no/a/lundberg/biografi.html, downloaded 28.07.2012.

Nordnorsk Kunstmuseum: www.musumsnettverk.no/nordnorsk-kunstmuseum/espolin%20 og%20holst.htm, downloaded 08.07.2010.

Bjarne Holst – "utdypning" (Norsk biografisk leksikon). In: Store norske leksikon, http://snl.no/Bjarne Holst.

http://viemoderne2.blogspot.no/2007/02/situationists-from-drakabygget-spiral.html, downloaded 29.07.2012.

# Istanbul's Architecture in Literature – From Le Corbusier to Orhan Pamuk

*Siri Skjold Lexau*

> This was a realm of squat-minareted and small-mosqued villages whose limewashed walls defined Istanbul neighbourhoods; a realm of sprawling cemeteries that at times dominated a panorama from edge to edge; a realm of fountains with broken ornamental fascia whose long-dry spouts nevertheless provided a cooling tonic; a realm of large Bosporus residences, of wooden dervish houses in whose courtyards goats now grazed, of quayside coffeehouses ... (Tanpınar 2008: 132).

## Istanbul on the edge

In 2011, it was exactly a hundred years ago that the famous Swiss/French architect Le Corbusier (his real name was Charles-Édouard Jeanneret) (1887-1965) did his Grand Tour through Eastern Europe, the Balkans, the Eastern Mediterranean, and Southern Italy. The journey lasted almost a year. He travelled by foot, on horse, by boat and by car. It took many years before his travel notes were published in a book entitled *Voyage d'Orient* in 1966, and an even longer period before a facsimile of his original "carnets" was published in 1987.

This anniversary prompted me to look more carefully into Le Corbusier's descriptions of Istanbul's visual appearance and its atmosphere at the time of his stay in the city. My purpose in investigating "Europe's Interior Other(s)" is to look into the long literary tradition of narrative accounts concerning the specific *otherness* of Istanbul's cityscape, urban quarters and buildings – and more specifically: the accounts of *loss* of certain structures belonging to the past of a rapidly changing city. Due to its location on both sides of the border between Europe and Asia, Istanbul is both part of Europe, and in certain aspects very different from other European cities. Turkey's borderline identity and difference from other countries in Europe is, among many examples, illustrated through appellatives such as "The sick man of Europe", originally thought to be uttered by Tsar Nikolai I of Russia. In the middle of the 19th century, the Ottoman Empire was increasingly dependent on financial support from the European powers, and had also lost territory through disastrous war defeats (Temperley 1936: 272). Even today, profound differences still exist, which is obvious in the controversies of Turkey's application for membership in the EU. Different interpretations of history are some of the main issues of disagreement.

But how does this presumed otherness leave its mark on people's minds? How do writers from various backgrounds convey this otherness to readers? My special interest as an architectural historian is to investigate how descriptions of buildings, streets, and topography, as well as light, sound, and water reflections of these structures are used to vitalize mental conceptualizations of Istanbul's morphology.

## The feeling of loss

Istanbul has maintained its own special identity in many ways. Several authors emphasize the conception of otherness, both physically and mentally, connected to the image of this city. One of these qualities is the feeling of both an on-going and a potential *loss*. This is most present in literary works describing Istanbul's complex identities, and several authors identify a specific kind of melancholy, *hüzün* in Turkish, as a significant feature of the city. According to such views, the inhabitants of Istanbul feel nostalgia for a glory of the past that still exists in some places, but which may soon disappear. They wish to decrease the pace of the continual change and modernization, to keep traces of a former existence alive, while also modernizing the city's infrastructure and their own lives.

Therefore, literary fiction may complete our impression of Istanbul's physical appearance and character as described by the architectural innovator Le Corbusier. Even though he was one of the world's most celebrated modernists, he was always open to aspects of architectural heritage. He wished to develop further the functional and aesthetic qualities of ancient building art and cityscapes, into architecture suitable to modern humanity of the 20th century. In 1911 this architecture was far from developed, and significantly the title of the well-known collection of written works by Le Corbusier published in 1923 was *Vers une Architecture*. In this book, the author demonstrates the possibilities of architectural innovations made by modern industrialization, and the temples of Parthenon and Paestum are shown as references on the same pages as contemporary car design (Le Corbusier 1986: 134-135). He also published his own drawings of the Ottoman architectural heritage, such as the Süleimaniye mosque (p. 181) and the Green Mosque of Bursa (p. 182). However, oriental architecture, especially Ottoman houses and religious buildings including the surrounding landscape, have also been key figures in many genre-creating works by authors writing fiction, poetry, and travel reports while living parts of their lives in Istanbul. One could mention Gérard de Nerval (1808-1855), Théophile Gautier (1811-1872), Pierre Loti (1850-1923), Yahya Kemal Beyatlı (1884-1958), Abdülhak Şinasi Hisar (1887-1963), Ahmed Hamdi Tanpınar (1901-1962) and Ferit Orhan Pamuk (1952-).

In the following text, we will look more closely into the authorships of Tanpınar and Pamuk. Even if Tanpınar is not so well known abroad, he has been called an icon of Turkish literature, as well as "the James Joyce of Turkey". His best-known book is *Huzur,* published in 1949, translated into English in 2008 with the title *A Mind at Peace.* Here Tanpınar writes about the colourful, but also poverty-stricken everyday life in various areas of Istanbul, and about the multitude of human personalities, mentalities, absurdities, and eccentricities that hide or are expressed in the city's streets and houses. Through his words, he provides the reader with images of the physical environments, the light, the sounds, and the weather surrounding the characters populating his texts. He describes how the main character, Mümtaz, "plodded through decrepit, grim neighbourhoods, passing before aged houses whose bleakness gave them the semblance of human faces". The narrow alleys are packed with people, and the downcast houses look abandoned and sick, "anticipating what the impending apocalypse of tomorrow held in store for them" (Tanpınar 2008: 23). Through *türkü* music and the voices of singers, which run through the novel as a way of experiencing life, Mümtaz also feels how Istanbul with all its intricacies, material objects and life fragments are present in the alleys, in the characteristic street structure with narrow spaces between tall, dark houses.

Tanpinar also underlines the differences and qualities of the diverse areas of the city, differences that we may also experience in distinct ways today. The descriptions are, however, pervaded by a clearly expressed compassion for this diversity, as in these words from his novel *Beş Şehir* (*Five Cities*) from 1946. I have only found it in French translation:

La véritable Istanbul, c'est-à-dire non seulement la ville des minarets et de mosquées enfermée dans ses murailles mais aussi Beyoghlu, Üsküdar, le Bosphore, les Iles, les parages d'Erenköy, de Bentler, de Çekmece, est constituée de paysages d'une grande diversité ayant tous leurs beautés propres. Ceux-ci éveillent en nous des sensations variées et nous font imaginer des styles de vie constamment différents (Tanpınar 1995: 31-32).

The true Istanbul, that means not only the city of minarets and mosques fenced in by walls, but also Beyoghlu, Üsküdar, Bosphorus, the islands, the area around Erenköy, Bentler, Çekmece, is constituted by landscapes of great diversity, each with their own beauty. They awake in us varied sensations and make us imagine lifestyles that are fundamentally different (author's translation).

Tanpınar clearly regards the city as a physical complexity where people live their substantial and varied lives. As readers, we may anticipate what it is like to move from one part of the city to another, to cross the Golden Horn or the Bosporus, to be transferred by boats from one part of the city to another – and how the physical and social qualities of the cityscape alter. Like the tactile quality of buildings and streets, the water is always present with its sounds, reflecting the light and facilitating marine traffic. Tanpınar's warm attachment to areas as different as old, crumbling Stamboul and chic Nishantashı, is clearly shown in these lines:

Tandis que vous êtes à Stamboul, vaquant à vos affaires, vous éprouvez le désir d'être à Nichantachı et, si vous êtes à Nichantachı, ce sont Eyüp et Üsküdar que vous souhaitez voir toutes affaires cessantes (Tanpınar 1995: 32).[1]

During the time you are in Stamboul going about your business, you are struck by the desire to be in Nishantashı, and, when you are in Nishantashı, it is in Eyüp and Üsküdar you wish to attend to tasks that have to be dealt with immediately (author's translation).

## Past and present

Tanpınar writes about the nostalgia he feels about his Istanbul and what is happening to the city. Instead of looking at the city through religion and memories "draped in the heavy caftans embroidered with threads of gold", he claims that the image of the city varies according to the state of the soul, and that the glow springing up inside the inhabitants of Istanbul is caused by memories and nostalgia (Tanpınar 1995: 31). It is evident that the profound changes of Turkish society after the revolution of 1923 must have affected the population of Istanbul in many ways. They had gradually lost their identity as

[1]    In the 19th and early 20th century, Stamboul was the name westerners used to denote the historic peninsula vs. Constantinople denoting the whole city.

inhabitants of the capital of a huge, theocratically administered empire. Many of the changes were welcomed by the Turkish population, but the reforms were imposed on the population at great costs. Neighbourhoods had been totally torn apart by the enforced emigration of substantial parts of the non-Turkish population, and the non-Turks who remained did not have an easy life.

The Turks themselves had to change their lifestyle, their clothing, their written and spoken language, and not least to abandon parts of their religious practice. The "Babel" diversity of languages in Istanbul was within a short time limited by law, signs, and public sanction into one language: Turkish. According to Pamuk, this Turkishness, put an end to "the grand polyglot, multilingual Istanbul of the imperial age; the city stagnated, emptied itself out, and became a monotonous, monolingual town in black and white" (Pamuk 2006b: 215). And the city's physical shape was rapidly changing, due to general modernization. The traditional Ottoman architecture was threatened in similar ways, as it did not meet the needs of the republican modernization process. Hardly any buildings of Ottoman architecture except mosques, the *medreses,* and the *hammams* were built of stone. The tightly built areas of Istanbul consisted of rows upon rows of traditional, Ottoman-style, wooden buildings. If they were not destroyed by fires, many of them were torn down to give way for modern road systems and property developments.

Eleni Bastéa argues that few contemporary literary works about Istanbul (and Thessaloniki) by Greek and Turkish authors, reflect each city's complex historical past (Bastéa 2004: 193). Instead, authors concentrate on the ethnic homogeneity of the present. According to her, authors avoid writing about the past, partly due to the population's traumatized relation to ethnic cleansing, and the compulsory exchange of minority populations between the two countries in the 1920s. She uses Orhan Pamuk and his book *Kara Kitap* from 1990, translated into English with the title *The Black Book* in 1994, as example. She finds that the book is oriented towards an international audience, and even if it gives a rich image of buildings, street corners, neighbourhoods, and the urban aura of Istanbul, it ignores the fact that also buildings have historical significance (Bastéa 2004: 205-206). This is interesting, as Pamuk in his next book, *Istanbul. Memories of a City,* published the next year, turns *buildings* into historical witnesses of Istanbul's past. In this book, Pamuk also confirms that both Kemal and Tanpınar wrote long articles that overlooked Istanbul's multilingual, multi-religious heritage to support its "Turkification" (Pamuk 2006b: 226). Perhaps Bastéa prompted Pamuk to comment on the ignorance of Turkey's multi-ethnic past?

However, it *was* characteristic that Turkish authors named persons by their ethnic identity as Armenians, Jews, Christians or Greek if they were not Turks, but this changed after the introduction of the republic in 1923. Even Le Corbusier must have been concerned about such issues, as he changed the words "greedy Greeks" of the original manuscript of *Voyage d'Orient* to "greedy merchants" in the 1966 edition (Le Corbusier 2007: 54, note 10). Anyway, this indicates that a practice of ethnic differentiation was the tradition before the "Turkification" politics were introduced, but that a conscious avoidance of the same was normal afterwards. Maybe most contemporary authors did not dare to contemplate the ethnic diversity of the past for political reasons, but in contrast to Bastéa's generalisation, Pamuk has several times done so both in writing and in public.

In 1995, he was among a group of authors taken to court for writing essays that criticized Turkey's treatment of the Kurds. In 2005, the year before he was awarded the Nobel Prize in literature, he was put on trial for making a statement regarding the Armenian genocide in 1915 and the mass killing of Kurds in the time of the Ottoman Empire. This resulted in the ritual burning of Pamuk's books in Turkey. In a BBC interview with Sarah Rainsford he states clearly: "But we have to be able to talk about the past" (Rainsford 2005). Probably Pamuk was also relatively alone with his daring criticism of the regime, as the persecutions of him in court might indicate. In his writings he has made great efforts trying to convey the combination of pride and shame with regard to the Turkish populations' view of their own history and identity.

However, Pamuk's novels concentrate mainly on the tensions between Eastern traditions and the wish to be modern and westernized, and less on internal tensions in the former or actual Turkish population. At the same time, however, his novels are interspersed with reflections on identity confusion and loss of former traditions that structure one's life. Pamuk has more than once claimed that he owes a lot of his literary perspectives to Tanpınar. One of them is obviously the notion of *hüzün* as discussed in Pamuk's novel *Istanbul: Memories of a City*. It has a different title in the American translation, *Istanbul. Memory and the City*. This difference in titles may indicate an intended variance. The first version signifies that the book is a collection of the author's memories of a specific city. The second focuses more on the profound analysis of a collective melancholy that Istanbul generates in temporary visitors as well as in inhabitants. Pamuk dedicates a whole chapter of the book to the phenomenon of *hüzün*, and extended reflections on the kind of shared sadness that he claims penetrates the lives of people living in Istanbul. *Hüzün* is "a feeling of deep spiritual loss", and at the same time "a state of mind that is ultimately as life affirming as it is negating" (Pamuk 2006b: 81-82).

## The notion of *hüzün*

Tanpınar calls *hüzün* "the Hydra-headed dragon of melancholy", probably meaning that if one tries to get rid of this feeling, it will respond by multiplying (Tanpınar 2008: 38). Songs also seem to convey *hüzün* to listeners. If we search for images illustrating this word on the internet, thousands of pictures of gloomy situations in black and white are listed (most from Turkish sources, obviously having a clear conception of this state of mind). The above-mentioned Mümtaz of Tanpınar's novel, thinking of the traditional and well-known "Song in Mahur", wonders whether "the *hüzün* of inexplicable melancholy" that had fallen upon him and his beloved Nuran walking on the hills of Çengelköy, emanated from the memory-charged twilight of the evening, or from the song itself (Tanpınar 2008: 62).

In many ways the city of Istanbul seems to be marked by this *hüzün*. Pamuk makes a profound analysis of this feeling as a quality shared by the population, "… the black mood of millions of people together" (Pamuk 2006b: 83). He claims that this is unique to Istanbul, and that such notions were imprinted on writers like Kemal and Tanpınar through the French author and critic Théophile Gautier, who stayed in Istanbul in the middle of the 19th century. Already at that time, Gautier characterized some of the city's views as "melancholy in the extreme", and meant it as a compliment (Pamuk 2006b: 84). Le Corbusier characterized the wooden Ottoman houses, the *konaks,* with their characteristic oriels (protruding bay windows), as architectural masterpieces. Obviously, he regarded this architectural heritage, of which he also made several drawings, as part of Istanbul's characteristic identity under threat of fires and neglect. Gautier likewise noticed this traditional feature, and Le Corbusier (also referenced by Vogt) noted that Gautier was obsessed by these *cages à poulets* (chicken cages) (Le Corbusier 2007: 167, Vogt 1998: 43).

Through the descriptions of people's feelings when they stroll through the old neighbourhoods of Istanbul, looking at the disappearing structures of former times, one can easily imagine their feeling of loss. Decay and dilapidation, especially seen through both the presence and disappearance of former beautiful buildings, are a significant documentation of life that once was. This also means loss of the feeling of belonging to the capital of a great empire and its architectural heritage. Transformations of society, disintegration of traditional family life, and the way in which his beloved city changes its outline, are key words in Pamuk's novel *Istanbul*. Lifestyle and habits among the Istanbullus are definitely close to European habits, but the urban quarters, the sounds and social life are also quite different, even if the contact has been intimate through the substantial number of European diplomats and merchants who have lived in the city.

The close physical connection between foreigners and the former Ottoman inhabitants of Istanbul gave local inhabitants a view into a culture that represented westernization and modernization. Turks wanted to be modern, and they wanted to shed their Ottoman habits and objects in favour of a more western life style. After the establishment of the Turkish Republic in 1923, this was also part of the political agenda of the nation as a whole. Pamuk gives us a view into this ambiguity, when he describes how his family's houses were furnished like museums filled with melancholy and mystery:

> Sitting rooms were not meant to be places where you could hope to sit comfortably; they were little museums designed to demonstrate to a hypothetical visitor that the householders were Westernised (Pamuk 2006b: 10).

One of Pamuk's subtitles in the *Istanbul* book is called "The Destruction of the Pashas' Mansions. A sad tour of the streets" (Pamuk 2006b: 24). Here he tells how the *viziers* and princes began to build big wooden mansions for themselves in the hills of nearby Nishantashı, when the Ottoman sultans abandoned the Topkapı palace for new palaces in Dolmabahçe and Yıldız. By the late 1950s, most of the mansions in this area had been burnt down or demolished. The rest were about to fall apart due to lack of maintenance. The Pamuk apartments, where he lived with his extended family, were built in the garden of such a pasha's mansion. He sees the melancholy of a dying culture around him everywhere: "Great as the desire to Westernise and modernise may have been, the more desperate wish, it seemed, was to be rid of all the bitter memories of the fallen empire [...]. But as nothing, Western or local, came to fill the void, the great drive to Westernise amounted mostly to the erasure of the past; [...]" (Pamuk 2006b: 27).

The destiny of the big *yalı*s alongside the shores of the Bosphorus was also a sorrow to the young Orhan Pamuk. These very characteristic, huge wooden mansions built during the 18th and 19th century, literally "hanging" out over the water, came in the 20th century to be seen as models of an obsolete identity and architecture. This duality between the expectations of an exciting, westernized and modern culture was juxtaposed with the sorrow of losing the old city's wonderful, outdated architecture:

What I enjoyed most about our family excursions to the Bosporus was to see the traces everywhere of a sumptuous culture that had been influenced by the West without having lost its originality or vitality (Pamuk 2006b: 46).

## A city in black and white

Various neighbourhoods in Istanbul are described with great love and affection. The tensions between old and new, tradition and modernity, but also between social classes, are omnipresent in Pamuk's narrative. He and his family belong to the upper classes of the city, but the life of less resourceful people is felt everywhere, even if the social distance is very obvious. As part of his descriptions of the sadness and vast social differences associated with the city's transformations, Pamuk claims that the poor neighbourhoods close to the family's apartments seemed as dangerous as those in a black and white gangster film. He feels an overwhelming melancholy and love when he looks at the walls of old apartment buildings and the dark surfaces of neglected, unpainted, fallen-down wooden mansions: "Only in Istanbul have I seen this texture, this shading ..." (Pamuk 2006b: 31). Pamuk writes about his mixed feelings for the city as visions in black and white, transformed into black and white illustrations, when all the derelict areas are protected by the darkness of the night or even by snow in the few days each year when the city is covered by a clean, white blanket of snow.

As I watch dusk descend like a poem in the pale light of the streetlamps to engulf the city's poor neighbourhoods, it comforts me to know that for the night at least we are safe from Western eyes, that the shameful poverty of our city is cloaked from foreign view (Pamuk 2006b: 32).

The line drawings of Istanbul's skyline made by Le Corbusier in his *carnets* during his residence in Istanbul in 1911, fit into this black and white portrayal of Istanbul, and these sketches are even described by Pamuk as "captivating" (Pamuk 2006b: 34).

Le Corbusier's sketches show his awareness of the city's outline, as well as its colours and topographic structure. This is not particularly original, as all European writers and tourists have been very aware of the qualities of this world-famous silhouette, enhanced by the shifting illuminations of the sky. Le Corbusier's swift notes give, however, a precious view of Istanbul anno 1911, as he describes how the city structure consists of dark wooden houses, green vegetation, and the "white" domes of the mosques. In fact, the domes of the mosques must have been more grey, due to the materials they are made of, but Le Corbusier's visualisation very clearly represents a city in three colours: Brown, green, and white. Before his arrival in Istanbul, he expected to find a "white" city reflecting the bright sunlight. He was very disappointed, when he actually arrived by boat, finding Istanbul to have "mosques dirty like old ruins" and "gloomy wooden houses" (Le Corbusier 1966: 67). The weather was also gloomy, the sky and the sea were grey, the Golden Horn was full of mud, and rain poured down for five consecutive days.

The imagination of Istanbul as a white city seems to derive from a certain book by Claude Farrère: *L'homme qui assassina* (published 1906). Le Corbusier repeats Farrère's exact words in stating that he had wished the city to be white, contrasted only by green cypress trees (Vogt: 35). Gradually, Le Corbusier came to terms with the qualities of Istanbul. He writes, however, of the *tristesse* he finds in the austerity of the graveyards, and comments on the structure of gravestones and cypresses lined up in rows. Of the women attending the graves, he says: "Des femmes sont/ brunes aussi. Elle sont/ comme certains de ces demons/ qui ornent la balustrade/ des tours de notre Dame/" (Le Corbusier 2002: 93). "The women are brown, too. They are like some of those demons decorating the balustrade of the towers of Nôtre Dame".

Like Pamuk, Le Corbusier also shows a mood of melancholy, when he comments on the frequent fires in the city. This was an effective way of clearing land for new, modern buildings, as it is even today. But of course it also meant a catastrophe for poor people losing their homes, and small merchants losing their shops and stocks of merchandise. Le Corbusier vividly describes the sounds accompanying the fires, from the alarms to the sound of the roaring flames. Strangely enough, he writes that he at last finds the grandeur and magic of Istanbul that he had dreamed of, watching the frantic work of artisans striving to save their goods, while others were pressing to get a better view of the contrast between "the black disc of a dome outlined against a brocade of fire and the solemnity of an obelisk" (Le Corbusier 2007: 157). He was very aware of the fact that the fires were destroying an important architectural heritage, as was the tearing down of buildings belonging to the cultural heritage of the Ottoman Empire. Some years later, he even warned Atatürk that the architectural heritage of Istanbul was disappearing, an act which he later bitterly regretted, because he put himself in a disadvantageous position with regard to the urban planning of the new capital, Ankara. In 1949, he mentioned this issue in an interview with S. Demiren for the Turkish journal *Arkitekt* (Bozdoğan 2001: 67).

## Architecture, memory and place

Le Corbusier also had difficulties understanding the Turkish soul, the soul that Tanpınar regards as an important precondition for exploring the images of the city of Istanbul.

> Je voudrais dire quelque chose de l'âme turque, je n'y arriverai pas. Il y a là une sérénité sans bornes […] une foi illimitée et souriante. Je n'ai connu, moi, hélas!, qu'une foi torturante, ce qui fait comprendre cette amitié que je ressens pour ceux de là-bas (Le Corbusier 2002: 66, Gruet 1997: 36).

> I would say something of the Turkish soul, but I am not able to do so. There is an unlimited serenity […] at the same time unlimited and smiling. I have not known it, alas! That which was once torture, now makes me understand this friendliness that I feel for those living there (author's translation).

One of the persons who tried to live as if he had a Turkish soul, was the French poet Pierre Loti. He stayed several times in Istanbul, including the year before and the year after Le Corbusier's stay in 1911. In 1910, he made a "pilgrimage" to places full of memories for him. His notes of how the city was changing could also have been written by Pamuk 95 years later. The beautiful wooden *yalı*s lining the shores of the Bosporus, plunging their "woodworm-riddled" pilotis into the sparkling water, were disappearing. They were replaced by "horreurs modernes", and he names what will happen in the future as "un noir projet" (Loti: 125).

## Melancholy – an architectural quality?

Should we try to analyse the architecture of Istanbul, we may turn to the Norwegian architect and theorist Christian Norberg-Schulz and his book from 1980, *Genius Loci. Towards a Phenomenology of Architecture*. His interpretation of phenomenology, heavily inspired by Edmund Husserl and Martin Heidegger, may be a way to investigate Istanbul as a place with a certain character. In classical Roman religion, a *genius loci* was the protective spirit of a place. In short, Norberg-Schulz has developed this notion further to indicate how people through traditional, vernacular and professional architecture have interpreted a place and its environments, its topography, and its natural building materials into built forms that are characteristic of a specific city or area.

However, I think Norberg-Schulz would have had a heavy task trying to establish a definition of the character of Istanbul, especially because of the diversity of 20th century Istanbul. He was continually searching for the architect's ability to interpret the building task and to *solve* the implicit qualitative challenge that might be hidden in a potentially *right* way to build. This approach may be valid when interpreting the traditional wooden architecture along the Bosporus that belongs to a certain tradition. One may well say that the *yalıs* of Bosporus are adapted to the specific conditions where they were built. These houses, often constructed around a central square, a traditional socializing space characteristic of Ottoman houses, the *sofa*, met certain standards and needs of a rich family's summer residence. The traditional *yalı* type was constructed hanging over the surface of the water, and was provided with window openings on all sides. The windows were equipped with outer sunshades, and were hinged at the top to be tipped outwards. In that way, they functioned as canopies providing shade from the hot sun, and fresh, flowing air cooled by the water surface could enter and circulate in the interior of the house. These mansions were built of wood, and constructed according to Turkish building traditions. They had broad roof eaves protruding out over the facade, to protect against harsh winter conditions and hot, sunny summers. The exterior visible to the public had latticed window openings to guard the residents', especially the women's, privacy. In such a way, these houses were designed with social, cultural and climatic traditions in mind, fitting well into Norberg-Schulz' theories of the *genius loci* – here of the Bosporus region.

However, probably his system would be of no use when characterizing the city as a whole. Pamuk's faded photos in black and white give a far better understanding of the multitude of elements that make up Istanbul's cityscape. Here we can see the dilapidated wooden buildings clinging to the city walls or tucked against the walls of the fabulous mosques – the tristesse of an everyday, neglected architecture that does not have a long life ahead. The poor people walking in the muddy streets seem to have long since lost every hope of better environments, but they still smile at the camera that depicts scenes from a disappearing cityscape. It seems like these neighbourhoods are just waiting to be destroyed, by more or less accidental fires or by directly intended redevelopment.

Perhaps we need to incorporate the quality of this second or multi-generations' melancholy, not present at the time of initial construction, to get a grip of this unique city's character. This melancholy has never been a quality that its architects and urban planners have wished to construct. It is part of the city structure's reception history, and we are talking about a *sentiment* that many authors have described. This is a kind of *otherness* in architecture that many western architects have been fascinated by, however, it is impossible to construct, and it would have had made no sense trying to do so. It implies cultural history and time, and it represents a kind of *loss* visualized by physical change. It definitely represents *another* quality in architecture than what was intended. Similarly, it is regarded as a sad, but all the same, positive quality – at least seen from a romantic point of view.

Julia Kristeva has written about Gérard Nerval's notion of melancholy in her book *Soleil Noir* from 1987. She concentrates on his poem *El Desdichado*, which means something like the unhappy, unlucky, ill-fated. The kind of melancholy that Nerval experienced, and which also Kristeva refers to, originated probably during one of his travels to Egypt (Kristeva 1994:137). Pamuk claims that what he himself experienced in the East, for instance on the shores of the Nile, is revealed in Nerval's poem *The Black Sun of Melancholy* (Pamuk 2006b: 199). Nerval feels simultaneously under the influence of, but is not in the position to grasp, what he longs for and loves. He is in the shadows, covered with ashes, compared to those who are in the position to reach the beloved phenomena (the Egyptians). According to Pamuk, Nerval had, like Gautier, an immense influence on how the Istanbullus have come to see themselves.

> In the last hundred and fifty years (1850-2000) I have no doubt that not only has *hüzün* ruled over Istanbul, but it has spread to its surrounding areas. What I have been trying to explain is that the roots of our *hüzün* are European: the concept was first explored, expressed, and poeticised in French (by Gautier, under the influence of his friend Nerval) (Pamuk 2006b: 210).

Pamuk shows that Tanpınar and his "fellow melancholics" Kemal and Hisar studied Nerval and Gautier. The French authors made an image of the city and a literature in which the Istanbullus could see themselves, and Gautier, writing for French newspapers, showed western readers that the poor neighbourhoods "on the wings of the famous sites" were just as important as the scenic views (Pamuk 2006b: 203). "Westernisation has allowed me and millions of other Istanbullus the luxury of enjoying our own past as 'exotic', of relishing the picturesque" (Pamuk 2006b: 217).

This is a really interesting point of view. If we pursue the logical reflections of such a conception, it presupposes a western identity and mode of imagination to sense the specific melancholy of places like Istanbul, where the tristesse and feeling of loss may be perceived as an *other* quality. People, who do not possess access to the beloved phenomena in the same way as native or long-residential Istanbullus, should in principle not be able to experience this precious sentiment. In this case, however, it is the individuals *not* having the intimate relation of the local population who convey the black melancholy to the city's inhabitants. The feeling of loss, of otherness, compared to other cities with a different past and a different heritage, is given back to its people. They have consumed and internalized this feeling produced by foreigners, and incorporated it into their own feeling of identity. Both the French poets of the 19th century, Le Corbusier and Tanpınar, and last but not least Pamuk, have tried to identify "the black sun of melancholy" as a painful, but rich and rewarding experience of memory and identity.

Tanpınar is trying to explain how this multifaceted touch of both past and present inhabits the identity and love of those having a close relation to the city of Istanbul, and I will let his words conclude this chapter:

> Mais ce sentiment de nostalgie n'est pas seulement tourné vers le passé et ne s'oppose pas obligatoirement aux modes de vie, aux mentalités actuels. Il s'agit d'un sentiment très complexe qui touche aussi, en partie, à notre vie de chaque jour, à nos rêves quotidiens de bonheur (Tanpınar 1995: 31).

> But this sentiment of nostalgia does not just reflect the past and it does not necessarily oppose itself to ways of life, to actual mentalities. It concerns a very complex sentiment that also touches our everyday life, our daily dreams of happiness (author's translation).

## Bibliography

Bastéa, E. (2004): "Storied Cities. Literary Memories of Thessaloniki and Istanbul." In: Bastéa, E. (ed.): *Memory and Architecture*. Albuquerque: University of New Mexico Press.

Bozdoğan, S. (2001): *Modernism and Nation Building. Turkish Architectural Culture in the Early Republic*. Seattle / London: University of Washington Press. Referring to an interview with S. Demiren for *Arkitekt* 19, no 11-12, 1949: 230-31: 'Le Corbusier ile Mülakat'.

Gruet, S. (1997): "Vers un non-lieu: pour une critique philosophique de la pensée corbusienne." In: Younès, Chris and Michel Mangematin (eds.): *Lieux contemporains*. Paris: Descartes & Cie.

Kristeva, J. (1994 [1987]): *Svart sol – depresjon og melankoli*. Oslo: Pax forlag.

Le Corbusier, C-E. (1986 [1931]): *Towards a New Architecture*. New York: Dover.

Le Corbusier, C-E. (2002 [1987]): *Voyage d'Orient. Carnets.* Milano: Electa Architecture / Fondation L. C.

Le Corbusier, C-E. (1966): *Le Voyage d'Orient.* Paris: Éditions Forces Vives.

Le Corbusier, C-E. (2007/1987): *Journey to the East.* Cambridge, Mass.: The MIT Press.

Loti, P. (2010): *Pasha d'Istanbul.* Texts collected and presented by Danièle Masse. Paris: Magellan & Cie.

Norberg-Schulz, C. (1980): *Genius Loci. Towards a Phenomenology of Architecture.* London: Rizzoli.

Pamuk, O. (2006a [1990]): *The Black Book.* London: Faber and Faber.

Pamuk, O. (2006b [2005]): *Istanbul. Memories of a City.* London: Faber and Faber.

Rainsford, S. (2005): "Author's trial set to test Turkey." Istanbul: BBC News. news.bbc.co.uk, downloaded 27.04.2012.

Tanpınar, A. H. (1995 [1946]): *Cinq villes. Istanbul-Bursa-Konya-Erzurum-Ankara.* Paris: Publisud/Unesco.

Tanpınar, A. H. (2008 [1949]): *A Mind at Peace.* Brooklyn: Archipelago Books.

Temperley, H. (1936): *England and the Near East.* London: Greens & Co.

Vogt, A. M. (1998/1996): *Le Corbusier, the Noble Savage. Toward an Archaeology of Modernism.* Cambridge, Mass.: The MIT Press.

# Authors' Biographies

**Knut Ove Arntzen** is Professor of Theatre Studies at the Department of Linguistic, Literary and Aesthetic Studies at the University of Bergen. His primary research interest and recent publications are on postmodern theatre, drama and performances in geo-cultural perspectives. Recent publications include: "Arktisches Drama und Landschaftsdialoge in szenischer Rezeption: Hamsun, Løveid, Iunker und Fosse – eine andere norwegische Dramatik" in *Die Gegenwart der Bühne. Aktuelles skandinavisches Drama und Theater* (Karin Hoff, Hrsg.) (Königshausen & Neumann 2012) and "A Metaphorical View on Cultural Dialogues: Struve's Meridian Arc and Reflections on Memories in Eastern and Northern Borderlands" in *The Borders of Europe. Hegemony, Aesthetics and Border Poetics* edited by H. V. Holm, S. Lægreid and T. Skorgen (Aarhus University Press 2012).

**Jørgen Bruhn** is Professor of Comparative Literature at Linnæus University. He has written monographs on Marcel Proust (with Bo Degn Rasmussen) and M. M. Bakhtin and has published articles on the theory and history of the novel, on intermediality as well as on medieval literature and culture. His latest monograph is *Lovely Violence. The Critical Romances of Chrétien de Troyes* (Cambridge Scholars Publishing 2010). In 2013 he edited *Adaptation Studies. New Challenges, New Directions* with Anne Gjelsvik and Eirik Frisvold Hansen, (Bloomsbury).

**Michael Grote** is Postdoctoral Researcher in German Literature. He has a degree in German studies and history from University Bielefeld, and has been a DAAD-Lecturer at the Department of Foreign Languages University of Bergen since 2002. In 2008 he received the degree of Doctor Philosophiae with the dissertation „Exerzitien. Experimente. Zur Akustischen Literatur von Carlfriedrich Claus" (Aisthesis-Verlag 2009). His research and publications are in 20th century German literature (i.a. Vienna Group, Oskar Pastior, Dieter Roth), the history and theory of autobiographical writing, and the aesthetics of media.

**Lillian Jorunn Helle** is Professor of Russian literature at the Department of Foreign Languages, Russian Studies, at the University of Bergen. She has published extensively on Russian 19th century literature and cultural history, Russian Symbolism and Modernism, Socialist Realism and literary theory (Belyj, Bachtin, Lotman, Jakobson). Her most recent research projects and publications are in postcolonial and interdisciplinary studies and center on the research field of "Russia's external and internal Other" and the relationship between literature and science. She is currently writing a book on Tolstoy's last novel *Resurrection*.

**Øyunn Hestetun** is Associate Professor of American literature and culture at the Department of Foreign Languages at the University of Bergen. Her main area of research is literary and cultural theory, including postcolonial theory and ecocriticism, and her most recent publications focus on migrant writing and environmental issues in recent fiction.

**Helge Vidar Holm** is Professor of French Literature and Civilization at the University of Bergen, currently co-leading the interdisciplinary research group "The Borders of Europe". His main research focus is on narrative theory and French novels from the 19th and 20th centuries, and his most recent publications include: *Mœurs de province. Essai d'analyse bakhtinienne de Madame Bovary* (Peter Lang SA 2011), "Soi-même comme un Autre: La judaïté chez Marguerite Duras" in *Revue Romane*, 47/2012, "Le rôle du destinataire chez Eco et Bakhtine" in *Plume: Revue semestrielle de l'Association iranienne de Langue et Littérature françaises*, 14/2013, "Etude chronotopique de *Madame Bovary*" in *Arena romantistica*, 13/2013 and "Flaubert og metropolen Paris" in Ahlstedt, Eva et al., *Metropoler: Reflexioner kring urbana rum i litteratur och kultur* (University of Gothenburg 2013).

**Sissel Lægreid** is Professor of German Literature and Culture Studies at the University of Bergen, currently co-leading the interdisciplinary research group "The Borders of Europe". Her research projects and publications are in modern hermeneutics, modernism, German-Jewish exile literature and Rumanian-German literature. Her most recent publications include: "Poems and Poets in Transit: Heterochronic Cross-Border Acts or the Aesthetics of Exile in 20th Century German-Jewish Poetry" in *The Borders of Europe Hegemony, Aesthetics and Border Poetics* edited by Helge Vidar Holm, Sissel Lægreid and Torgeir Skorgen (Aarhus University Press 2012), *Diktatur og diktning. Herta Müllers foratterskap* edited by Sissel Lægreid & Helgard Mahrdt (Tiden 2012) and

*Dichtung und Diktatur. Die Schrifstellerin Herta Müller* edited by Sissel Lægreid & Helgard Mahrdt (Königshausen & Neumann 2013).

**Siri Skjold Lexau** is Professor of Art History at Department of Linguistic, Literary and Aesthetical Studies at the University of Bergen. Her primary research activity is connected to architectural and urban studies. She has published widely on the history and development of cities and places and the recent transformation of industrial sites. Her most recent contributions within these topics are: "From Production Site to Postindustrial 'Architexture'" in *Global Heritage, Local Context*, Spartacus forlag (forthcoming) and "A University Site for the Future. Master plan for the Nygård Hill in Bergen, 1965" in *Festskrift for Ingebjørg Hage*, Orkana Akademisk forlag (forthcoming).

**Torgeir Skorgen** is Associate Professor of German Literature at the University of Bergen. His primary research interests are in addition to German literature, philosophy, and in particular hermeneutics, dialogism, multiculturalism, nationalism and racism.

**Željka Švrljuga** is Associate Professor of American Literature at the University of Bergen. Her research interests are in African American literature, the experimental novel and the aesthetics of suffering. She is the author of *Hysteria and Melancholy as Literary Style* (Edwin Mellen Press 2011) and a series of articles on the rhetoric of pain and the contemporary novel of slavery.